DO GREAT EXPLOITS

Saying Yes to Your Dreams When It's Easier To Say No

H. Michelle Johnson

authorHOUSE®

AuthorHouse™ UK
1663 Liberty Drive
Bloomington, IN 47403 USA
www.authorhouse.co.uk
Phone: 0800 047 8203 (Domestic TFN)
 +44 1908 723714 (International)

Scripture quotations marked AMP are taken from The Amplified Bible. Old Testament copyright © 1965, 1987 by the Zondervan Corporation. The Amplified Bible. New Testament copyright © 1954, 1958, 1987 by The Lockman Foundation. Used by permission. All rights reserved.

Scripture quotations marked MSG are taken from The Message. Copyright © 1993, 1994, 1995, 1996, 2000, 2001, 2002, 2003 by Eugene H. Peterson. Used by permission of NavPress Publishing Group. Website.

Scripture quotations marked NASB are taken from the New American Standard Bible ®, Copyright © 1960, 1962, 1963, 1968, 1971, 1972, 1973, 1975, 1977, 1995 by The Lockman Foundation. Used by permission.

Scripture quotations marked NKJV are taken from the New King James Version. Copyright © 1982 by Thomas Nelson, Inc. Used by permission. All rights reserved.

Published by AuthorHouse 06/19/2019

ISBN: 978-1-5246-6352-0 (sc)
ISBN: 978-1-5246-6354-4 (hc)
ISBN: 978-1-5246-6353-7 (e)

Print information available on the last page.

Any people depicted in stock imagery provided by Thinkstock are models. and such images are being used for illustrative purposes only. Certain stock imagery © Thinkstock.

This book is printed on acid-free paper.

Dedication

For those of us with ideas above our station.

In loving memory of James Howard:
the first person who taught me to dream;
and who told me I could reach for great things.

Endorsements

'Michelle last night…I finally started reading your book…And I ABSOLUTELY LOVE IT!! I love the way you write, so clear, so very logical, great style, embroidered with really fascinating, telling examples of people and facts. It truly is a great read – very motivating. Well done, Lady J!" Mary Stretch, Director of Executive Search Business. Former BBC TV 'Breakfast Time' Current Affairs Correspondent/Presenter, BBC Radio 4 Producer.

'It's true! Having gone through a long, hard journey to see my dream become reality, so much of what I read I thought "Yes! That's exactly it!" For those contemplating stepping out, they are going to find real, practical, wise advice to help them do it. Why didn't I have this book 8 years ago…?!' Beth Moran, award winning Author of *Making Marion*, *I hope you Dance* and *The name I call myself.*

'I got this book for someone who was going through some challenges at work and she said it really encouraged her. She went out and got herself a new job at a higher level! Really fantastic! If you want to move forward with boldness and confidence into the future, you need to read this book!' - Joan Myers OBE, Founder Rehoboth Children's Home Charity

'I love the stories in this book. They're inspiring and motivational. It's empowering to read about some of the difficulties that accomplished people experienced on their personal journeys, yet still moved forward to do great exploits. This book is basically saying, if they could do it, you can too!' – Lynette Philips OBE, Coach and Wise Women Award winner 2016.

'*Do Great Exploits, Saying Yes to Your Dreams When It's Easier To Say No* is a book that everyone, regardless of age, should read and study if they want to breakthrough to new levels of impact and influence in life. It breaks things down and gives really practical insights for breaking free of limitations of the mind and of the past that may be holding you back.' – Pastor Muyiwa Olubowale, God's Vineyard Church

'I've known Michelle a long time and she has always had a desire to see people mobilised and moving forward in purpose and achievement. She has a passion for people, mentoring and coaching them to set the right foundations in life so they could maximise their impact. I'm delighted to finally read this book, which she has been carrying in her heart for some time. I'm inspired by the insights included in *Do Great Exploits* and I know you will be too.' – Pearl Moses, Free Range Chicks

'This book is so easy to read. It's packed with life lessons from the stories about real people. I'm sure *Do Great Exploits, Saying Yes to your Dreams when it's easier to Say No,* will challenge and motivate readers like it did me.' – Reverend Noel McNamee

Contents

Endorsements vii

Introduction xi

Part I 1

Self-Mastery

1. People who do great exploits connect with why they're here ...3

2. People who do great exploits can see their future 21

3. People who do great exploits believe that they can 39

4. People who do great exploits think positively 62

5. People who do great exploits take personal responsibility 86

6. People who do exploits develop their influence 104

Part II 131

Maximise your talents, gifts, abilities, and ideas

7. People who do great exploits recognise their potential 133

8. People who do great exploits overcome limits to their potential 150

9. People who do great exploits release their potential 171

Part III 195

Never Give Up

10. People who do great exploits befriend their fears 197
11. People who do great exploits are passionate 217
12. People who do great exploits are willing to pay the price 235
13. People who do great exploits keep going 255

About the Author 283

Introduction

Ever wondered what your life's about? If so, you're not alone, many people are searching for meaning and a sense of fulfilment. For a while, I too had the same restless feeling. Life was good, but something was missing. I wasn't convinced that I had discovered my '*It*'. And I almost constantly wondered what my '*Why?*' was.

What I knew was that I was on this earth for a reason and had a sneaking suspicion that it was one of significance. Today I believe that more than ever and I believe that it's the same for you. When I learned that I could discover my '*It.*' and connect with my '*Why.*' through the application of incredibly simple principles, it changed everything -and I mean everything.

When I learned not to dismiss other's achievements as mainly luck; and discovered that I was thinking and doing a number of things that were contrary to my success in some areas of life, it was an irresistible opportunity for transformation. It was like stepping out of a fog and finally seeing the path clearly. Yet, being able to see clearly, was just the beginning. There was still the path ahead that had to be followed – and that is the real work.

Here's a little story that might illustrate what I mean. Imagine you inherited a piece of land; a vast acreage of wild forest territory. Underneath, there's a waterbed of fresh water that flows down through a mountain from it's very peak. There are people living in the foothills of your land, who need that water. You have the answer to their thirst. Their need, is your call and the water that flows beneath your land is the answer.

The only thing standing between the villagers and the water is you. If you had the means and ability to provide the water, would you deny them the water? Yet that is what we do, when we don't take the necessary action to fulfil our dreams.

You dream of using your resources to make progress. You want to make a difference but getting what you have to offer out to where its impact would be most valued seems like a complicated proposition. There are all types of obstacles, pitfalls, dangers and risks involved. And there's you. Are you really up for it? You're reasonably comfortable being where you are and doing what you're doing – except for when you think about your dream, that is. Your life is safe. You know your comfort zone like the back of your hand and how your life pans out daily. If you decided to step out in the dream – to get that promotion, start that business, change your career, challenge the system - you don't know how that will pan out. You remember what it feels like to fail. You have people who remind you about that. They tell you not to stick your head above the parapet - again.

As though all that wasn't enough, there are external factors to consider. You've heard the legends of the giants and beasts that roam about the land. Are you a match for them? The outside world is cold and harsh, the ground, not easy to break. All in all, the odds seem stacked against you. This is why it's just easier to say, *'No!'* to achieving your dreams.

The water represents your gifts, talents, abilities and potential. The wisdom your experience has taught you. The obstacles represent, anything keeping you from saying *'Yes!'* to stepping out to do what you dream of doing. They make it easier for you to say *'No!'* to the call to achieve. Some of the obstacles include fear, mindset, misuse of time, the past, what other people think, not knowing what to do, and a host of other progress assassins, whether real or imagined.

But this is your life; and you have only one chance to live it. It's your territory. It's your future we're talking about. Your impact. Your legacy. Your call. Why not say, '*Yes!*' and live it? Embrace it? Do Great Exploits with it?

I believe you're reading this book because you want to discover meaning and purpose in life. You want to do more with your life and you want more out of life. In other words, there's a longing to do great exploits. You've seen others do exploits and long to do some of your own but recognise there are things that hold you back. Perhaps you just don't know where to start. You may be reading it because have done exploits in the past and are about to reach for more. Whatever your reason, keep reading. This book is designed to take you forward.

To be effective in life, you don't have to reinvent the wheel. There is much that can be learned from those who are successfully accomplishing what you want to accomplish. With this principle in mind, I've used a range of people from historic to contemporary times who have done great exploits to show you how they did it. Their lives provide great examples of what's required for exploits. They are as human as anyone. They struggled with some of the issues that commonly hold people back from doing great exploits. But they overcame those issues and still did exploits. For example, they did exploits because they discovered purpose, put aside fear and become bold, changed their thinking, and embraced the power of taking action. These requirements for exploits and more are discussed in the chapters of this book. Plus, practical insight is provided regarding how to break free of the things that may be holding you back.

The essential difference between people who do great exploits and those who don't is that the former develop self-mastery; maximise their gifts, abilities, and ideas; and keep going until they achieve their goals.

Doing exploits is a journey that is as demanding as it is rewarding. People who are successful have developed a particular set of strengths and overcame certain weaknesses. If you want to succeed you will need to do the same. Remember those obstacles I mentioned above, in the analogy? Any one of them is enough to defeat the best of us if we let them. To avoid being broken or defeated during the journey, takes a particular set of strengths. King Solomon, of ancient times, who was believed to be the wisest man who ever lived, wrote that, 'A cord of three strands is not quickly broken.[1]'

Therefore, *Do Great Exploits* is organised according to these three strands: Self-Mastery, Maximising talents, gifts, abilities and ideas and Never giving up. When you begin to embed the principles of each strand into your life, you will be able to do great exploits. Whatever age you happen to be, if you start practicing the keys in his book, you will be able to do great exploits. Regardless of your past or present circumstance, when you apply the solutions offered in this book, you will be able to do great exploits.

The first of the three strands you must conquer if you want to do great exploits is *self-mastery*. This means discovering who you are and finding your purpose. Next, you should develop a vision that's aligned to your purpose, believe you can fulfil it, take responsibility for establishing it, grow your ability to influence others, and think constructively about problems and challenges. The second strand is to *maximise your gifts, talents, abilities, and ideas*.

Many of us do not recognise our own potential even though we can recognise easily the potential others have. Yet great exploits find their foundation in healthy self-belief. You must believe you are fully equipped with the potential to fulfil your dreams. The gifts, talents,

---

[1]   Ecclesiastes 4:12, The Amplified Bible.

and ideas you were endowed with are customised to suit your purpose perfectly. You'll need to release that potential if you're going to fulfil your purpose. The final of the three strands is to *never give up*. It deals with one of the biggest threats to purpose: fear. It looks at the importance of passion when it comes to doing great exploits, paying the price to obtain the goal, and adhering to the call to keep going even in the face of failure, setbacks, delays, and even success.

Part I
Self-Mastery

Discovering the purpose for which you were created is the foundation for exploits. As a volunteer youth mentor, one of the most common questions young people asked me was, 'What am I supposed to do with my life?' Even grown men and women struggle with this question. For as long as the answer escapes them, they remain confused about life drifting from one day to the next without a clear sense of purpose or direction. Yet the pages of biographies, history books, newspapers, magazines, bristle with people who found direction for their lives once they connected with purposes. Their stories tell of seemingly ordinary men and women who arose with a sense of calling (passion) and accomplished more than they had dreamed possible. In chapter 1, I take a good look at the importance of connecting with the why behind your life and share a number of insights that will help you discover purpose.

People who do exploits can see their futures clearly. In chapter 2, I discuss the issue of vision and the need not only to create one, but also to ensure that it's aligned with your purpose.

Every person who does great exploits has vision. I share examples from the lives of those whose vision became the basis for their exploits. Vision has the power to transform ordinary people into extraordinary people. Having a vision empowers you to do great exploits; without one, the future perishes.

Chapter 3 highlights one of the big reasons people end up saying no to their dreams. More than actual reality, what we believe defines who we are and the boundaries of our world. It doesn't matter how capable or talented you are, self-limiting beliefs will stop you from doing the exploits you were put on earth to do. Many of us believe we're not capable of doing what we're called to do – nothing is further from the truth. A famous example is the life of a man called Moses, considered one of the greatest leaders in antiquity. He resisted the call to set his people free from the tyranny of prejudice and slavery because he believed he didn't have what it took to speak to the Egyptian rulers who enslaved them for generations. How wrong he was. Even when he had someone to do the speaking for him, Moses didn't let that person speak! He did all the speaking himself and accomplished his dream. If you have self-limiting beliefs, you're in the company of great heroes such as Moses. You can break free just like he did.

People who do great exploits tend to take personal responsibility. In chapter 4, I show that; though taking personal responsibility is a tall order, it has many great benefits. For dreams to become reality, you must take action.

Action must be preceded by the will to do them. That will is personal responsibility. Though we may have a vision, we have to take responsibility for manifesting it. We need to commit to doing what is required to create the outcomes we desire. The truth is that no one will do your exploits or fulfil your purpose for you; only you can do that. Therefore, if you want to do the great exploits you called to do, accept that you must take personal responsibility. This chapter provides numerous tips on how to do that effectively.

Negative thinking is a guaranteed way to short circuit the future. That way of thinking aborts every good plan, destroys every good intention, blocks every step you might want to take towards fulfilling your purpose. If you want to do great exploits, you should avoid negative thinking like the plague that it is. In chapter 5, I share a range of ways to overcome negative thinking and build positive and constructive thinking habits to tackle the inevitable challenges that arise while pursuing your purpose.

Doing great exploits invariably involves other people. Often, we have to persuade others to buy in to our plans or help us push our assignment forward. To do this, you need to develop your ability to influence. Influence is discussed in depth in chapter 6. There, I explore the sheer importance of communication and share a long list of ways to communicate your vision effectively with those whose help or support you need. That way, those people become willing (and even passionate) about helping you move forward.

Part II
Maximise your gifts, talents, abilities, and ideas

Part II of the book looks at potential and the fact that, you are equipped with the gifts, talents, and abilities you need to fulfil your purpose. First, we need to Recognise the potential we carry to do great exploits using the talents, gifts, and ideas we have. These are all suited to the unique purposes we're meant to fulfil. People who do great exploits are extraordinary because they step off the beaten path, rise above the norm of everyday life and make a difference for themselves and others. At some point in their lives, they become aware that they have a gift, talent, or idea that uniquely positions them to make that difference. One of the many traits such people share is *recognition* of their potential.

Chapter 7 outlines the steps needed to discover your potential. It looks at how people such as some Olympic gold medallists and others discovered their potential.

Chapter 8 acknowledges that, even if you recognise you have potential, there might be things from the past that present a challenge to achieving your potential. In this chapter, I share ways that well- known figures overcame these challenges. Beethoven experienced the slow deterioration of his hearing, which eventually led to deafness. His diagnosis came before he had composed some of his greatest musical works. Nevertheless, he struggled against these forces and became one of the greatest composers who ever lived.

The final chapter in Part II is focused on techniques for releasing potential. Potential has to be tested and tried before it is maximised for great exploits. I reference people who maximised their gifts and ideas, all of whom are still alive and doing great exploits today. In chapter 9, I provide some key methods for releasing potential.

Part III
Never give up

Part III contains four chapters: the first, chapter 10, deals with one of the most significant obstacles to doing great exploits: fear. Fear is a paralyzing force and stops talented people with vision and purpose from actually doing the things they need to do to bring about exploits.

But fear can be managed in such a way that it never stops someone from doing what they dream of doing. The good news is that everyone feels fear, even the people who do great exploits. The difference between people who do exploits and those who don't succeed is that they have made fear an ally. They use fear as motivation to spur them to creativity; they allow fear to drive them towards solutions rather than defeat them. Not only have they learned to master their fear, some even refer to fear as their friend.

Chapter 11 shows that passion is as important to doing great exploits and fulfilling your purpose as having a vision of what you want to achieve. Without passion, you won't be tenacious. You'll be more likely to give up pursuing your purpose if you lose your passion. Through the ups and downs on the road to purpose, passion is the fire that can go out. The fire – enthusiasm for your dream – has to be fanned and sustained if you're going to complete the course of your race.

The principle discussed in chapter 12 is that whatever you're seeking to accomplish in life will demand payment up front. Payment is usually made through consistent and correct action underpinned by dogged tenacity. Many of the people who do great exploits worked for years, paying the price in obscurity. Their success might appear suddenly and seemingly out of nowhere to the outsider, but it took them a combination of time and hard work – decades in some cases – before they achieved success worthy of celebration. The great exploits done by people usually mask the years of effort, dedication, and sacrifice that went into making their accomplishments possible. If you want to live a life filled with great exploits, resolve to pay the price required. In chapter 12, I provide guidance to accomplish these sorts of exploits.

People who do great exploits take a long-term view of life. Each day provides a fresh opportunity to move forward and make progress. They operate from a premise of optimism, even when things are challenging or not going the way they had planned. An important key to their success is that they don't give up; whatever life throws at them, they find a way to keep going. In chapter 13, lessons are shared regarding how to be tenacious and how to cope with failures and setbacks so they don't derail you from your purpose. But we must be mindful that success can also be the cause of stagnation.

Do Great Exploits: Saying Yes to Your Dreams When it's easier to say no is written for those who want to discover and then fulfil the purpose for their lives. I hope you find something in the pages of this book that will help you move forward in answering the call.

Part I

As you think, so you are.

Self-Mastery

Purpose
Vision
Belief
Personal responsibility
Positive thinking
Influence

1

People who do great exploits connect with why they're here

Live, not just your whole life, but each moment, on purpose.

Packed full of cheering students, the university sports auditorium buzzed with excitement the day of the intercollegiate basketball final. The players were on the court warming up in a pre-game match. All along, Garvin Brown, a well-known centre from the visiting team, had been keeping up a steady stream of pep talk directed at his fellow teammates – while trying to intimidate and distract the home team players. The moment Brown saw Wayne Coors, the home team star shooting guard, heading unto the court, he shouted, 'Hey Wayne, go put on a bigger shirt so we can see your number better!' Coors, glanced at him, but gave no reply.

When Coors hit the court, the temperature increased. He was on point for all his passes scoring 100% on jump shots from the peripheries. The crowd roared each time, chanting his name. In the end his team won 78-62, with Coors scoring a game high of 34 points. When they got back to the benches, Coors' name was still being chanted from the bleachers. It filled the auditorium like thunder. Coors turned to Garvin Brown and said, 'I didn't come here for a fashion show.'

An important difference between people who do great exploits and those who don't is that people in the former group know exactly what they're here to do. Successful people understand that there's a correlation between knowing purpose and doing exploits.

Finding out your *why* can lead to a life of fruitfulness and impact beyond your wildest dreams. People who do great exploits discover their unique purpose in life and then order their lives around it. They know that they were born to do certain things; and with that knowledge comes focus and energy to get those things done. If you want to live a life of great exploits, you must connect with why you're here.

Purpose and great exploits

It doesn't matter which walk of life they desire to make their mark in, people like Wayne Coors do exploits because they know their purpose. Purpose is central to doing exploits. Whether its business, science, charity, art, ministry, medicine, or some other field, people who do exploits have a strong conviction about what they were born to do. That conviction is a sense that they are called to do a specific thing; and they are clear about what that thing is. Indeed, that call becomes their reason for living.

Discovering purpose inspires people to take action that results in exploits. Famous examples are Nelson Mandela and Gandhi, both of which campaigned to change laws that revolutionised countries and lifted people's lives. Mother Teresa started missions around the world that met the needs of countless people in poverty. Some, such as Louis Pasteur, locked themselves away in laboratories for many years, experimenting and searching for cures to diseases. Others, like Rick Warren, planted churches that changed the shape of communities. Billy Graham began a ministry that impacted the world. And then there're the types like Sir Richard Branson, who started businesses that changed industries. Mary Kay Ash pioneered a great business idea that created opportunities for women to take control of their own financial future. Steve Jobs and Bill Gates created technological inventions that altered the way we communicate and connect with our world. Chris Gardner, in his *Pursuit of Happyness* blazed a path out of poverty and now empowers others to do the same. All these people are humans like you and me. Many of them started out with less than some of us have. One thing they each discovered at some point in life (which so many have not yet discovered) is the knowledge of their specific purpose in life.

What each of these people, and others like them, have in common is that they signed up to a purpose they considered bigger than themselves. Purpose focused their hearts and minds on a bigger picture. While others go to their graves never having found meaning in life, people who do great exploits discover meaning in service to a compelling purpose in life. For them, the meaning of life entails providing some type of benefit to others: family, community, countries, or humanity as a whole.

Why you need to discover your purpose

To achieve anything great in life, you must begin with purpose. President Kennedy said, 'Efforts and courage are not enough without purpose and direction.' Effort and courage are both necessary to do exploits (as we'll see in later chapters), but if your effort isn't channelled towards a predetermined purpose, it will be wasted. King Solomon, said to be the wisest man who ever lived, put it this way in the book of Proverbs: 'Ignorant zeal is worthless.'[2] You can put in

---

[2] Proverbs 19:2, The Message Bible

a lot of time, energy and effort doing many things, but are they the right things? Will what you're doing now lead to the outcomes you desire? Knowing your purpose will help you to effectively choose what you ought to do and when.

There are several reasons why knowing your purpose is important. Here are some of them:

1. Knowing your purpose brings clarity

When I was a voluntary youth mentor, one of the most common questions young people asked was as follows: 'What am I supposed to do with my life?' Even grown men and women struggle with this question. For as long as the answer eludes them, they remain confused and drift from one day to the next. Many stand on the basketball court of life focusing on their tee shirt because that's what someone else told them they should do; however, they ought to be in the thick of their game scoring goals. They get into difficulties because they aren't clear about why they're on the court of life in the first place and so have no idea how they should spend their time and energy. As a result, they spend these precious resources in the wrong way or on unfruitful pursuits. Many things easily distract them: whether good or not so good. Whereas clarity of purpose safeguards us from the many distractions life throws at us.

Purpose has become a hot topic for many businesses in recent years. Organizational research shows that, when employees have an understanding of the purpose of the company they work for, they become clear about how to align their actions towards achieving that purpose. Such organizations tend to do exploits in their respective markets. On the other hand, employees who don't know their company's purpose find it much more difficult to decide on the most appropriate actions they need to be taking. Therefore, they are less productive and their organisations perform worse than their market rivals. When you know your purpose, you better understand yourself and why you're here. It enables you to order your activities in a way that will produce the kind of outcomes you want to achieve in life.

On the other hand, not knowing what you want to achieve makes it impossible to know what you're meant to be doing. That results in confusion, chaos, and frustration. Dissatisfaction with the outcomes achieved in life is often rooted in a lack of clarity about purpose. That lack of clarity can lead to a life spent going round in circles, lost time and wasted opportunities for people. But, if you know your purpose, it gives you direction and you can then effectively maximise the use of your time, resources and every appropriate opportunity that comes your way. Thus, you will be more likely to achieve the outcomes that you desire.

2. Knowing your purpose gives direction

Imagine you saw a friend wandering down a long road as you drive past. You stop and offer them a lift. They accept and climb in. You then ask, 'Where are you headed?' But they reply, 'It doesn't matter much. Just drop me off anywhere you think is best.' People without purpose are a bit like that. Because they don't know where they want to go in life, it doesn't matter much which direction they go in. My father, who has one of the strongest work ethics I've ever come across, describes them as bottles in the sea. Such bottles are adrift, bobbing passively in the waves. The winds and currents carry them wherever they will. People without direction are carried along by life wherever life wills.

On the other hand, the pages of the biographies, newspapers, magazine features bristle with people who found direction for their lives once they had connected with their purpose. Ordinary men and women arose with their newfound sense of calling and accomplished more than they ever dreamed possible.

7

For example, Saul, who later became Paul the apostle, found an entirely new direction in life after he discovered his purpose. Until then, he went around killing and persecuting Christians. After a life changing experience in which he got a revelation of his life's purpose, Paul made a huge U-turn in life. He went on to pen many books of the bible's New Testament, advanced the movement of a fledgling new faith, which started out with a few hundred and now reportedly has a third of the world's population as followers today. Purpose turned a killer into a preacher. Paul went from fruitlessness to incredible fruitfulness when he found direction through purpose. All this he did despite some extremely difficult challenges in his life.

3. Knowing your purpose keeps you focused on the big picture

Life is full of distractions. Plus, it comes with inevitable challenges, setbacks, and disappointments. I've found that those with a strong sense of purpose find a way to handle distractions as well as any difficulties they face effectively because they keep their eyes fixed on the big picture. Much like Wayne Coors, the star player, in the story at the start of this chapter, they don't take their eye off the ball or the goal they have in sight no matter what's happening around them. This is often the reason why they're able to reach the finish line when others fall by the wayside and drop out of the race. The obstacles and distractions they encounter along the course of their race do not derail them because they learn to focus on the end goal. When distractions arise, they don't lose their focus. When they meet with opposition, they stand their ground. The prize set before them is of far greater worth than the price of any current sacrifices or hardships.

4. Knowing your purpose can prolong your life

Everyone wants to know that his or her life matters, that it counted for something while here on earth. We want to be able to measure the effect our lives had through some difference we made; otherwise, what would have been the point? People who discover their answers to these questions live extraordinary lives. Doing great exploits becomes a habit for them. This sense of having something to live for is so critical to human beings that research shows that people who have a sense of purpose live longer. There are research studies, which show that people who live for a purpose that is greater than themselves tend to be healthier and enjoy longer lives than those who simply drift along in life. Such people, when followed up, are found to have established effective habits. They often take better care of themselves - because they have something to live for. People who pursue a purpose they're passionate about, enjoy increased longevity. Some studies even show that living for purpose has a positive effect on brain functioning. The evidence powerfully supports the hypothesis that having a higher purpose is crucial to life, impacting the body *and* the mind. Connecting with our purpose prolongs our lives.

Further studies discuss findings that people with purpose tended to do different things compared with people who didn't have a purpose they were working to achieve. For example, women with a higher purpose are more likely to get a mammogram than their counterparts who lack that higher purpose.

Healthy behaviours aside, people who have a higher purpose engage in many other activities that people without a higher purpose don't engage in. While the latter are living each day as it comes, individuals in the former group do exploits, which take them ever closer to the fulfilment of a higher purpose. Their lives are productive and fruitful. Some prefer to believe that these types are winners because they're blessed; because they have a special helping of divine favour and grace that makes things work out for them more often. In reality, what a person sows is what he or she will reap. A fruitful and productive life of exploits springs from knowing one's purpose in life and sowing your life into achieving it through consistent and correct action. In other words … work!

People do better in life because they have a higher purpose in mind that they are living for. This single commitment to consistently engaging in a specific set of actions towards a predetermined purpose is what accounts for the outcomes these people achieve in life.

5. Living your purpose makes you effective and creates a life of impact

It is the glory of kings is to search out a matter.[3]

Man was born to have measurable impact in the world. People who do great exploits grasp this principle and habitually put it to work. If you want to do great exploits you need to discover why you were born. You need to discover the hidden resources, both in yourself as well as externally that can be harnessed and utilised to have an impact on the world around you. Discovering these resources is discussed some more later on in this chapter and in the chapters on potential.

Great exploits are linked to discovering and living out purpose. You, too, have your own range of gifts, talents, abilities, and experiences to bring solutions to your world. But in a world of over seven billion people, it's tempting to wonder whether you can make any difference. We wonder whether what we have to offer is of any real value. Does it really matter that I am here or that you are here? Does it matter whether you fulfil your purpose or not? It's easy to think that there are more talented and gifted people out there – that they are far better connected, have better financial backing, have greater ideas. They are taller and better looking and better at communicating and more educated. It's tempting to believe that the world doesn't need what you have. But such ideas are more catastrophic than we realise.

Some creatures in the animal kingdom provide us a good illustration of the purpose and relevance everyone has in the world. For example wolves and beavers have been described as *ecosystem engineers*. It's

---

[3]   Proverbs 25:2, The Amplified Bible

simply another way of saying that they are world changers in their own realm.

Their presence in the wild is transformational. They have impact because when they unleash their unique set of instincts, talents, and abilities – plus the skills they acquired through learning and experience they bring ecological and environmental balance to the physical world. For example without wolves, deer overrun some natural areas. Their population will multiply unchecked. When these high numbers of deer graze they turn vast grasslands into barren wastelands. Most other creatures then migrate because they can't survive in the area. However, when wolves are present, the deer numbers remain in balance and they curtail their grazing territory to avoid the wolves.

In the world of ecological study, this is called 'trophic cascade'. It happens when an animal at the top of the food chain establishes the right balance that allows many species to thrive. Wolves are one type of creature that possess this transformational power. The knock on effect is that as deer numbers remain healthy, many plant species are allowed to grow up from the ground. Trees and foliage flourish. All sorts of birds then come and occupy them. The roots of the trees and grasses stabilise the soil and keep it from being eroded. This affects the rivers and waterways passing through the land. Riverbanks don't collapse as often. As a result beavers come and build their homes on the banks. Their presence in turn allows for water living creatures to thrive. As wolves kill off some deer and leave behind their carrion, bears arrived to feast on the leftovers.

On and on the cycle goes: natural areas are transformed into places that teem with life and variety. They become havens where many different species of animal can live. And all this because wolves do what they were created to do. They execute their purpose. By doing so, they make room for others. They make it possible for other creatures, further down the food chain, to have habitats where they can thrive and carry out their own unique purpose in the ecosystem of life.

This trophic cascade is the service wolves bring, not just to the animal kingdom but also to humans, whose survival is dependent on an environment that is in balance.

You and I are called to be world changers in our own realms. We're called to trigger our own transformational 'trophic cascades' in the arenas where we're called to have impact.

By making a difference in our places of work, families, neighbourhoods, and communities, we alter the environment. You don't have to try to do or be anything that we're not. To discover who you are, connect with the power of your potential and be willing release that potential – whatever it might take.

There may be over seven billion people in the world, but not one of them is like you. Within you is deposited a combination of gifts, talents, and abilities that, when released through your unique personality, produces fruit other people need. The world is crying out for the particular gifts and talents you carry. We each have a responsibility to bring what we have been given to make a difference in the world. What you have counts. The unique combination of your gifts, personality and experiences matters. Without wolves the natural world would cease to flourish and a host of animal communities would perish. When we do not fulfil purpose, the world suffers.

Living without purpose results in a tragic waste. It's the number one reason some people do not do the exploits they wish they could. If you never discover your purpose, that potential remains trapped and no one benefits. Some of the fruit of our gifts include products, services, works of art, charitable acts, and businesses. Some people were created with the gift of song such that their voices can move others emotionally, releasing them from sorrow or stress and filling them with peace. Others are great organisers. The release of their talent creates order, causing systems to run smoothly, decreasing risks, and safeguarding the future of households, organisations, or even countries. Joseph, in the Bible, was that sort of person. Although a slave, he brought order to his master, Potiphar's house. When falsely accused and thrown in prison, Joseph still found avenues to apply is talents and gifts, becoming the chief aid and advisor the governor of the prison. At the right time, his gifts were brought to the attention where it really counted – the king himself. That got him his release and positioned him at the pinnacle of government. In Egypt he was second in power, with just Pharaoh above him. He continued to apply his talents and abilities and serve with the diligence and accountability that he began nurturing way back when he was obscure - a mere servant in a private estate.

People who do exploits are like that. They don't despise, or take lightly, their small beginnings. Small beginnings are not an indicator or where you can end up. They do not prescribe the future. You want to be great? You want to rise through the ranks of your organisation? Then mind your own business – work on yourself. Focus on developing and expanding your abilities, skills, knowledge. Strive for excellence and distinguish yourself as the person who is sound.

Some people are gifted with an ability to relate to children and become successful teachers. They're able to capture a child's imagination with their creativity and communicate so that the child learns and develops successfully. There's no shortage of talent on earth. Abundance is reflected everywhere. Our gifts, talents, and abilities can only serve us so far. When we connect them to purpose, that's when we step into the abundant life and our lives make a difference on earth. It's the beginning of a life that has meaning, adds value, and makes a difference.

How to discover your purpose

There are many common ways people can discover their purpose. For most people, it's a collection of clues that forms a pattern, which points towards their future. Some of these clues are listed here:

1. What attracts your interest?

One of the most common ways people find purpose in life is feeling drawn to a subject. This can manifest in a strong desire to learn that subject or find work in that field. Others are drawn to a problem and feel passionate about solving it. For example, Mother Teresa experienced a compulsion to do something about street children in the developing world.

The reason people are powerfully drawn to a particular issue is that they were born to address it in some way. Within them exists the solution to the problem. It's like the force that exists between a magnet and metals; particular problems draw particular people. For instance, I have several friends who are scientists and engineers. When I listen to them talk about their experiments or some new breakthrough in their area, I'm more excited about their excitement and passion for their discovery than I am about the problem that was solved! That's because I'm not wired for science or mathematics. But I find pleasure in the fact that my friend is fully enjoying being who they were created to be and fulfilling purpose. I know that their work matters greatly, even though it doesn't fire up my imagination or get the blood running through my veins. I'm drawn to different problems and flow naturally when I'm solving those.

To discover your purpose in life, ask yourself, *Which problem do I want to solve that will make a difference for other people?*

2. Purpose will unfold when you strive to always do your best and attune yourself to the needs around you

This is a very common way that people discover their purpose in life. A famous author and philosopher, Vicktor Frankl, found purpose in very difficult circumstances. He was taken as a prisoner during the reign of Hitler and was imprisoned in a Nazi camp. In the camp, he witnessed and experienced all kinds of atrocities and thought a lot about the impact of the harsh realities of the camp on the prisoners. When he became free, Frankl wrote books about his experiences, which gave powerful insights into the human need for meaning. Frankl's books continue to challenge and inspire millions of people around the world.

I hope you never find yourself in a situation where you're enslaved like Joseph was or imprisoned like Viktor Frankl. But it's not uncommon that people find themselves in less extreme situations where they have little or no alternatives. In such cases, they can work to become excellent people where they are, that in itself represents a worthy purpose. If you happen to identify a need that resonates with you, why not see what you can do about it? I know of people who set up orphanages in developing countries, set up charities here in the UK because of a need that they personally identified with. To discover purpose train yourself to be attuned to the needs around you that you could do something about.

3. Identify your gifts and talents

Many of the people who do exploits begin to manifest their particular talents early on. While in junior school, Usain Bolt, the Olympic gold medallist and record holder, was playing cricket when his physical education teacher noticed his talent for sprinting. He was encouraged to try track and field. By the time he got to high school, his natural talent was so obvious that it attracted the interest of a former Olympiad, who began to coach him.

Each person has particular gifts and talents. A gift or talent is some ability you have that naturally shines through. For example you may have the ability to sing better than the average person, or do numerical tasks or even the ability to bring joy and encouragement, through your personality, to others – or all the above! Whatever your gifts and talents, they are given to you to use, don't let them go to waste, use them! If you haven't already done so, you should become clear about your abilities and begin to think about how you can use them to have an impact where it matters most. These form the basis for doing exploits in life.

As you'll see in the chapters on potential, our talents and gifts play a huge role in the fulfilment of our purpose.

4. Find your passion; discover your purpose

My mother retired early after twenty-five years as a music teacher in schools. Although she was a great teacher and mentor to many of her students, some of whom are still in touch with her, she had a passion in her heart to do something else. Therefore, when the opportunity to take an early retirement package presented itself, she grabbed the chance with both hands.

All along she'd pursued gardening as a hobby. My mom has an amazing green thumb. As children we always had a beautiful yard to play in, with hedges and pockets of colourful, tropical shrubbery and trees. She had a way of creating landscapes, even in small gardens, that were a botanical feast for the eyes. She won prizes for plants and landscapes in competitions and had articles written about her gift of transforming wild spaces into botanical havens in the newspaper.

Mom took her retirement fund and started a horticulture business. In little time, she began doing exploits, winning contracts from private individuals to transform their gardens, plus commercial and public organisations to do interior and exterior landscaping. Mom's contacts and business grew and grew. It was hard work, but doors just seemed to open up. I think that though she was a good teacher, her true passion lay in horticulture; and in her business, she had found her true purpose. She's also passionate about music. In chapter 11 I tell the story of the great exploits she did taking 80 people (70 of them where her students), who had never travelled before, on a performing tour in Canada. Mom is a great inspiration when it comes to finding purpose through knowing your passion and utilising your gifts in service to God and others.

People who do great exploits are passionate about purpose. Their passion drives them forward, giving them a compelling urge to keep searching until they find what they were born to do.

To discover your purpose, ask yourself, *What am I truly passionate about?*

5. Your purpose is suited to your personality

As a young person, I attended church. I listened to sermons that said, 'God's got a great plan for your life. You need to find your purpose!' I had dreams and desires for my life, but I was half-convinced that they weren't what he had in mind for me. My secret fear was that if I really opened myself up and asked him what his purpose was for my life, I would end up having to become someone I was not.

For instance, I thought, *Maybe I'd be sent on a mission to some remote island where Christians are a staple food for cannibals.* I imagined I'd be burned at the stake like Joan of Arc, if not slow roasted over a fire to provide meat for hungry, heathen bellies. Even if I weren't martyred, the best I could hope for would be to live in a grass hut with no running water or electricity and the maddening whine of mosquitoes for music!

Such a life was completely at odds with the person I thought I was. Thus, whenever I heard a sermon or happened to read anything about purpose I shrunk back. I was afraid of finding out what the purpose for my life might be.

Yet my assumption back then only showed how little I knew about this topic (or the diversity of mission fields, and the work missionaries do, for that matter!). The reality is that specific people are drawn to specific works.

I saw things very differently when I finally had one of those moments. You know the ones where something that has been bothering you suddenly becomes clear and makes perfect sense. This happened one day when I was looking at a beautiful magnolia tree that was just outside the window of my bedroom. The magnolias were in full bloom, their scent filling the summer air with sweet perfume. I could see the sunlight reflecting off the leaves, and it struck me that all things in nature are connected and interrelated. Everything from a tiny ant to a great elephant to the moon to the stars – they're all interdependent. Each aspect has its unique role to play in the delicate balance of life. That day, I realised that everything was made fit for its specific purpose; and in the simple fulfilment of that purpose, it thrives.

Whales never clamber up a beach and head down the road to find a job. Whales don't try to be something they're not. These magnificent creatures tend to stay in the water, swimming the depths of the ocean. There's a reason for that: that is what they were created to do. It's why they fascinate us and we spend millions of pounds and dollars on research to discover more about their ways. There's so much beauty when something functions the way it was intended to function. There's so much harmony as it makes its unique contribution to life, like a piece of a puzzle that fits perfectly into God's big idea. When any piece is missing or in the wrong place, the big picture looks out of whack. It suffers because of it. If you're called to be a corner piece in the puzzle, be a corner piece. If you're called to be a centre piece, don't try to be an edge piece. Likewise, as intelligent creatures, monkeys never climb down from their trees, put on suits, and try to run corporations. The simple reason is that they were not created for that. Only humans fear connecting with the purpose for which they were born and doubt that it could be the very thing they dream of doing.

I don't think I am alone in assuming the worst when I thought of this thing called purpose. So many of us think that, if we hand over the reins to God, he's going to do something really weird with us – we'll be forced into being something we're not and doing things we don't want to do. Like the whale, we'll become fish out of water. This couldn't be further from the truth. The reality is that you are who you are and your impact is create by who you are. Purpose is fulfilled through your uniqueness, often ignited and driven by the sum of your experiences, gifts, abilities, and everything built into you. Through their lives and everything that makes them who they are, you can fulfil your purpose. There isn't anything you're called to do that will be contrary to your deepest longings and knowledge of yourself. Sometimes the way in to purpose, may seem strange, even distasteful to you, just like it was to Joseph the slave. But even that is part of the journey that may be required to get you to where you're going.

Trust your instincts, that inner voice that has constantly nudged you in a particular direction. Just like Garvin trying to tell Wayne what he should do at the start of the chapter, there are many other voices trying to tell us what we should do or which direction we should be heading in. They are not necessarily right. They often have their own agenda just like Garvin did, when he tried to distract Wayne. But if Wayne hadn't already formed a solid connection with why he was standing in a packed auditorium holding a basketball, Garvin would have been able to distract him from the issue at hand. Knowing your *Why* in life will enable you to remain focused and do great exploits. Trust the voice inside you. Your purpose is written in your DNA – only you can hear what your spirit is telling you.

6. *Listen to feedback from others*

Having said all that, the voices of others can confirm what you are hearing on the inside. Throughout school and university, different teachers told me I would write, but that wasn't really a new idea for me. I had discovered my passion for writing long before any of them told me that. I also received prophetic words at different stages of life about writing. Various people began to notice my ability in this area and encouraged me to develop my natural ability. This confirmed that I was on the right track. What others are saying should always resonate with what you already know about yourself based on your passion, your natural inclination, your talents, experience, and so forth.

Reflection on exploits

Do you know what you're here for? Have you discovered your purpose? All the people mentioned in this chapter discovered a purpose they were passionate about and then lived it out. In the rest of this book, there are dozens of great examples of those whose lives have made a difference because they discovered their purpose. It led them on to do exploits. Like them, you'll need to start at the beginning. Find out who you are and what you were created for. To do great exploits, begin by connecting with why you're here.

2

People who do great exploits can see their future

Janice Wright, a business woman who I've heard speak several times at events says, 'Vision is about thinking big while doing a host of small things. Keeping your overall vision in sight helps you make sure all the small things are heading in the right direction.' Wright knows about the importance of making sense of all the small parts so that they contribute to the bigger picture in an organised way. Her interest has been digital technologies for over two decades and she speaks on how businesses can organise and prepare themselves to exploit the on line revolution. That quote sums up the beauty of having a vision that is aligned to your purpose and guides all the small things you do every day.

Life will have us running around doing countless small things. But a life of meaning and purpose, a life of great exploits, is one in which those small things fit into a predetermined, bigger plan – in other words, a vision.

You might have heard the story about three bricklayers who were working on a wall beside each other. It supports Wright's view well. The story goes something like this:

A passerby came up to one of the bricklayers and asked him, 'What are you doing?'

'What does it look like I'm doing?' He replied sarcastically. 'I'm laying bricks!'

The man turned to the next bricklayer and asked him the same question. The second bricklayer replied, 'Can't you see what I'm doing, buddy? I'm building a wall.'

Finally, the passerby turned to the third bricklayer and asked, 'And what are you doing?'

The last bricklayer exclaimed, 'I'm building a great cathedral for God!' Vision helps us make sense of what we're doing and why we're doing it. Without a vision you may be doing many small things – laying bricks or building walls – without knowing the purpose behind it. It could turn out that the way you laid the bricks, or the length of the wall, isn't what was needed for a cathedral. Without a vision of the end product, you risk wasting precious resources, time, energy, and money doing the wrong things. People who do exploits always have an end product in mind before they take action. They are people with vision who are on a mission. They convert their vision and mission into plans, and they break down their plans into goals.

What having a vision does for ordinary people

César Castellanos, now the author of several books, including *Dream and You Will Win the World*, began pastoring a small group of people. Within a year, the church had grown to six hundred members. Today, Mission Charsimatica Internacional (MCI) is one of the largest churches in South America – there are over two hundred thousand members and forty five thousand cell groups in the city of Bogotá. The discipleship programme, which he teaches to ministries around the world, is the framework for his cell church. The inspiration for the programme came from a clear vision of pastoring 'multitudes', which Pastor Castellanos says God gave him in 1983.

A vision is a dream. It's a mental picture you develop of an ideal situation you want to accomplish in the future. You can create a vision for anything: marriage, career, business, ministry, or physical health, for example. Vision isn't all you need to do great exploits, but great exploits can't be achieved without vision. Dreams are accomplished by the many exploits, big and small, that must be done to fulfil them. The small things that Wright talks about make up the exploits, and they produce the dream. Once you have a vision or dream, you can direct your time, effort, and other resources to achieve it.

Dreams are what transport ordinary people from where they are to where they can be, from who they are to who they can be. People perish without a vision. They remain as and where they are, and their purpose in life goes unfulfilled.

Make it a big one!

The Microsoft founders had a big vision of a computer in every home when they started the company. In the UK, this ambitious vision is close to being a reality (if we use Internet access as a proxy for access to a computer). In 2015, 86 per cent of households (22.5 million households) had Internet access, which was up from 57 per cent in 2006[4]. In developing countries, the picture varies widely but,

---

[4]   Office of National Statistics. (2015). Statistical bulletin: Internet Access - Households and Individuals: 2015. Use of the internet by adults in Great Britain including mobile access, activities, shopping, security and storage. [online] Available at: Http://www.ons.gov.uk/ons/rel/rdit2/internet-access—households- and-individuals/2015/stb-ia-2015.html. [Accessed 20 Jul. 2016].

as the years go by, there has been a steady increase in Internet access. No doubt the founders of the technology giant wouldn't have fully imagined the scale of impact having such a vision would have in the world. Vision can set you up for success beyond your wildest dreams. It gives you a focus, something to live for and work towards. It's the finish line in the race set before you. Once you know it's there, it engages you like nothing else can. For as long as you choose to focus on it, it will order everything you do so that you can reach it.

Some people have a vision of travelling to the moon and achieve it. Others have a vision of travelling round the world and manage to visit many countries of the world. Those with no vision have never travelled outside their hometown or country. Even if you don't fulfil your vision, you are still better off having one because you're likely to accomplish some of it.

Why have a vision?

I hope I've managed to convince you about the merits of creating a vision if you want to become someone who does great exploits. But if not, here are some additional reasons you should develop one that's aligned with the purpose for your life.

1. If you can see it, you can do it.

Given that each of us has a calling in our lives, yet so many do not even approach it (and fewer still fulfil it), there must be reasons why. I believe that one of the common reasons is that some of us doubt our dreams are possible. Not believing a dream is possible, makes it easier for some to say *no* to the call to do the exploits the dream demands (see chapter 3).

It's true that knowing your calling and actually doing it are two different things. Knowing what you are supposed to do and believing that you can do it are also two very different things. Again and again, however, people who have done great exploits have shared the secret that anyone can do exploits, including ordinary people like you and me.

One key asset that helps create a belief that you can do something is being able to see yourself do it. If you can imagine it, it means you can actually do it. The more you hold a picture of your dream or vision in your heart, the more convinced you become that it can be accomplished. You may need to go through some training, or experiment, or work hard, but you can accomplish what you see if you are willing.

Sometimes, when I hear kids say, 'I can't do that,' I suspect they're really saying, 'It's too hard. I don't want to put in the effort (or sacrifice) it's going to take.' In their hearts, they're thinking, *I'd rather watch TV than do the research needed to write that essay.* Or, *I'd rather be out playing than take that piano lesson! These swimming classes, these chores are too hard!*

I once mentored a teenaged girl who grew up in foster homes and was at the age where she was leaving the care system. My role was to support her in transitioning from the care system, into independent life as a young adult. She was enrolled in a local college but wasn't enjoying it as much as she thought she would. I asked her what the issue was. She said one of the teachers didn't like her and she felt he was always picking on her and embarrassing her in front of the class. That got me concerned and I asked for more details. As it turned out, this particular teacher taught the first class of everyday which started at 9am. However, she often got there after 9, sometimes 5 minutes past or even 20 minutes past!

Each time she arrived late and tried to slip in quietly, the teacher made a point of drawing attention to her. When I'd confirmed that she wasn't late because of the bus or some other logical reason, I asked her what time she woke up in the morning. She said she often overslept. 'But you have an alarm clock,' I pointed out. 'Don't you set the alarm?' 'Yes,' she replied. 'But when it rings I'm still tired, so I switch it off and go back to sleep. It's really hard getting up at 7 in the morning!' I could hardly believe what I was hearing. 'My dear,' I told her. 'When the alarm goes off in the morning, most of us want to switch it off and go back to sleep, but responsible people don't. You're always telling me you're an adult and want to be independent. Well adults get up and do what they have to do, whether it's hard or not.' It was a little funny. As adults, we sometimes do the same thing: rather than do what's needed to do great exploits, we say, 'It's too hard!' and switch off. People prefer to settle back into the default position of what's comfortable for them and then don't do exploits.

The fact is we are more capable than we think. Or perhaps it's truer to say that we are more capable than we are willing to put in the work to demonstrate!

2. Vision inspires discipline

> Where there is no vision [...] the people are unrestrained;
> but happy is he who keeps the law.[5]

King Solomon said that, without a vision, people tend to live life without direction. Their approach to life is an anything-goes-anytime approach. Decisions are made based on what's convenient, easy, or pleasant rather than what's necessary for a good future. Without direction, any path is taken; people end up anywhere. But this approach to life is the complete opposite of the way people who do exploits live.

Some young people I've spoken to said they wanted to be like Richard Branson or Bill Gates. When I asked why, they said they want to be rich. I asked why they wanted to be rich. Their view was that rich people like Branson and Gates are free to do anything they want,

---

[5]   Proverbs 29:18, The Amplified Bible

whenever they want – they don't have to listen to anyone. They then went on to list what some of those things might be. The list included sleeping in late every day, not having to go to work, and having staff they could give orders to. This was their perception of what it meant to be a rich business person!

I explained to them that business people are usually hard working people. It's not uncommon for them to work every day, often from early in the morning to late at night. The majority of them possess a strong sense of responsibility, which drives them and guides every decision they make. They bear the weight of providing jobs for their employees who rely on their business for their livelihood.

Furthermore, these people surround themselves with advisors. They are always keen to be taught something new. I read about a famous preacher who, after hiring a team of advisors, walked into his first meeting with them and announced, 'If at anytime I start to know more than any of you, you're fired!' And then he left the room. Effective leaders surround themselves with people who have expertise they don't have. That way, they learn from them. People who do great exploits in their chosen field value listening to other people – not just their advisors, but ordinary people who use their products and services.

People who do great exploits are usually very disciplined, methodical, and precise people. They live lives according to a predetermined vision, which guides their decisions and activities each day. Time is valued highly by them, and they do not waste it. People who do great exploits do not live unrestrained lives because they have a compelling vision that they have held for a long time and remained committed to living out every day. Sacrificial service to that vision has brought them to the level of success they have accomplished.

Their willingness to sacrifice their pleasures to their cause is what sets them apart from the people who do not do exploits.

One of the wealthiest men in the world is reported to still live in the same house he bought long before he accumulated his vast wealth. He seems to have no appetite for expensive toys or luxury cars. Despite his status as a billionaire, he is known for his frugality and love of simplicity.

I believe the key to such a life of restraint lies in loving what he does. Pursuing his vision for the company he founded, keeps him focused on what really matters. Because he enjoys running his business, he doesn't feel any need to escape. We'll look at the power of passion in a later chapter. For people like these, the passionate pursuit of their purpose provides them with pleasure, fun, and all the excitement they need. Therefore, instead of ever wanting to avoid hard work, they throw themselves into it. They don't need to spend lots of money and time on distractions, relaxation, and other ways to escape the misery of working at something they don't love. Their passion for what they do goes some way to creating that restraint naturally.

3. Vision transforms purpose into action, revealing the direction of all the small things you need to do great exploits

By the end of the decade, we will put a man on the moon.
John F. Kennedy

Following a speech by Kennedy in 1962, which included the statement about putting a man on the moon, the US space programme went full throttle. President Kennedy challenged Americans to see America as a leader in the space race with the superpower Russia, which was already making huge strides in space exploration. Kennedy sowed the vision that the US could land a man on the Moon before the end of the decade, before the Russians. The vision galvanised one of the greatest mobilizations of resources and work in US history. Huge amounts of resources were channelled into a full programme of training, research, and development, and the right workforce and saw several shuttles built and missions flown into space in the ensuing years.

By July of 1969, in line with Kennedy's vision, astronauts Neil Armstrong and Buzz Aldrin flew the first manned moon-landing mission in the famous Apollo 11 space shuttle. Armstrong poignantly summed up his experience of standing on the moon with the following timeless words: 'That's one small step for man, one giant leap for mankind.'

Kennedy's defining of a clear vision compelled the US government to make plans and take action to make it happen. Vision triggers action. It translates purpose into a discernable shape and then animates and mobilises you. Your vision will enable you to become clear about which activities, resources, help, and people you need in order to make your dream happen.

3. Vision gives the present pain meaning and purpose

For those who do great exploits, the prize or vision have in mind becomes the motivation for everything they do. Each day, they live a life which is restrained by the boundaries of purpose, denying themselves many of the pleasures, distractions, and comforts that people who do not do exploits always choose. There's an internationally recognised financial guru who even relinquished the basic human need for shelter, sleeping in his car while he built up his business. A well-known film maker as did the same. Others went hungry in times of voluntary and involuntary fasting. Whatever the cost, they committed themselves to go through whatever hardship they had to go through to establish their vision. In other words, they made their life an offering. They were fully persuaded that their vision was worth the pain they endured. People who do great exploits are willing to pay the price that their vision demands. Paying the price is discussed in greater depth in chapter 12.

Others, including actors, film-makers, and authors endured trials and hardships for the sake of fulfilling their dreams. They were so determined to make their vision a reality that their difficulties and setbacks didn't deter them. For example a now famous playwright and filmmaker saw his first musical debut to an audience of fewer than thirty people and run for about one week. The pain of disappointment didn't stop him from trying again. He sometimes lived out of his car in the early days of starting in the business. Though very difficult, people like him could endure hardships because they were convinced they were on their way to realising their dream.

4. Vision will train you

Pursuing a vision trains you for success. The bigger the vision the more demanding it will be to achieve it. Pursuing a vision changes you. Meeting its demands stretches you. It takes you out of your comfort zone. When you're in the presence of someone who does great exploits, you'll notice that there's something different about them. They have a certain posture. They're confident, bold, decisive, patient, skilled, clear-headed, and effective executors. Here's a secret: they weren't born that way. They became like that on their way to accomplishing their dreams. Those traits are hard won through experience, the fire of trial and opposition, setback and disappointment, failure and mistakes. Such experiences, as you'll see in Part III, are all part of becoming a successful person. Working towards a vision prepares you for success.

To do exploits you have to be willing to change, to lose sight of yourself and do away with the way of life you lived before you had a vision. Being flexible and making the necessary sacrifices are all part of the price of achieving your vision. But the prize set before you is worth it.

You need a season of preparation to do the exploits that will fulfil your purpose. Vision is your trainer. It's a picture of your future that should inspire you, creating a drive within, to pursue that future. As you pursue it, you develop the ability to actually take possession of it. This was the case for people like Mother Teresa, Mandela, Ghandi, scientists, inventors, business people, athletes – anyone who has made their mark in their field. It is still the case for everyone who has a vision for their life. A vision is conceived followed by a process of training, trial and error, mistakes and failure, refining, and preparation that leads to skill and maturity. There are many small tests along the way that we must pass in order to qualify for the next level.

Having a vision triggers that process. If you're determined to fulfil the vision you have, it will bring about experiences that change you for the better. By this I mean, it will develop your character, but also, it will bring you through experiences that increase your skill, wisdom, knowledge, and understanding of your field of endeavour. That is how you can effectively master or have dominion over the works you are called to do. Paul, the Apostle described the commitment required to learn, adapt, grow and transform so that we can achieve the future we see, as being 'faithful to the heavenly vision.' Paul's vision to spread to message of Christ, transformed his life from that of a killer and persecutor to one who preached life. It gave him a new mindset and a deeper understanding of spiritual things.

Vision has to become a part of you that transforms who you are. It becomes the voice that gets you up in the morning. It's the voice that orders your day. It determines where you go, who you see, what you do. It teaches you everything you need to learn, shaping your instincts and releasing all of your potential for its fulfilment. When your vision has become the trainer in your life, you will do great exploits and ultimately manifest your dream.

> The pursuit of vision is the greatest moulder of
> character, ability, and human potential.

5. It inspires passion

People who do great exploits are passionate about their vision. Vision gives birth to passion. It creates a magnetic force between you and the picture you hold in your heart about the future you can have. Passion and vision go hand in hand.

Of the three bricklayers in the story at the start of this chapter, which do you think is likely to be the hardest worker? Which do you think will give of his best work? Clearly, it's the one who had the vision that he was building a cathedral. Vision had created a sense of destiny in the third bricklayer. His knowledge, skill, and experience as a bricklayer found their perfect inspiration. It was the reason he was a bricklayer. Vision creates drive and inspires love in people. It stirs strong emotion and can even become like a virtual romance or a marriage for the person who has one. I have heard my mother, whose story I told in chapter 1, speaking to her plants from time to time. When a new flower begins to bud on a plant, she actually tells it how beautiful it is and where she will position it in the next project she is envisioning! That's not crazy, it's a symptom of the passion she feels for the possibilities she sees in her mind, i.e. her vision.

Vision creates a sense of destiny. People become motivated and committed like never before. It focuses them on a bigger picture and breeds a sense of significance. It energises and mobilises you to dare to reach beyond the limits of what you can do to what you believe God can do.

Developing a vision

In developing a vision, it will help if you focus on these keys:

1. It's in you

First, discover it. Vision is birthed from within you; it springs from your purpose or calling. You can create it by looking inward. What are your talents and gifts? What ignites you, fires you up? What gets you excited, interested, frustrated, or moved? What do you want to change in your personal life: family, community, church, or the world at large? What problem do you want to solve as discussed in chapter 1? What experiences have you had in life that can help you shape your vision? What do you or others need? For example, Mother Teresa saw the needs of the poor in Kolkata and her vision to care for them was born. Think of your particular gifts, abilities, and talents – they will point you towards your vision.

2. Write it down and refine it

> Write the vision and engrave it plainly on [clay] tablets so that the one who reads it will run. For the vision is yet for the appointed [future] time. It hurries toward the goal [of fulfilment]; it will not fail. Even though it delays, wait [patiently] for it, because it will certainly come; it will not delay.[6]

Your vision is like a snapshot of what success would look like to you. Writing down your vision will create momentum and a drive to achieve it. The most effective vision statements tend to be short and simple. That vision statement of the Microsoft co-founders is a great one and has had a huge impact since its creation several decades ago. It was written down before the company even made computers. Computers were far from commonplace back then – the majority of people didn't even know what they were. But the vision made them commonplace. Today, computers are largely considered essential and can be found in the majority of offices and homes around the world. Like any great vision, this one gave people a glimpse into what was possible in the future. When you write your vision down, make sure it's simple, short, and tells you what the future holds. Your vision also needs to be somewhere where you can see it. It's important to write it down. Your vision should be captured or recorded somewhere that you can easily see it on a regular basis.

There are many tools you can use to ensure your vision is visible to you. You can write it in your journal if you keep a journal. Or you

---

[6]   Habakkuk 2:2-3, The Amplified Bible

can hang it on the wall of your office or bedroom. A very popular method is creating a vision board. Vision boards are made of images you cut out of magazines, newspapers, or other sources, and they represent what you want to acquire or achieve. You then paste the cuttings onto a board. Some people use sketchbooks as their board. I know many people in different age groups who have used vision boards to help them remain focused and motivated to pursue their goals. For example, a few years ago, my friend's thirteen-year-old daughter really wanted one of the popular brand name mobile phones. The upgrade model was due to come out a few months down the line, just after her exams. Her parents promised her the phone if she got *A*s on at least half of her exams. She got the idea of cutting a picture of the new phone from an advert and stuck it on the mirror of her dressing table. She saw the picture every day while she combed her hair. It motivated her to pay particular attention in class and to put in extra time studying and preparing for her exams. She confided in me that there came a point when all she could think about was that phone. When she wasn't doing the things she had to do to get the phone, she felt like she was cheating herself. The vision of the phone became such a part of her that she began to feel as if she already had it in her hand. A few months later, she sat her exams and got *A*s in not just half, but all of her subjects! Her parents went out and got her the phone she asked for immediately. That's the power of recording a vision and putting it somewhere where you can see it daily.

You'll be surprised how many successful people use visualisation techniques – from business people to celebrities to pastors. There are about as many techniques to use as there are people! For example Diego Maradona, the famous footballer from Argentina, had a habit of visiting the football field in the hours preceding every game. He would run around the field and imagine himself scoring goals. This technique, is a popular one and easy to do. From time to time I've been invited to give talks or run workshops. I always visualise myself delivering a talk before I do it. When I'm finally on stage speaking live, I feel more at ease because I've visited that spot many times already in my imagination. Many popular personalities credit their success to visualisation, whether they've done exploits in acting, sports, the music industry or business. Visualisation is a way of imprinting your vision in your memory.

Recording your vision involves having a visible and tangible representation of it. For example writing it down, creating a vision board as described before, collecting objects which symbolise what you want to achieve, such as trophies or pictures, using your imagination to dream of what you want to happen and capturing it in a drawing; or a combination of all these! One gospel singer I know confided that he first heard of vision boards when he was a teenager. He decided to make a vision board of his dreams and aspirations to become a singer. One of his cherished pictures on the board he created was of Kirk Franklin the famous American gospel singer, holding his first Grammy award. My friend eventually went on to produce several gospel albums. It thrills me to hear his songs on the radio because I know the background story of his struggles to get to where he currently is and I know he will go much further. Similarly, my neighbour's daughter wants to be a professional athlete. The wall of her bedroom is lined with posters of Olympic swimmers and other athletes, plus pictures of medals and trophies. She competes in swimming meets up and down the country and does very well, winning gold or silver from time to time.

Recording your vision is an important part of achieving it. This is a scriptural principle, which when applied has become a measurable reality in people's lives. Dreams are not achieved by default, they are achieved by the consistent application of specific principles, many of which are discussed in this book. To achieve a vision, you have to immerse yourself in it. A key way to do that is to surround yourself with the imagery of the dream realised so that it's the thing you see everyday. The quote at the start of this section says put the vision somewhere it can be *easily* seen. It goes on to say that anyone who is seeing it regularly in the natural routine course of his or her daily life will run with it. Corporations commonly use this approach. When you enter their reception area, their mission statement or vision is sometimes captured on a wall. Staff coming and going are reminded of it, on a subconscious level it shapes their behaviours and bring them into alignment with the vision. To run in this context means to set oneself to fulfil a predetermined plan i.e. the vision they see. You need to be able to see your vision until it alters your behaviour and becomes something you make your life an offering to.

This principle bears fruit for whoever applies it consistently.

3. Develop a plan

In addition to vision, doing exploits requires a workable plan. The purpose of planning is defining the actions needed to translate your vision from an aspiration into a measurable reality. After the vision, the next step is to plan. I shared the example of President Kennedy's vision for America to be the first country to put a man on the moon. Following that, plans were created to include key elements such as actions, responsible people, goals, timelines, and financial resources.

In the book of proverbs, King Solomon wrote, 'Without consultation, plans are frustrated, but with many counsellors they succeed[7].'

In planning how you will go about fulfilling your vision, whatever it may be, it's always useful to do some research and speak to others who have knowledge about what you want to achieve. The insights you gain are likely to increase your chance of success (see chapter 6 for ideas of how to do this). President Kennedy would never have gotten his vision started without consulting a range of experts. In the first place, such a vision would have been informed by intelligence from scientists and other experts to test its feasibility as an aspiration. The plans that were then generated were contributed to by people with specialist knowledge, ability, and experience that the president

---

[7]   Proverbs 15:22, New American Standard Bible

did not have personally. He would have failed if he'd planned it in isolation.

There are discussions about seeking information, training, enlisting the support of others and mentorship in the chapters on developing influence and potential.

4. Create goals to support your vision

In the 70s, a graduating class was surveyed to find out how many of the students had goals and how many had written those goals down. The results were 100 per cent and 5 per cent respectively. Twenty years on, the alumni were followed up. It was found that the 5 per cent who had written their goals down were worth more financially than the 95 per cent who had not

Goals are long, medium or shorter-term objectives – 'small things,' to use Wright's terminology. They are your vision broken down into smaller aims that can be measured by time and effect. Because they have a shorter timeline, they can lend a sense of urgency to achieving your vision – especially if a vision is very big and will take years or even a lifetime to accomplish. They act as powerful motivators because, when achieved, they give a sense of accomplishment and success, which creates momentum and encourages you to strive for the next level. Though they are smaller aims, you should still set them at a level that will challenge you.

Be creative and flexible when you set goals. When starting a new job, a friend of mine approached key people in her organisation and won their buy in to change certain approaches and processes. It led to a marked increase in product quality and sales. The company began to get new business from other organisations who had never approached them before. Her colleagues, though they admired her for the impact she had, were also unsettled by her approach. Although they had ideas of their own, they had never had the courage to simply stop a senior executive in the corridor and share them, the way Abbey had done. They were incredulous that senior management had simply picked up on her ideas and gave her the mandate to implement them. With senior backing, Abbey achieved her goals quite quickly, had an unusual impact and was promoted in no time. Her more long standing colleagues tended to adopt the ideas that cascaded down from the top of the organisation. Abbey told me that though she was ambitious and wanted to do well in the job, it hadn't been her intention to blaze a trail. Her approach was based on the fact that she didn't know enough about the way things were done in the company. Fortunately, her ideas were great and impacted positively on the profit bottom line. She now encourages people to think outside the box when planning and setting goals and says, 'Don't discount your ideas just because you're a new kid on the block. Your approach may well be a better way to go about things.' Setting short-term goals that are challenging may force you to be more creative and innovative.

Even though you've written down the plans, be flexible about how things unfold. Those who have been successful often have very different stories regarding their process. Their paths were different. Be prepared to throw out plans if you need to and try new ones, but make sure to stick with your goals and vision.

Reflection on exploits

Without vision all the countless little activities we participate in daily add up to little. People without vision live unrestrained lives. They can be as busy as those who do great exploits, but they may never do any exploits themselves. An unrestrained life is one where anything goes whenever. In the end, such a person looks back over the course of his or her life and wonders what it was all for. If you want to do great exploits, develop a vision for every area of your life, and then spend your time, energy, and every other resource you possess to fulfil it.

3

People who do great exploits believe that they can

If you can believe, all things are possible to him who believes.[8]

People who do great exploits believe they can achieve their vision and fulfil their purpose in life. No one attempts exploits without a certain amount of faith or self-belief. Successful people appreciate that success isn't always guaranteed. In fact, they experience failures just like everyone else. But they also know it's impossible to succeed if you don't first believe that you can. (Strategies for handling failure are discussed in chapter 13). It's important to develop the types of beliefs that will enable you to fulfil purpose. To do great exploits you need to get your mind working for your good.

---

[8] Mark 9:23, New King James Version

Belief and great exploits

I described the ecological phenomenon referred to as the trophic cascade in chapter 1, using the impact wolves can have in their realm. I became fascinated by this idea of trophic cascade some years ago watching nature programs about predators. Predators tend to be animals at the top of the food chain in their territories. But in bringing their innate gifts, skills and instincts to bear, they create a harmony in their environment by making it possible for other creatures lower down the food chain to co-exist. I love the idea of trophic cascade in relation to wolves because it challenged my thinking in many different ways. It changed my beliefs about wolves and, more importantly, it showed me how wrong beliefs, whether about others or ourselves, can put limitations on potential. Potential is critical to fulfilling purpose. The concept of potential is explored more in Part II of this book.

I always had a negative view of wolves; I believed them to be the bad boys of the animal kingdom with little to offer. I never imagined they could have a positive impact in any environment. Where did my belief about them come from? All the stories I was told about wolves when I was a child created those wrong beliefs. *Little Red Riding Hood, The Three Little Pigs,* and all the werewolf films aimed at adults today have painted wolves in a very bad light. The wolf eats vulnerable old grannies and blows down houses so he can gobble up defenceless little pigs. In the stories we're told, the wolf is always the bad guy. He's portrayed as a trickster, a con artist, a good-for-nothing menace. We can't help but believe he can never amount to anything useful.

These beliefs left me blind to the gifts, talents, and potential usefulness of wolves. I had unconsciously put the wolf into a small box. However, as a result of learning about trophic cascades, I was able to see wolves the way God sees them: animals doing great exploits according to the purpose for which they were created.

In a similar way, the stories people tell themselves about themselves create beliefs about what they can and cannot do. Some of these beliefs are self-limiting. Those who hold on to self-limiting beliefs find it difficult if not impossible to do great exploits. But people who do great exploits choose beliefs that break the limitations off.

There's a story my friend Kay tells about an eagle, and it illustrates the power self-belief has in shaping our present and future lives. I've expanded the story here.

One day, an eagle was out hunting, soaring high in the sky. With razor-sharp focus, she scanned the terrain below for prey. Eventually, she flew over a farm and spotted a bunch of chickens scratching around in the yard. She swooped down, hoping to catch one of them. But as she neared the ground, the eagle spotted something that looked very odd. As she got closer, she saw that one of the birds roaming around in the dust was an eagle, not a chicken.

It was behaving very strangely: he was plucking seeds from the ground and behaving like the chickens that surrounded him. Amazed by what she saw, the older eagle swooped down and expertly caught a large grey chicken in her talons. Terrified, the other birds squawked loudly, dashing every which way. As it took to the sky again the old eagle took a good look at the young eagle who dashed away looking for cover like the chickens.

The next day, the older eagle headed back to the farm. When she spotted the younger eagle, she swooped down, landing between him and the entrance to the chicken coup. The chickens ran for their lives, leaving the young eagle outside.

'What are you doing here? Why are you living among chickens?' she asked the young eagle.

Trembling, the young eagle replied, 'This is my home.'

The older eagle shook her head and said, 'Your home is up among the cliffs. You should be soaring near the sun, not crawling in the dust down here with chickens.'

'But I am a chicken,' the young eagle asserted. 'And besides, I'm afraid of heights.'

The older eagle didn't know whether to laugh or cry. She'd never heard such a thing before. 'You are an eagle,' she insisted. 'Come with me and I will teach you to soar.' The young bird seemed to consider her words very carefully. A few moments passed before he looked at the old eagle with a gleam in his eye and said, 'Give me a minute; I want to say goodbye to my friends and mother hen. She taught me everything I know.'

The old eagle bristled. There was so much waiting, and she wanted to begin his training without further delay. But if she argued, he'd only refuse to follow her. With a sigh, she gave her consent. *Once I have him up on the cliffs, I will retrain him, get rid of his chicken mentality and teach him how to think like an eagle,* she thought. She would then release him into his full potential. The old mentor could already see her new student excelling at gliding high above the clouds. She imagined him becoming even better than she was at hunting. There were so many things she wanted to teach him, just as she had done with her sons and daughters. There was so much wisdom she wanted to pass on. And as she thought about these things, she stepped aside and allowed the young eagle to pass. The young eagle then dashed full speed into the chicken coup, slamming the door shut behind him.

Inside, the chickens cheered. A large hen folded the young eagle into her voluminous wings. 'My son! My son!' she clucked, 'I'm glad you didn't believe her. You can never soar the way she said. You would break your neck! You are a chicken and belong right here with the rest of us.'

Turning to face the old eagle from the safety of the chicken coup the young eagle sneered, 'Ha! You wicked, old eagle. I know who I am. You thought you could outsmart me, but I outsmarted you!'

Why is what you believe about yourself so important?

The story above shows the impact of wrong beliefs on an individual's life and future. The young eagle's beliefs made it impossible for him to fulfil the purpose for which he was created. In reality, he was a great and powerful bird, a dynamic creature capable of doing things no other type of creature could do. Because he believed a lie about himself, however, his identity was grossly distorted. That one wrong belief limited him to becoming one of the least dynamic birds in creation.

What beliefs do you hold that may be keeping you back from fulfilling the purpose for which you were created? Are you posing as something you're not? Are you avoiding who you are called to be because you've accepted an identity that is not yours?

Developing a healthy self-belief is about recognising any beliefs you hold about yourself that are contrary to who and what you are called to be. If you have a vision, you are called to do exploits and achieve that vision. Doing great exploits involves many different types of struggles. It requires one to overcome various forms of resistance. If you go around believing you're not a conqueror or cannot be victorious, you won't even attempt exploits. Because somewhere in your heart you believe you are the opposite of a conqueror i.e. a victim or loser, then you will indeed be defeated. What you believe is who you are and who you are creates your circumstance. Healthy self-belief means that you value yourself, what you can do and will become.

Self-limiting beliefs cost the young eagle in the story everything. His beliefs had already cost him time in his past that should have been used for his development. But the loss also carried over into his future when he closed the door on the possibilities that lay ahead. He believed he was incapable of being what he was created to be, that it was impossible to fulfil his unique purpose. This erroneous belief kept him from doing the great exploits for which eagles are known.

But imagine what would have happened if he had just believed the old eagle. Imagine how different life would have been had he said *yes* to her offer. He would have fulfilled his purpose as an eagle; he would have learned how to do all the great exploits that eagles do.

Certain beliefs hinder the fulfilment of purpose in people's lives. If you want to be a person who does great exploits, search your heart. Are there any beliefs that might be limiting you? Take a look at some of the consequences of self-limiting beliefs:

1. You become what you believe

> For as he thinks in his heart, so is he.[9]

As a manager, I had young woman in my team who refused to carry out a task I asked her to. The task involved creating a budget. When days had passed and she still had not returned the work I asked for I scheduled a one to one meeting with her. Creating and managing small budgets for projects was part of her job description. She was performing very well in every other area of work. She was punctual, courteous and respectful and everyone liked her. So this recent behaviour seemed really uncharacteristic to me and I was curious to get to the bottom of it. 'Well I can't be perfect, I can't do *everything*.' Came her reply. 'This isn't about you being able to do everything. What's the problem? Don't you know how to create a budget?' She looked at me briefly and said, 'No, I can't.' 'Why not?'

---

[9]   Proverbs 23:7, New King James Version

I asked. 'Because I just can't! I lost my last job because of this. Are you going to get me fired too?' 'No,' I answered. 'I'm just going to send you on some training.' With that offer she felt she could be a bit more open about her experiences. She explained that she was 'a bit stupid' when it came to math, having struggled with math in high school and then failing her GCSE math exam. Then in her first job, when she couldn't prepare a budget for a project, she overheard her boss telling another manager that he thought she was stupid. That really hurt and it affected her confidence, sealing her belief that she was in fact 'stupid' when it came to numerical work. As a result, although she managed to get other jobs, she learned to avoid carrying out tasks were numbers were involved. She generally shied away from numerical challenges of any kind, even handing over all responsibility for managing their household money to her husband. This was the first time someone had offered to address the issue through further training. I told her I was glad she felt comfortable enough to share her experiences and said that far from thinking she was stupid, I actually considered her to be among some of the most capable people I'd come across, which was the truth. She did outstanding work in other areas and was very good at helping others in the team to deliver on their work too.

People with self-limiting beliefs often have them because of something they were told by other people. You may have heard about the parent who told her child, 'Why can't you be more like your sister? She's a better person than you'll ever be.' Or the teacher who said, 'You're a poor student. You'll never amount to anything!' Words like those can turn into beliefs, which the person then carries throughout life. They shape and limit what people achieve as they believe themselves unworthy or incapable. In the latter part of this chapter, I share many techniques for neutralizing wrong beliefs and breaking free of their limitations. Getting rid of wrong beliefs will set you free to do great exploits.

2. Your limiting self-beliefs stop you from putting your gifts and talents to good use

The right self-belief is vital to doing exploits. Many people have not done things or won't try things because they don't believe in themselves.

Although he was actually an eagle, the young eagle had the mentality of a chicken. His self-belief was limited to the thoughts chickens have. Thus, he couldn't exercise any of the actual gifts he had. Eagles were created to soar higher than any other bird. They come nearer to the sun than all other creatures; they can see further than any bird; they are more skilled at hunting than any other bird. The young eagle never allowed himself to put any of these talents to use, and his purpose went unfulfilled.

Such an attitude in humans can be very costly. It affects people in two ways: first, they miss the purpose for their life and second, other people are affected.

Missing purpose has many implications. One of the great things about life is fulfilling the personal mission to which you are called. I can't imagine any greater joy. If living out your mission releases joy, it follows that not living out your mission produces a lack of joy. It's the reason so many people are restless and feel unfulfilled. Non-discovery of their life's purpose and mission is a source of emptiness and frustration for many.

Some people lose their passion for life because they are not exercising their gifts in the fulfilment of their purpose. They have avoided purpose for reasons including wrong beliefs about who they are and what they're called to do. This renders their gifts dormant. Your gifts are critical; you won't be able to complete your assignment without using your gifts.

3. When you refuse to use your gifts, it leads you away from purpose

If you're not on the road to your assignment, what road are you on? Being off course can be dangerous. You may of heard the story of a man called Jonah who found himself in the belly of a whale because he chose to go in a direction that was opposite to the direction he was called to go in. His gifts were desperately needed in the city of Nineveh. The population there was about to be destroyed and as a great prophet he was called to exercise his gift and warn the people so they could change their ways and be spared. However, Jonah wouldn't use his gift for that purpose. A lack of self-belief wasn't the motivating factor for him – in fact the opposite was true: he was too self-confident! But his is a good example of the personal consequences that can be suffered when we refuse to use our gifts in service to others. Some people experience all sorts of negative environments and frustrations in life, it could be that they are not in the right place, moving in the direction of their purpose – like Jonah in the belly of the whale!

Being in the belly of a whale wasn't comfortable. Jonah didn't belong in that environment. Straying from away from your pre-determined purpose or vision means that you're in the wrong place. Being in the wrong place produces discomfort and regret. When they're in the wrong place, people feel the pain of missed opportunities. They're tormented by memories of roads they should have taken but didn't. They regret the things they could have accomplished but didn't when they had the chance. Jonah lost three days while in the belly of the whale. Time is lost when we're in the wrong place. And as time passes, peace, satisfaction, and joy slowly erode.

4. Self-limiting beliefs produce a life of regret

At the end of their life, people don't look back and wish they had done less with their life; they tend to look back and regret the dreams they never fulfilled. While working as a nurse in a private hospital, I had a conversation with a grand old lady who had been left very well off after her husband died. She was 78 when I first began nursing her. In the evenings when the ward had quietened down, I'd spend time with to her in her room. She loved to talk about her past and the great life her husband's business had given them. She'd met and befriended many famous people in her lifetime – big American film stars – a couple of whom had indeed visited her during her stay on our ward. All in all she'd had a good life but she still had a number of regrets. There are many things she wished she had done differently. For example she'd had a dream of becoming a nurse herself when she was a girl. However, because she got married and then began a family soon after, it was a longing she'd never fulfilled. At the time she believed she wouldn't have coped with raising a family and pursuing a career. But she regretted it because so many others had done it. Instead, she focused on giving significant amounts to charities doing work in developing countries. But still that didn't satisfy her and she regretted never having started a charity of her own, when her children were grown. She wanted to know if I was content in my profession as a nurse or if I had any other dreams for my life. I confided that though I enjoyed caring for people, I wanted to be a writer. Her words to me were, 'If you don't go after your dreams, you'll eventually regret it. You'll always wish you'd tried.'

5. People lose their rewards

Self-limiting beliefs hinder people from doing what they were born to do, which causes them to lose the rewards that are stored up for them. There are certain rewards waiting for us when we complete each stage of our assignments. These are lost when we don't make progress. God wants to reward his children for using their talents. Jesus told his disciples the following parable: there was a businessman who gave his three servants varying amounts of talents before he went on a business trip. When he returned and asked for an account of how they used the talents, he discovered that one of the servants had not done anything with the talent he was given. The businessman demanded an explanation. The servant revealed some wrong beliefs he had about his master, and used them as the reason he did not exploit his talent. The other two servants, however, invested their talents and maximised their rewards. Overjoyed and proud of the two successful servants, the businessman rewarded them further by giving them a promotion and even greater access to him as a mentor than they had before. As for the servant with limiting beliefs, the businessman called him wicked and took away the one talent he had, giving it to the most successful of the three servants. Using your gifts and talents is discussed in this book's chapters on potential.

6. Your limiting self-beliefs affect other people

If the first consequence of holding self-limiting beliefs is that you don't use your talents and gifts, which then leads to regret as you grow older, the second consequence for not using your gifts is that others peoples' lives are impacted adversely. Purpose is about service to others, as explained in chapter 1. When purpose goes unfulfilled, the consequences for people are extensive. The longer Moses believed he was incapable of speaking and therefore couldn't possibly go back to Egypt and lead the slaves to freedom – as was his life's purpose - the longer they remained in oppressive captivity. Moses' self-limiting belief had consequences for over a million men, women, and children. Imagine a world with no trophic cascades, where wolves are extinct and disorder was allowed to reign. Imagine if the Wright brothers had not discovered a way to fly. What if Nelson Mandela and others hadn't challenged apartheid? What if the inventors of the computer or the Internet hadn't invented them? If you're holding any self-limiting beliefs that keep you from doing what you're called to do, how many people's lives are you affecting?

All the innovations, discoveries and inventions we know and enjoy today came about because someone put their talents and gifts to a predetermined purpose, a problem they wanted to solve. They didn't always know whether they would succeed or how things would turn out but, invariably, they had enough belief in themselves to try.

7. Self-limiting beliefs close doors on opportunities to learn

The old eagle in the story volunteered to be a teacher and mentor to the young eagle. She had done many exploits in her time and was willing to pass on her years of knowledge, wisdom, and experience. But the young eagle rejected the opportunity because he didn't believe he could learn what she was there to teach him. Because he didn't believe he could fly, he never learned to fly. He could never learn the thrill of hunting; he would forever miss out on knowing the fulfilment that can only come from maximising one's gifts and abilities.

How to change your beliefs

Can people do exploits without changing the way they think about themselves? If you lack self-belief, it hinders your ability to do exploits. Therefore, the way you think about yourself must change. You must align your self-belief to your vision. You couldn't have sensed your call and created your vision if you didn't have the potential or ability to fulfil it. Each of us is equipped to fulfil purpose despite any shortcomings. In his spiritual awakening, Paul discovered this wonderful compensation for any weakness: 'I can do all things, [which he has called me to do] through him who strengthens and empowers me .... I am ready for anything and equal to anything through him who infuses me with inner strength and confident peace].[10]'

There are a number of things you can do to change any limiting beliefs you have about yourself.

1. Learn a new set of beliefs

When you were born, your brain was empty. Nobody is born with any beliefs. Whatever beliefs you have now were learned. They can be unlearned, too, and replaced by new beliefs. To change them, you need to learn new ones that work better for you.

---

[10]   Philippians 4:13, The Amplified Bible.

Earlier on, I shared the story of the girl who worked in my team. In our conversation I challenged her belief that she was stupid and it became a turning point in her life. Her first manager's words were like a seed that was planted in her mind. Fortunately, she was willing to let go the limiting view she had accepted about herself when it was finally challenged. When I told her that in my opinion she was one of the smarter people I've ever had in my team, it set off a chain reaction in her mind. It challenged the way she saw herself and she learned to see herself differently, which boosted her confidence. Therefore she became more willing to take the risks that were necessary to advance her professional life.

When our limiting or wrong self-beliefs are challenged, it's an opportunity for us to learn new and better ways of thinking. It takes some time and effort to develop a new vision of ourselves, but if we persist it can pay off in ways we can't anticipate. This young woman is now a senior manager in another organisation responsible for her own budget with several staff reporting to her. If, like the young eagle, she had insisted on holding on to what she'd been told earlier in her career, she wouldn't be doing the great exploits she does today.

In most cases, all it takes to begin changing a limiting belief is to challenge it. Each of us has limiting beliefs in some form. They are like thorns in our side. A large part of us knows we can be better and do more, but we're held back because of what we believe. Fortunately, we don't have to wait for anyone to challenge these beliefs for us – we can challenge them for ourselves when we become aware of them.

Another great thing is that, as you challenge any limiting beliefs and replace them with beliefs that boost your confidence, other people will begin to notice and start believing in you. The people in your life will eventually give way to your emerging new self when you choose to throw off limiting labels and become who you were born to be.

2. Create a new vision of yourself

Once you've identified a self-limiting belief that keeps you from doing exploits, the next step is to choose a new set of beliefs. After that, go to work embedding them in your mind. To do this, you'll need to create a vision of yourself as someone who is capable of doing what you need to do to accomplish your dream. Whatever your dream might be, whether writing a book, moving forward in ministry, starting a business, landing your dream job, becoming a speaker (or all of the above!), you should begin to see yourself doing it. This is referred to as visualisation.

Visualisation is scriptural. There's an account about a man called Abram who lived thousands of years ago in the Negev, whose wife was barren. Abram was led out of his tent one night and his gaze drawn to the stars. Scripture writes that God told him that his future would be such that, if Abram could number the stars, his descendants would be more than them25. This created a powerful image in Abram's mind about the lineage that would come from him and the impact his descendants would have on the earth. If you research this man's descendants, you'll find that today, their numbers are in the hundreds of millions. Vision is more powerful than you can imagine. Vision represents the future in a person's mind. It gives hope for the future, an assurance that they could have that future. In short, it draws people up from their current position to a higher one.

Visualisation as discussed in the previous chapter is a great technique for creating a vision and then imprinting it in your memory. But is also a proven and effective technique for strengthening people's beliefs about themselves. Two famous personalities in business and politics have been open about using visualisation techniques to motivate themselves to achieve their goals and dreams. For instance, one of them encourages fans to, 'Imagine your life as you wish it to be. Visualise yourself becoming what you want to become, because you become what you believe.'

Another effective technique that can be used to create and reinforce positive beliefs about the future is affirmation. A high school friend of mine who is now a lawyer grew up in relative poverty. He watched both his parents labouring with little or no tangible reward at a local factory every day of their lives. For them, it was a constant struggle to keep up with rent payments and providing the needs of their five children. He and his siblings often went without. In those days Greg remembers saying to himself, *My life won't be like this. I will have a different life.* In those affirmations, he was rejecting any beliefs that his parents' difficult life would automatically be the life he would live. At the same time, they built up beliefs in his mind about the future of great exploits that was in store for him in the field of law. More of Greg's story is told in chapter 5, which looks at the importance of taking responsibility for your future. Choosing affirmations in line with the future you want to have, or the exploits you long to do, is a simple start to taking responsibility for the way that future turns out. You can make up affirmations of your own or search the scriptures and find the ones that you can use to empower and motivate you. They will challenge your mindsets and any self-limiting beliefs you may have that are holding you back.

Greg is also a strong believer in visualisation. In the times when he affirmed that his life would be different to the life his parents had, he began to imagine the alternative life he wanted. It wasn't void of hard work, but it was a life where the rewards were more tangible, where he could earn his living using his mind, rather than physical labour earning a wage that barely met the needs of his family. He imagined sitting in an office, arguing cases in court, driving his dream car and providing a spacious home for his wife and children. He saw himself taking his family on holidays to exclusive resorts, paying for extra classes and training that enabled his children to develop their natural talents. He imagined himself being in a position to give them choices in life. Greg did exploits and broke the cycle of poverty in his family becoming the first person to go to university. He has fulfilled all of those childhood dreams and has been doing exploits as a senior partner in a law firm ever since.

When we meditate on words - spoken or read - they form pictures in the mind. Writing your vision, reading it and meditating on it forms a picture of who you can become. Meditating involves thinking deeply on the word, as opposed to just a casual reading of it. It allows you to form and hold that ideal picture in your mind. As you regularly meditate on your vision, the more your behaviour aligns itself to create that outcome in reality. Similarly, speaking it out loud, reinforces it. Hearing it spoken builds your faith, or belief that you are capable of achieving it. When we use the word as affirmations, they become our beliefs. An example is the one Paul discovered, which I quoted earlier – that he could do anything he was called to do and equal to every task required of him to fulfil his purpose. Whatever your calling may be, create a clear picture of it in your imagination. It's the model you should visualise as often as possible. It will eventually overcome any limiting beliefs you have and also become your reality if you remain faithful to it.

You can learn to visualise by finding a quiet space and getting into a comfortable position. Close your eyes and form a picture of you being and doing the things you want to be and do. You can imagine yourself being decisive and making the right choices. See yourself behind the counter of your business or sitting at the desk of your dream job. See all the smiling faces of the people you want your life to impact. Make a mental movie of yourself acting in a confident way and carrying out all the behaviours of a successful and accomplished person in the area of your calling. Make it a habit to practice these visualisation techniques, if you do, you'll find that you naturally become the person in your mental movie. The truth is, the person you are today is the person from the mental movie you've been playing in your mind until now. Why not change that movie so that it's more in line with your vision?

3. Be your own motivational coach

My life really transformed when I took a life-coaching course many years ago. It taught me how to speak to myself (and others I would coach) using language that was positive, accepting, inspiring, and motivational. I had dreams, yet my life felt stagnant. I wasn't doing any exploits at all, and I was unsure about what my purpose was. Learning how to speak positively to myself enabled me to move forward. Getting rid of thinking habits that were doubt filled removed fetters in my mind. I was then able to tackle those things had been dormant for a long time because I was telling myself I couldn't do them or that I would upset the people in my life if I did.

Most of us find it easy to encourage and motivate others, to boost their confidence and self-belief when they are feeling insecure. Yet we rarely think to speak to ourselves in the same way when we have doubts about our abilities. The same mother who says to her daughter, 'Jacqui, you are a talented person. You can do anything you dream of doing. Don't let fear get in the way. You are more than able to do this.' Is the same woman who would tell herself, *I'm not that smart. I remember how I messed up in the past. I'm so stupid; there's no way I can figure out how to do this.*

Negative self-talk was typical of me before my coaching class helped me become aware of my inner voice and the harmful things I was habitually telling myself. I took that course with the sole aim of helping other people overcome their obstacles, but the course taught me how to overcome my own! Now, when I feel doubts about my ability to take on a challenge, I use those coaching techniques on myself. I think of what I would say to a client or friend to help them think in a way that enables them to accomplish their goals, and then I say those things to myself – at times out loud. I've been doing that so long that it's no longer a conscious effort; rather, it's a reflex.

The moment I sense any limiting thoughts trying to creep in, my mind automatically kicks in with affirmations. Or I remember a success I've had, or some positive feedback I received. It's impossible to think about two things at the same time, so in order to expel one thought you just need to replace it with another. To expel an image, all you need to do is replace it with the image you prefer to hold in your mind. This will become automatic once you make a habit of it. I see negative thoughts like crows or shadows: when they approach, I don't let them find a place to land in my mind. I use the weapons I just listed (and many others) to chase them away.

A simple example of the effectiveness of self-coaching is when I used to be terrified of interviews. Back then, I used to say these types of things to myself, *They probably won't think I'm good enough. There's bound to be someone else better than me on the interview list. No doubt I'll forget half of what I planned to say about my experience and skills.* No wonder I got more and more depressed during the days running up to the interview and was a bundle of nerves on the day itself. I had a mindset of failure. No wonder it made me anxious and worried – who wouldn't be if they really believed they were about to make a fool of themselves in front of people whose approval they craved? By learning to think differently my mindset has been revolutionised. I now believe, that I can do anything I put my mind to – and you should too, because it is the truth. Now, before I go into an interview, having done my preparation in advance, I tell myself: *I'm going to wow them at this interview. They'll really like me because I'll show them how much I know about the organisation and all the knowledge and skill I can bring to add value. These people better be smart enough to spot that I am their preferred candidate. More importantly, they had better show me why I should come work for them. It's not just about why I should want to be employed by them!* As you can imagine, I do exploits in my interviews and tend to be offered the jobs I apply for.

Another easy coaching technique I adopted is, whenever I do something well or perform an act of kindness towards someone else, I always congratulate myself. Just like that mother would tell her daughter, Sarah: 'Well done, honey. I'm really proud of you for doing that so well.' I tell myself the same thing: 'Well done, Michelle. I'm really proud of you; you did very well!' And then I allow myself to enjoy the pleasant feelings that come from being complimented. I stay as long as I can in that moment; I stay until it becomes a part of me. This technique creates an important memory tool I can draw on in those moments when I need to boost my self-belief.

Let's face it: there are more negative messages and people speaking negatively than there are positive sources. Negative voices come to us through parents, siblings, teachers, colleagues, peers, bullies, etc. We learn to criticise ourselves based on those voices. That criticism undermines our self-belief. You can learn to make your inner voice work for you using the techniques I've described and many others. The one voice you can control is your own. Why not make your inner voice the one that's on your side?

The next chapter really speaks to this negative inner voice and all the thoughts it produces.

4. Remember David

If anyone makes you feel inferior, it's by your own consent.

We all know the story of David and Goliath. I first heard the story when I was a kid and attended Sunday School. It made quite an impression on me. Decades on, I still often recall David in the moments he stood in front of the giant determined to bring him down. Goliath's insults were intended to force David to see himself as inferior. They were meant to take away his power and undermine any belief that he could overcome the obstacle standing in front of him.

57

When I'm up against a giant, regardless of whether it's a person, a problem, or a task, I think of David. I think, *If David was able to slay Goliath, I can tackle this.* It gets rid of doubt and boosts my confidence and boldness.

5. Remember your last success

As I alluded to before, I keep a memory bank of things I did well and projects in which I succeeded. It's important to take a moment and reflect on these accomplishments when they occur. Reflecting helps you commit them to memory with sufficient detail that you can retrieve them when you need to do so. You can recall your successes whenever you like. But they are particularly useful in boosting your self-confidence when you've just experienced a failure. Remembering past successes helps you separate the failure from who you are. The memory provides proof that you are not a failure because you have succeeded in the past. It clarifies that failure came because something didn't work out this time and that whatever it was can be adjusted so that it is unlikely to cause a failure in future.

Another good time to call up one of your memories is when you are about to do an exploit that looks intimidating. David did this when he was going to face Goliath. He told King Saul that he had succeeded in killing a lion and a bear. Therefore, he was confident that because he had accomplished those things in the past, he could do the exploit that was looming in the present.

6. Believe you are worthy of doing exploits

You are as worthy as the next person in terms of doing well in your life. Exercising your gifts is an important part of that. Our gifts make us relevant, of value, and necessary in the world. In Proverbs, King Solomon wrote, 'A person's gift opens doors for him, bringing him access to important people.'[11] I see this as the Creator, giving each

---

[11]   Proverbs 18:16, International Standard Version.

of us a peculiar resource that will enable us to thrive, flourish, and make our mark in the world. He did this so that my life and your life would matter, that our lives would count for something, and that no one could legitimately deny our significance. Often, we look to others to open doors and provide opportunities. Instead, we ought to focus on doing our best and developing the gift that was given us. Your gift in operation causes you to shine and draws the attention of two types of people: those who are in a position to help and promote you, and those who will try to contain you. This is exactly what happened to Joseph, the slave who became a ruler, and whose story I told in a previous chapter. During the early years of his life, because of his gift, he experienced more people trying to limit him than make room for him. He experienced more signs of unworthiness than signs that he was worthy. Those types of people did all they could to ruin him. But little did they know that the very devices they employed to try to destroy Joseph, were the ones that brought him in sight of people who would help him fulfil his purpose. The further his enemies drove him, the nearer he came to his ultimate calling. As a slave in Egypt Joseph first came into the house of Potiphar, an influential and mature man, who began to notice his difference without feeling threatened by it. Potiphar, the prison warden, and the butler all played a critical role in facilitating Joseph's transition from one level to the next. But these men only acquiesced because they saw his gifts in operation and couldn't deny their value in meeting particular needs. Joseph's gifts made him worthy of doing exploits. Likewise, you and I are worthy of doing exploits because of the gifts we carry.

I've met a couple of 'crown princes and princesses' in my time – those who have the banquet laid out for them regardless of whether they are worthy of it. This was not Joseph's privilege once he arrived in Egypt. For most of us, it's not our privilege either. It's up to us to believe we worthy to achieve the highest and best life has to offer regardless of the circumstances and situations we face. But as Joseph maintained a humble, respectful attitude and continued to employ his gifts, which included administration and interpreting dreams, they made room for him time after time. In Potiphar's house, his gifts gave him authority that was second only to the man of the house. Likewise, in the prison, his gifts promoted him. Those who benefited from them remembered his gifts. His gifts were his bridge into the palace, where he found his ultimate relevance. Joseph's gifts did not merely make room for him; they laid the world at his feet.

Your gifts and talents are proof of the reality that you are called to do exploits. They are one of the criteria for a life of significance.

7. Know that you give God pleasure when you pursue purpose

God gave us gifts because he takes pleasure in watching us express them. There was once a British Olympic gold medallist called Eric Lidell. Lidell was born in 1902 to Scottish missionaries serving in China. He was very open about his personal faith in Christ, and he returned to China as a missionary himself. In the 1924 Olympic games, Lidell opted out of the 100-meter race because it was scheduled on a Sunday. He did, however, run the 400-meter race and broke the record. Lidell said, 'I believe God made me for a purpose, but he also made me fast! And when I run I feel his pleasure.'

I experience that same pleasure when I'm writing. There's an inspiration that comes which has an unearthly feel. At times I'm convinced God whispers wisdom to me, and I write it down. When I'm not writing, his ideas come to me in a flash. I've learned to carry my tablet or a notebook with me wherever I go so I can jot down the words he gives me. It pleases him when I use what He gave me for his glory and make a difference to those who benefit from it.

When I write, I feel his pleasure.
Michelle Johnson

Reflection on exploits

You become what you believe. Many of us go about life carrying wrong beliefs about who we are and what we're capable of doing. Such beliefs end up hindering and limiting us so that we cannot perform the works we are called to do. Doing great exploits becomes impossible without the belief that they can be done. If you have any self-limiting beliefs, the good news is that they can be changed to the types of beliefs that break all limitations. People who do great exploits believe that anything is possible, that they have the gifts and talents to fulfil their purpose.

4

People who do great exploits think positively

Employ positive and constructive thinking about
your life, your purpose, and your problems

Many of the things we think are needed to do great exploits don't matter nearly as much as we think they do. It's often the things we pay less attention to or place less value on that hold us back from fulfilling our purpose. The way we think is a prime example: the difference between people who do great exploits and those who don't is the way they think about the issues of life.

I once read an article that featured a man who was doing exploits in business. As a child he grew up on the streets of a city in Eastern Europe. He dropped out of school to fend for himself. Though he's now in his late forties and running a multimillion-pound company that he built from scratch, he never learned how to read.

People who do great exploits come from a variety of backgrounds and have different types of personalities. Their circumstances are varied: some had a good start in life; others were abused and neglected. Some are highly educated; others didn't finish school. The majority came from average backgrounds but emerged as doers of exploits for all the reasons discussed throughout this book. You can be one of them.

People who do great exploits may come in all sorts of packages, but one thing they all have in common is that they think positively about the future or the problem at hand.

What's negative thinking?

The way we think decides the outcomes we get in life. Those who do great exploits are not blind to problems; rather, they think about them with the express aim of finding solutions to them. Positive thinking is thinking that believes in possibilities. It is hope-filled thinking that is driven by the expectation that there is always a way forward. On the other hand, the negative thinker blocks out possibilities and is unable to see a way through to victory.

Case in point: the difference in outcome experienced by the Israelite army and David when confronted by the same problem (namely, Goliath). The men in the army thought Goliath was a problem they could never solve. As a result, it paralyzed them and stopped their progress. David, on the other hand, revealed a way of thinking that led him to a solution. His thought process proved very effective in bringing him success where the majority refused to try. David's way of thinking is the perfect antidote to negative thinking patterns – and anyone prone to negative thinking can learn it easily. If they put it into practice, they'll find that, in very little time, their thoughts will be transformed. Once someone's thoughts are transformed into positive ones, the results of their life change for the better. They will be released to do great exploits and fulfil purpose. The secrets to

David's exploit that day can be observed in his thinking. I'll share them later on in this chapter.

> Negative thinking is costly – avoid it like the plague
> that it is. Avoid indulging in negative thinking about
> yourself, your purpose, or other people.
> It's a luxury that will cost you everything.

Negative thinking is an expression of doubt that stifles belief and hope that good things will happen for you. Here are some additional examples of how negative thinking works:

'I have a really good idea for a new business, but I know I'll never convince anyone to invest in it. Besides, I'm going to have to work really hard and put in long hours just to get it off the ground – I don't think I can do what it takes.'

'Someone visited my church and heard me sing solo. They invited me to sing at their church's anniversary celebration, but I don't want to sing for a bunch of people I don't know. I don't think I'm good enough for that!'

'I wish I could start a training organization to help young people get into the job market, but without the skills and experience, what would be the point of trying to do that?'

Negative thinkers commonly mistake their negative outlook on life for reality or a wise analysis. In each of the examples above, the thinker took inventory of the facts: starting a business takes long hours and hard work, singing at a new venue means singing to strangers, starting a training organization requires certain skills. However, they chose to believe that those facts were insurmountable, that trying to realise their dream was hopeless. I believe it's important to be realistic, to make an assessment and understand what the actual facts are. But I do this only for the sake of preparing myself to manage a circumstance more effectively and achieve the goals I have in mind.

Negative thinking can also disguise itself as analytical thinking, bottom-line thinking, or reflective thinking. These and other ways of thinking are good because they are all geared towards solving problems, creating ideas, and learning from past experiences. They are the types of thinking that can take you forward in life and help you become successful. However, negative thinking will produce none of these outcomes and will end in defeat.

Negative thinking is like the thief who comes to kill, steal, and destroy the future. That type of thinking makes it easy to say *no* to your purpose and harder to say *yes*. However, if we learn to think differently, it becomes easier to say *yes*.

Why get rid of negative thinking?

It's impossible to do great exploits when you're thinking negatively about yourself, your situation, or your dream. Negative thinking will block your progress for the following reasons:

1. Negative thinking breeds fear

At age 15 I left home to finish my schooling in Canada. I was sent to a boarding school in a little town outside Toronto called Oshawa. As a child I had opportunity to travel quite a bit to various countries, however, it was the first time I was moving away from my family to live more or less on my own. Although I looked forward to it, the prospect also filled me with apprehension. I arrived at my new school (and home) in the dead of the Canadian winter in January 1986. The snow was beautiful, but the weather was bitterly cold. My uncle drove my mother and me to the halls of residence and we were ushered into the office of the women's Dean in charge of the dormitory where I would spend the next two years. Mom was asked to sign some papers and then she gave me a hug and kiss and said goodbye. I watched as she got into my uncle's car and drove off on her way to the airport.

In the days that followed I tried settling in as best I could. So many things were very different to what I had been used to in my short 15 years. School started at 7:30 am every morning long before the sun came up. Breakfast was at 6. I had to trek through three hundred yards of knee-deep snow to get to the school building. When at last the weekend came, I ventured into Toronto, to do some sight seeing and walk around. It was a big bustling city and I felt very tiny in it. It was vastly different to anything I'd seen or experienced in my hometown. There were many skyscrapers, traffic filled the busy streets, crowds of people moved like mighty rivers up and down the sidewalks. They all looked so serious, not like the warm and smiling faces I was used to seeing back home. I didn't know how I would ever fit in and feel at home there.

I felt privileged to be there but wondered whether I had what it took to make it. Plus, I was already missing my friends, family and the familiar comforts of home. One afternoon, I got back to my room, and announced to my roommate that I decided to return home. I said, 'I don't think I'll enjoy being here. It's too scary being away from home and I don't know anybody in Oshawa.'

My roommate listened to me as I told her all the negative things about the town and why I wasn't going to stay. When I was done, I waited for her sympathetic reply; instead, she laughed and said, 'Girl, get over it, besides, you know me, don't you?'

That conversation forced me to find a way to overcome my negative thinking and adjust to my new life in Oshawa. Many years later, I returned for the funeral of one of the many good friends I eventually made there. As I drove from the station to the church near the campus in a taxi, I stared out the window at the passing sights. Everything that had once loomed so large and alien when I was 15, now seemed small and familiar. I asked myself, *What had I really been so scared of?* At the time, my roommate's advice seemed harsh, but it was the greatest advice. It had made me look out across the city of Toronto the next time I was there and say, 'You're going to be my city in no time; I'm going to conquer you!'

Moving forward in the purpose for your life can be a bumpy ride. Purpose will uproot you from perfectly comfortable places and land you in tight, difficult spots. So many things changed for me when I left home for the first time. My parents had sacrificed to provide me with a great education. It was essential to my development but it presented many negatives. I wouldn't see my family for a long time. There would be no home-cooked meals waiting for me when I got home; there would be no family to talk to and laugh with in front of the television. I'd have to endure the long, lonely months of bitter winter; whereas, in Trinidad, the temperatures soared all year round. I would have to get used to being relatively anonymous, which was very different to living in a town where practically everyone knew my family and me and adjust to a new culture and people.

Many people take their first steps in the direction of a dream only to turn back because the initial change seemed fraught with difficulties or sacrifice. Like this experience was for me initially, stepping out of your comfort zone to do something new can be intimidating. Venturing into the unknown makes most people feel vulnerable, weak, and exposed. The temptation is to see those inevitable changes in a negative light and then doubt that you have what it takes to be successful.

Because I stayed, I discovered that I did have what it took. If you don't allow negative thoughts to overcome you, you too will discover that you have what it takes to fulfil your dream. We're never exposed to more than we can handle. At every stage life puts us in places that will challenge and stretch us so that we can rise to the occasion. We discover strengths and abilities we didn't know we had, assets that have been instilled in us. But if we give up, we will never find out what we're made of and fail to accomplish any great exploits.

2. Negative thinking blocks your creativity

We only need to do great exploits because problems and obstacles to the fulfilment of purpose confront us. Exploits are what we do to overcome or get round a problem so that our mission can be realised. Finding solutions to problems requires creativity. But when we think negatively it closes the mind and shuts down creative thought processes. Thus, we are unable to come up with fresh ideas for moving forward. Yet creativity is a necessity, as is finding different approaches when needed. People who do exploits often find new ways to reach people and get things done. Our creative ideas often are what see us through the stages of progress. Negativity hinders the flow of good ideas and creativity.

Creativity is one of the most valuable assets anyone can bring to their life's work. Jesus was a master at using creative approaches to engage both individuals and crowds of people with his message. His mission was to preach the good news. But there were many other speakers in his time – Pharisees, Sadducees, rabbis, philosophers, and politicians – all warring for the minds of the masses. Jesus understood he would need to get creative in delivering simple messages that would allow his ideas to stick. He made this creative approach a priority. He used techniques such as parables and enriched his talks with metaphors, symbolism, and even humour to keep people interested. Many world-class speakers use his techniques today.

3. Negative thinking blinds you to the possibilities

Nothing limits achievement like small thinking,
Negative thinking is like a pair of scissors destroying great ideas.

People who do exploits are possibility thinkers. They are continuously scanning the horizon for fresh opportunities for growth and achievement in their areas. Our purpose on earth is to use our potential, which includes our unique combination of gifts, talents, abilities, and experiences to solve particular problems others have. Possibility thinkers recognise that purpose is about pushing boundaries and creating new frontiers. It's about advancing their cause on earth. To advance, we need to be tuned into opportunities for advancement as they present themselves. We need to be forward-looking thinkers. When nothing much seems to be happening, possibility thinkers either create the opportunities they desire or wait with a sense of anticipation to seize an opportunity that arises. Another characteristic of possibility thinkers is that they identify and explore their options. They do not believe that anything is impossible and will test every possible option for achieving what they desire. Should they ever arrive at a dead end, they will look for another road to go down. They are not afraid of failure because they know there are always other options. Possibility thinkers see openings that others don't see. Possibility thinkers are hungry; impossibility thinkers are not.

On the other hand, anyone prone to negative thinking inevitably becomes a short-sighted person who is unable to look up and outward to the horizons. Often, they are only able to see one way of doing things. If that way fails, they give up. Because they are impossibility thinkers, they can't embrace the opportunities that come their way. If they see an opportunity to solve a problem, even when they are fully equipped to solve it, they will always find a reason to deem it impossible. Often, they misinterpret the potential of opportunities – just like the salesman in this illustration.

You may have heard the old tale of two British salesmen who were sent to a large developing nation by a shoe manufacturer. Their mission was to investigate the potential of the market for shoes and bring back a report.

The first salesman arrived and, upon seeing the masses of men, women, and children in the country, reported, 'There is no potential here because nobody wears shoes.'

Upon finding these huge populations in the country, the second salesman became very excited. He could hardly wait to report back,

'There is massive potential here because nobody wears shoes.'

Regardless of the great future that is possible for them, negative thinkers will find a way to render it impossible. Negative thinking blinds people to possibilities.

Like that shoe manufacturer, Moses sent men to investigate the Promised Land and bring back a report on the potential of the land. The twelve spies returned with different reports. All twelve of them agreed that the land was filled with good things: an abundance of fruit, waterways, and beautiful country space for raising families and producing crops. There was just one snag: the current inhabitants of the land were giants. Interesting how this theme of giants runs through the early scriptures in the Old Testament. These were the giant tribes that the likes of Goliath descended from. We don't have giants today, and that fact alone should provide us with sufficient proof that giants can be defeated! But in the time of Moses, the giants were many and they were intimidating. Thus, the spies disagreed on this one point. Ten of them thought the giants could not be overcome; they told Moses that they felt like grasshoppers when they saw the giants. They thought it would be impossible for the Israelites to defeat them and take possession of their dream. But two of them, Joshua and Caleb, thought that, though the giants were large, the Israelites could do great exploits, overcome them, and fulfil their purpose.

The negativity of the ten spies, however, spread throughout the camp like a virus. As the story goes, the people wept all day and all night, feeling sorry for themselves. They had come very far. They had endured the harshness of the desert, the soaring heat in the day, the plummeting temperatures at night, the sandstorms, the reality of having no homes to call their own. Now, at last, on the edge of their breakthrough, someone told them their dream was an impossible one and they believed it.

But Joshua and Caleb were able to see the possibilities because they remembered all that had been achieved previously. They reminded the people of how the impossible had been made possible for them in Egypt. But the people were so overcome by negative thinking that they couldn't see the possibility they could do exploits again. As a result, they couldn't fulfil the dream. With the exception of the two possibility thinkers, Joshua and Caleb, that generation never fulfilled its purpose and did not enter the Promised Land.

Possibility thinking entails having a faith-filled attitude. Faith is necessary for great exploits. If negativity blots out the possibilities, you won't be able to do great exploits.

Once a fluffy term that was easy to dismiss, positive thinking is now recognised as providing a profound set of advantages for individuals who think in this way. Research reveals that this way of thinking entails much more than being in a happy state or having an upbeat attitude. Positive thinking creates value in people's lives and is strongly linked to building important skill sets, which enables people to achieve in life and fulfil their potential. We can experience the benefits of it in our work, health, and life.

A lot of research on the impact of negative thinking on a person's ability to problem solve and take action has been carried out. For example when a group of people were exposed to images considered negative or that instilled fear or anger, they were unable to come up with any good solutions to the problems they were asked to solve.

Their results compared a lot less favourably with another group who were exposed to positive images producing joy, hope or love. The people in the second group were able to come up with many more workable solutions to the same problems and took much less time to do so than those in the first group. What this shows is that, when we are in a positive frame of mind, our ability to see more possibilities and come up with ideas is greater than when we are in a negative state. Negative mindsets are disempowering and block our ability to take action that's necessary to achieve desirable goals. In other words, negative mindsets make it easier to say no to the call.

Is it any wonder that the Israelites became stuck after visualising images of Goliath parading around and making threats? David, however, came to the field with a heart filled with happy memories of victories past. He also had empowering memories of how he killed a lion and a bear (and the satisfaction those previous exploits had given him). His positive thoughts paved the way for him to take faith-filled actions. A very similar situation is described in the next section, where Rahab saw things very differently as compared to the people of Jericho, and she did a great exploit because of her positive thinking.

When we hold negative thoughts in our minds or focus our imaginations on the things that could go wrong, we become fearful and immobilised. Thinking positively on good things as Philippians 4:8 tells us, unblocks our creativity and unlocks our ability to solve problems that appear in our path. It enhances our ability to develop and apply skills and abilities that are useful and add value to everyday life. A positive mindset makes us open, and this leads to behaviours that provide opportunities for us to develop or enhance skills and abilities we would not have if we were shut down by fearful attitudes.

The following scripture reads like a cool drink of water on a long hot day. Whenever, I get into a place of negative thinking, I read this passage and it allows me to reset my mind to focus on the things I should be thinking about. Before long, the problems that seemed insurmountable, or the things that might have gone wrong, give way to solutions and strategies for going forward. Applying the following technique is one of the most powerful weapons at your disposal to clear your mind of wrong thinking. Paul's inspired words have been proven by modern day research.

Finally, believers, whatever is true, whatever is honourable and worthy of respect, whatever is right and confirmed by God's word, whatever is pure and wholesome, whatever is lovely and brings peace, whatever is admirable and of good repute; if there is any excellence, if there is anything worthy of praise, think continually on these things [centre your mind on them, and implant them in your heart].[12]

4. Negative thinking keeps you from trying

Should you ever find your mission in life or your dream facing genuine threat, negative thinking will keep you from trying to find a way out. When faced with great difficulty, many people give up and think, *What's the point?* or, *I can never win against these odds.* These types of thinkers set themselves up to fail in life. They never do great exploits and their purpose goes unfulfilled.

In around 1250 BC, a woman named Rahab found herself cornered with no obvious way out. She lived in a city called Jericho in Canaan. We do not know the full history of her life, but she is described as a harlot in the Bible. She also provided lodging for travellers. About this time in Jericho's history, the atmosphere in the city was very tense. The city was about to be invaded by a foreign nation under the leadership of Joshua, son of Nun, who had succeeded Moses, the prophet, as leader of Israel. People throughout the land were afraid because they had heard of all that happened to the Egyptians and their Pharaoh. They had also heard of how Joshua vanquished the Amorite kings Sihon and Og. Joshua now had his sights on Jericho.

One day, two Israelite men appeared at Rahab's door. They said they were passing through, but Rahab knew they were spies sent to scout

---

[12]   Philippians 4:8, The Amplified Bible

out the city. She welcomed them into her home and negotiated a deal that would see both her life and the lives of her family spared during the invasion. The spies agreed to her terms and she hid them, saving their lives when the king of Jericho sent out a search party to find them.

When Joshua and the Israelites finally invaded Jericho, they saved Rahab and all her loved ones. Rahab got a new start and found a good future among the Israelites. She even married and had a son. She produced a long line of kings, beginning with David, Israel's greatest monarch. Jesus Christ was also one of her descendants.

Thus, Rahab did a great exploit in her time and went on to discover a great purpose for her life. I think Rahab is one of the great women in scripture for many reasons. She entered the Bible narrative from a very low position – a harlot. She was singular in her time because she was unmarried and created income for herself running a hostel of sorts. It's likely she had a dream to be married and have children, but her situation in Jericho would never permit that. Just when it was all going to come to an end, she saw an opportunity to change her life and took it. Although, negative, defeatist thinking paralyzed everyone else in Jericho, Rahab thought positively about her problem and found a solution that took her beyond anything she had ever dreamed possible for someone like her. She dared to try something, and it paid off massively. The king of Jericho didn't even try to find a way out for his people. He, along with all the other negative thinkers in Jericho, perished during the invasion.

Doing great exploits can be risky business. Rahab put herself in grave danger when she hid the spies in her house. If the king of Jericho had ordered a search and found the foreign spies on her premises, she would have paid for it with her life. If the spies did not keep their end of the bargain, she would have perished. The stakes were high, but because she was a positive thinker, she was willing to try, which took real courage. Negative thinking never produces courage in us;

rather, it magnifies fear and stops us from trying to realise our goals and dreams.

While pursuing purpose, we may find ourselves in vulnerable positions from time to time. But great exploits sometimes involve taking calculated risks. When we try something new, we risk failing or making mistakes. This is often the reason some people refuse to try. But there can be no progress without taking these risks. And there are ways to minimise them or eliminate them altogether.

Apart from being potentially perilous, some of the problems we face on the road to purpose can appear hopeless and insurmountable. In this circumstance, negative thinking will make it easy for us to accept defeat before we've even tried. Sure enough, thinking that there's no hope makes it likely that you won't even try to do anything about a problem. But if you don't try, you'll never discover, as Rahab did, that (even in apparently hopeless situations) trying makes all the difference in the world. There is always a way out. No situation is ever hopeless when it comes to your purpose. Trying will lead to all the possibilities that are waiting for you once you dare to take that first step.

> Fortune favours the brave.
> Alexander the Great

Providence seems to smile on the people who dare to try. The ones who, by faith, not knowing exactly how things will go, dare to take a risk and seize an opportunity to try something to advance their cause in life. The Rahabs and the Davids were at risk of failure or even death, but they showed a willingness to try and push past an obstacle or conquer a giant to get to achieve their destinies.

> For the eyes of the Lord run to and fro throughout
> the whole earth to show Himself strong in behalf of
> those whose hearts are blameless toward Him.[13]

---

[13] 2 Chronicles 16:9, The Amplified Bible, Classic Edition

If God is actively looking for people to help, why not show him you're the one he should help? A blameless heart is a heart that is full of faith. By faith, make a move that will give him a reason to show himself strong on your behalf. The bible says that by faith the men and women of old did many great exploits: they 'subdued kingdoms, administered justice, obtained promised blessings, closed the mouths of lions, extinguished the power of [raging] fire, escaped the edge of the sword, out of weakness were made strong, became mighty and unbeatable in battle, putting enemy forces to flight.[14]' Many times I have acquired assets and seized opportunities having little resources of my own, taking action by faith, and seen things come together as if by a miracle. I have seen doors opened that shouldn't have opened based on my qualifications or experience, but I stepped up to them by faith, and they did. Rahab is my kind of woman. Having nothing of her own to recommend her, by faith she took action and subdued enemies and caused those same enemies to open the door to her new life. When you are at last prepared to take the necessary action by faith, opportunities will come knocking on your door, just as those spies came to the one door in the whole of Jericho where there was still someone with hope who was willing to take a risk.

5. Negative thinking disempowers

Positive thinking is often viewed as fluffy thinking that avoids reality. It's perceived by many as thinking that allows people to bury their heads in the sand without an honest assessment of the facts. But this isn't the case at all. Truly positive thinkers have an awareness of critical facts. The difference is that, instead of being overcome by them, they use them to plan the future they prefer to have. Negative thinkers tend to look at the same facts and conclude that there's no hope. Therefore, they lose their power to act.

---

[14]   Hebrews 11:33-34, The Amplified bible

Both types of thinking are a response to facts. We have the power to choose which response we make as individuals. This power to choose will be explored in the next chapter on taking personal responsibility.

Here's an extreme example of a positive and negative response to the same problem from the Bible. When David lived in the wilderness, he and his men offered protection to vulnerable shepherds[15]. For weeks, he watched over the shepherds of a rich man called Nabal. Eventually, David sent word to Nabal about the services he had rendered to him and asked whether he would compensate him and his men in some way. When Nabal refused, David became very angry and set off with his men to kill Nabal and his entire household. When word about the approaching danger reached Nabal's wife, Abigail, she responded very quickly. Abigail prepared food and drink to feed David and his men. And then she hurried along to meet him before he got to her homestead. She negotiated peace with David and he agreed to relinquish his plan. When Abigail returned home and told her husband what had happened, he collapsed and died! Abigail and Nabal had two distinctly different responses to the same facts. Abigail didn't avoid reality; instead, she assessed its implications and took actions to mitigate it, eventually doing a great exploit. That's how positive thinkers operate.

Everyone can change the way they think

The great news is that, if you're prone to negative thinking or have developed negative thinking patterns, you can change the way you think. It will take some practice, but if you do it consistently, you will become a positive thinker. Becoming a positive thinker has a beneficial knock-on effect on the rest of your life. Your perspectives will become broader, which means you'll begin to understand life in way that helps rather than limits you. You'll be better able to accept other people as they are and find ways to work with them more

---

[15]   1 Samuel 25, The Amplified bible.

effectively. That will, in turn, increase your influence with them. Influence, as you'll see in chapter 5, is paramount to doing great exploits.

Earlier on, I mentioned David's secrets to success that day that he conquered Goliath. Here they are, plus a couple more keys to positive thinking:

1. Assess accurately

> For who is this uncircumcised Philistine that he
> should defy the armies of the living God?[16]

In 1 Samuel 17, when David arrived at the battleground and saw the situation, he assessed it more accurately than everyone else. He saw things more clearly because he tapped into the bigger picture to interpret what was really happening. Seeing things from a higher perspective altered the dynamic and empowered David. It didn't matter that Goliath was a giant and a skilled warrior because he was not in a covenant relationship with God. Plus Goliath was directly opposing God's will by resisting the people. That put the philistine in the proper perspective. David understood that being in a covenant relationship with God, and aligning himself with what God wanted to do, gave him the advantage over Goliath. Anything or anyone outside that covenant was in a weak position. Anyone who set himself in opposition to God's will was skating on thin ice – in a sense, they were already defeated.

This insight then gave him the impetus to take the necessary action to do his great exploit because he knew God would give him the victory.

You'll meet many giants along the way to fulfilling purpose. Some will be in the form of personalities and others might be problems or needs. I've dealt with the issue of challenging personalities in chapter

---

[16]   1 Samuel 17:26, The Amplified Bible, Classic Edition.

6. Assess them in the light of your big picture and those you're called you to impact. It will disarm the power of negative thinking and empower you with the right perspective. You'll see that, whatever it is you're called to do, you will be enabled to do ... if you are willing to make a stand. Starting with an accurate assessment of the problem is key to positive thinking. After all, it empowers you to do your great exploits.

2. Find the motivating factor

'What shall be done for the man who kills this Philistine and takes away the reproach from Israel?' David asked the men.16 When we do what is right, there is a reward. Focusing on the reward is a powerful antidote to negative thinking. Knowing there's a prize waiting for you on the other side of your exploit will stimulate you and get you excited about tackling the problem at hand. When you think about the prize, you're more likely to want to turn your energies towards finding a solution to the problem. Identifying the prize or reward on the other side of the problem is another key to positive thinking. It will motivate you to do your great exploits.

3. Don't flock with other negative thinkers

> And David turned away from Eliab to another
> and he asked the same question,
> and again the men gave him the same answer.[17]

Once David had accurate knowledge of the challenge and identified why he wanted to take it on, he cut off the doubters. David refused to give any airtime to Eliab or those who had a negative view. He was only interested in those voices that would encourage him, boost his confidence, and strengthen his resolve.

---

[17]   1 Samuel 17:30, The Amplified Bible, Classic Edition.

Often, when we are called to do something, we listen to people, who aren't doing much themselves, for advice on what we should do. If you are serious about saying *yes* to purpose, you'll likely have to turn away from some of the company you normally keep. To be successful in the pursuit of your purpose, you have to guard your mind from sources of negativity. You should seek the views of people who will say, 'You can do it!' instead of, 'You can't do it; it's impossible.'

Withdrawing from naysayers is important to keeping your thoughts positive. It will free you to do your great exploits.

4. Begin to testify

> David said, The Lord Who delivered me out of the
> paw of the lion and out of the paw of the bear, He will
> deliver me out of the hand of this Philistine.[18]

David found himself surrounded by negative thinkers, including his brothers and the men in the army. As he stood his ground and resolved to move forward, he gained the attraction of King Saul himself. King Saul's voice was the most powerful and carried the most authority. When we set out to pursue purpose, we will attract higher authorities than we've previously encountered. As the preacher said, 'New levels, new devils.' Be sensitive and aware of what is happening; be cautious and weigh up what is being said to you and by whom.

Saul said to David, 'You are not able to go to fight against this Philistine. You are only an adolescent, and he has been a warrior from his youth.'[19]

At this point, many people turn back from pursuing their dreams. When someone with authority says, 'You can't do it,' the average person believes that naysayer. This is why so few people lead lives

---

[18]   1 Samuel 17:37, The Amplified Bible, Classic Edition.
[19]   1 Samuel 17:33, The Amplified Bible, Classic Edition.

of great exploits and fulfil their purpose. When I was in my final year at university, I took an elective course purely out of interest in the subject. It wasn't necessary to my degree. One day after class, the lecturer asked me to meet her in her office. When I arrived, she said, 'I'm concerned that you will fail and won't be able to graduate this year. Your writing lacks the maturity of a level 3 degree student.' That very year, I graduated with first-class honours; I was in the top three students in my class, and the only woman. The lecturer's negative views didn't destabilise me at all because I recalled that, I had done exploits up to then in my other courses.

Confronted by Saul's negative views, David's positive thinking shifted to the next level. He responded with testimonies of past exploits. He spoke about the times when the Lord helped him. He told Saul about how the impossible had been achieved in the past – more than once.

Rational arguments, even from the highest authority, will sooner or later give way to a powerful testimony. Because of his testimony, Saul couldn't prevent David. Though he started by saying David couldn't do exploits, he eventually had to give in to him. This is as much a spiritual principle as a physical one. David's testimony silenced all the arguments of the doubters and they stopped trying to contain him. There's an effective tool[20] to overcoming any negative arguments brought against us.

Negative thoughts are like an accuser, who accuses us day and night. They undermine our confidence and faith that we can do all things. The accuser manifests in negative thinking – both our own and that of others. One sure key to overcoming it is the word of our testimony.

Speaking your past success out loud is one way to dispel negative thinking. It will arm you to do your exploits.

---

[20]　Revelation 12:10b–11.

5. *Choose to believe you were appointed you for such a time as this*

> And David said to Saul, I cannot go with
> these, for I am not used to them.
> And David took them off. Then he took his
> staff in his hand and chose five smooth
> stones out of the brook and put them
> in his shepherd's [lunch] bag. [21]

People who do great exploits believe they have been appointed for certain exploits because it's who they were born to be. Each of us has been appointed for certain times to do certain exploits. We are uniquely fashioned and prepared for our assigned tasks. We each have the particular combination of personality, talents, skill, and knowledge for what we are called to do.

If we devalue what we have been given, it inevitably results in failure. When we think what we have isn't good enough, or if we think negatively about our gifts and abilities, we will never be able to do great exploits. If we decide to do exploits by trying to copy others or by trying to be like someone else, we will fail as well. We can learn from others, as the chapters on potential will show, but learning from others and trying to be them are two different things. Don't covet the gifts others have; value and utilise your own gifts.

True freedom from negative thinking comes when you accept yourself and love and cherish who you are. You are empowered to succeed when you value the unique resources you've been given. Your freedom, strength, and successes are multiplied when you can recognise and love others in the same way.

Saul offered David his armour. Fortunately, David was secure enough in the person he was created to be – and in the gifts and skill he had been trained in – to politely decline Saul's offer. Because you're appointed

---

[21]   1 Samuel 17:39b–40a The Amplified Bible, Classic Edition.

know that you can succeed by being yourself. You can bring your gifts, talents, and skills to bear upon the issue, and do great exploits. But these successes can only happen if you use what you have. It won't if you try to use someone else's gift. Therefore, trust your uniqueness and respect your gifts – don't criticise, devalue, or belittle them.

The key to positive thinking here is appreciating and believing in the gift you have. It will give you confidence to do your great exploits.

6. Speak positively

The next secret of David's positive thinking is that he spoke the solution, not the problem.[22] He made declarations speaking to the problem, Goliath, and told him that he was already defeated. Earlier, I shared my experience of moving to Toronto – I moved away from family for the first time and found it intimidating. I had came from a strong Christian upbringing, but my new environment filled me with negative thoughts. The big city proved to be my first of many Goliaths in life!

One day, however, I looked out across the city and told it I would conquer it. Everything began to change for the better following that proclamation. As it happened, I not only conquered my fear of that big city, I went on to travel to many big cities in the world, even as far as Tokyo by myself.

When we make positive affirmations and declarations, they put negative thoughts to flight. Speaking or prophesying what you desire destroys negative thoughts; doing so will give you the power to do your great exploits.

7. Run your thoughts by someone who thinks positively

Fortunately, my roommate at boarding school was a positive thinker. Coming from Ohio, in the US herself, she did understand what it felt

---

[22]   1 Samuel 17:45–47.

like being on her own a long way from home. But she was a year older than I was and she believed we would both settle in to our new home and be fine. We both had what it took to thrive – I just needed a fresh perspective. Her response forced me to do some rethinking that was more constructive, and this led to my ultimate victory.

To become a positive thinker in any situation, talk to another positive thinker. It will give you the right perspective needed to do your great exploits.

8. Think creatively

People who do exploits think creatively about solving problems. In Jesus' time, he faced the problem of numerous other teachers competing to win the hearts and minds of the people he wanted to win. Instead of thinking it was impossible to impact the masses in Galilee, Judea, Samaria, or Jerusalem, he chose to think creatively.

Negative thinking would have focused his mind on the fact that the people were uneducated and probably wouldn't be able to receive his message (or that they were too busy with the activities of life to want to stop and listen to him). Negative thoughts would have led him to believe the other speakers were more skilled, had more experience, and had more resources. If he had settled on this way of thinking, he wouldn't have tried to reach out the way he did. He would have failed in his mission and not fulfilled his purpose. Instead, he came up with a creative solution to reaching them through the many parables and stories he told to capture their attention and deliver his messages.

Creativity is often necessary to the positive thinking process. Creativity will bring a dimension of fun to your great exploits.

Reflection on exploits

Negative thinking is often the default for many people. It can become a part of us in such a subtle way that we don't even realise we're thinking negatively. It can even disguise itself as realistic thinking. Try not to be seduced by negative thinking because it does nothing but limit and hinder you.

Positive thinking isn't a frivolous pop psychology idea. Research is proving its benefits. The impact of positive thinking is played out by the great characters whose stories instruct us regarding what it takes to do great exploits.

5

People who do great exploits take personal responsibility

In dreams begin responsibilities.
W. B. Yeats

To accomplish a dream or vision, you first need to have one (as discussed in chapter 2). But having a dream or vision is only the beginning. You must believe you can do the exploits needed to fulfil your purpose, and you must develop the habit of thinking positively when faced with the inevitable challenges or problems that crop up. But in addition to all that, you must accept personal responsibility for ensuring that your vision is fulfilled – that is the next step to do exploits.

Life doesn't owe us anything. No one is entitled to have his or her dream come true. The difference between people who do great exploits and those who don't is that they know and accept that it's up to them to make their dream come true. No one else will do your exploits for you. Successful people do not have any sense of entitlement when it comes to their success – no matter how great their idea, vision, or dream might be. They understand that if they do not take personal responsibility to make it happen, it will not happen.

One of the biggest choices any of us has to make is whether to take personal responsibility to fulfil the purpose of our lives.

Defining personal responsibility

Personal responsibility is about commitment and taking ownership for one's life and the conditions of one's life. When I read the word *responsibility,* I see two words: *response* and *ability.* Therefore, for me, personal responsibility is a person's own ability to respond to life and the situations he or she faces in life. That ability to respond varies from person to person in its effectiveness. There are a lot of factors mitigating that ability. My hope is that the topics covered in this book will give my readers the keys to increase the effectiveness of their responses so they are able to do the great exploits they long to do and fulfil their purpose.

Here's a story that illustrates the power of taking personal responsibility. Greg, one of my close friends in high school, lost his father suddenly towards the end of our graduating year. He was the eldest of four kids. His mother was a low-income worker at a local factory. The family was devastated by the loss. His mother was worried about the family's survival because his father was the main breadwinner.

Greg had already been accepted at university with a full scholarship. He had a dream to be a lawyer. But, desperate to ensure they could pay their rent and buy food and clothing, his mother suggested he get a job instead of going to university. Greg thought about his mother's request for a few days.

He loved his family very much and understood the situation. As the eldest boy, he was expected to take on more responsibility now that his dad was gone. But Greg looked far into the future. He saw that if he gave up on going to university and took a job at the factory, he would probably never have the future he dreamed of. He saw how hard both his parents worked and, even with both of their incomes, the family always struggled. If he chose to take the job his mother got him, his future would likely be like hers.

Greg had a decision to make. He sat his mother down and told her that he was not going to give up the scholarship and take the job. He made her a promise that, if she allowed him to continue living at home, he would get a part-time job to help out. After university, he explained, his degree would enable him to get a job at a law firm and his income would be much greater than if he took the job she had organised for him. Seeing how serious Greg was, his mother reluctantly agreed to his plan.

Over the course of the next three years, Greg worked harder than he had in his life up until that time. He attended his lectures and worked his part-time job as a night security guard. The job enabled him to put in many hours of study during the night. He graduated at the top of his class. In no time, he was selected as an intern by a reputable firm. Even as a junior at the firm, his starting income was almost three times what he would have earned had he taken the full-time job at the factory. True to his word, Greg helped his mother and siblings with monthly cheques to help cover some of the bills. Today, Greg is a successful tax lawyer and is very well-off. He's happily married with children of his own. He never regretted making the choice to take personal responsibility for his future following the untimely death of his father. His mother never shied away from telling him how proud she was of him before she passed away many years later.

People who do great exploits have a set of traits and attitudes that stand out. Taking personal responsibility for what happens to them in life (instead of allowing circumstances or external factors to decide) is a distinguishing feature they all have. They are people who want to decide for themselves the course they will take. That desire doesn't spring from arrogance or a view that they are better than anyone else. In fact, it's usually the opposite: it comes from a deep understanding of themselves and what they came into the world to do. They tend to be humble about it because, when they measure themselves against their sense of purpose in life, they feel small and inadequate. They are humbled to be charged with such responsibility.

Like my friend Greg, they are often faced with tough decisions. But they are less likely to choose options that appear to be easiest, more convenient or that provide present solutions at great cost to the future. When faced with the pressures of life, whereas the majority choose the course of least resistance in the present, people who do exploits make avoiding the long-term consequences their priority. They tend to avoid bowing to pressure, preferring instead to sacrifice their present comfort to have the future they dream of having. This uncommon form of pragmatism is a hallmark of people who do exploits, and it's discussed further in a later chapter.

We do not have to be governed by our circumstances. We can take responsibility for how we respond in the moment. We can take responsibility for the outcomes in the present and for the future. This ability, when well trained, becomes key to doing exploits.

When Greg was confronted by the tragedy of his father's death at a young age and the implications of that event for his mother and siblings, he assessed his options based on a future he imagined and chose his response to his circumstances based on the future vision of the life he wanted. That vision, not the circumstance or its pressures, enabled him to decide what he needed to do in the moment. But it took courage to choose that future over what seemed more expedient at the time. It took courage to tell his mother he wouldn't do as she asked. It took courage to work by night and attend lectures by day for three years when his classmates were free to do as they pleased. To me, that showed that, even as a young man, Greg was able to take personal responsibility for his own future. He could have given up on his dream to become a lawyer in response to the urgent needs of his family; instead, he took control and found a way to help his mother while still going ahead with preparing for what he believed was his calling in life.

You can't do exploits without taking personal responsibility. Every successful person I know of succeeded because they had this particular quality. They didn't look to others, they didn't think they were entitled. They just got up and got on with doing whatever they needed to do, in order to achieve what they needed to achieve.

Personal responsibility is making a commitment to a future outcome we desire and following through with the appropriate actions until we have that outcome. During those years at university, life was hard for Greg, but he was willing to stick it out and do what was necessary to succeed. The life he desired was not going to be handed to him on a platter. If he wanted a future as a lawyer: a future where he didn't have to struggle the way he saw his parents struggle, it was entirely up to him to put in the effort to make it happen. No one could make the sacrifices that were needed on his behalf - they had to be his sacrifices. Greg learned at a relatively early age that, in life, stuff happens. People encounter problems, tragedies, and setbacks. But the people who take personal responsibility, those who appreciate the reality that it is up to them to accomplish their dream, tend to find ways to move past them and keep heading towards their dreams and goals. In other words, they take ownership over how they respond.

When you own your response, you are better able to choose one that leads to the future you want to have instead of the default or the one others think you should accept as your lot in life.

Seizing an opportunity

I find the story of Rahab to be one of the most interesting stories in the scripture. It's a great illustration of personal *response-ability*. I told her story in Chapter 4 illustrating how her ability to think positively enabled her to solve a life and death problem. Rahab's approach can also teach us a lot about taking personal responsibility. When the Israelite spies came to her, Rahab said to them, 'I know that the Lord has given you the land, and that the terror and dread of you has fallen on us, and that all the inhabitants of the land have melted in despair because of you.'[23] She then told them that she and everyone else in Canaan had heard that Israel had destroyed the armies that challenged them previously.

Everyone in Jericho, including the king, was gripped by a fatalistic terror. But despite her own fears, Rahab decided that she was going to try to find a way out; after all, she still had a life she wanted to live.

Rahab said to the spies, 'Now swear by him that you will treat my family as kindly as I have treated you, and give me some sign that I can trust you. Promise me that you will save my father and mother, my brothers and sisters, and all their families! Don't let us be killed!'

The men replied, 'May God take our lives if we don't do as we say! If you do not tell anyone what we have been doing, we promise you that when the Lord gives us this land, we will treat you well.'[24]

When Joshua invaded Jericho, he spared the lives of Rahab per the agreement with the spies. Rahab did a great exploit. Her life and the lives of her family were saved because she chose to take personal responsibility to ensure a good future rather than passively allow circumstance to determine her fate.

---

[23]   Joshua 2:9, The Amplified Bible.
[24]   Joshua 2:12-14, The Good News Bible.

By accepting personal responsibility for what happens, you become empowered to take control and do great exploits. It enables you to influence your future so that it becomes the future you prefer.

> Whatever we decide to do, for good or bad, the
> choices we make are our own responsibility.

Vision without action is a daydream

Personal responsibility doesn't only come into play when tragedy strikes (as was the case for my friend Greg) or when one is confronted by a difficult situation (as was the case for Rahab); rather, it is equally relevant when life is comfortable or easy. Without it, even in the most conducive circumstances, dreams won't come true.

The following Japanese proverb sums it up nicely, whatever your circumstance: 'Vision without action is a daydream.'

It takes action for dreams to become a reality. The book of James says, 'Faith without works is useless.'[25] Action must be preceded by the will to do it. That will is personal responsibility. Though we have a vision, we have to take responsibility for manifesting it. We need to commit to doing what we need to do to create the outcome we desire. Actions lead to exploits. They are the only way to demonstrate your commitment to your dream.

Paul was very interested in Timothy, his protégé, committing himself to certain achievements at the church in Ephesus. In a letter he wrote to him, he stated, 'I remind you to stir up the gift of God which is in you.'[26] Your gift, your dream, your purpose needs activation, and the only person responsible for activating it is you.

---

[25] James 2:20, The Amplified Bible.
[26] 2 Timothy 1:6, New King James Bible

Personal responsibility strengthens your sense of having been called to something. It engenders the belief that you can make a difference, that you count, that you can have an impact.

Why take personal responsibility?

1. People who take personal responsibility are empowered to succeed

While in the middle of his situation, Greg told me that he kept asking himself, *What can I do to make sure I become a lawyer and still help my mother?* Answering such questions became his motivation in life. He quickly came up with a solution that worked for everyone. Many people would have given in to the circumstances, but asking questions such as, *How can I fix this?* or *How can I make this work out in the long term?* empowers you to take control of the outcome. When you feel in control of what happens to you, you are more likely to choose what is best. This then motivates you to put in the effort needed to achieve it – just like Greg.

Once the solution was clear, Greg knew it was entirely up to him to see things through and make it work. The ball was firmly in his court. He had put his cards on the table, and now he had to walk the talk. Although the responsibility was daunting, with the decision came determination and power to see it through.

Greg says he had to change in many ways. He had to reinvent himself to meet the demands of his dream and sustain his mother's faith that he knew what he was doing. He wouldn't have been able to pull it off if he remained the boy he was initially. He had to demonstrate his commitment through a series of attitudes: things such as the way he managed time, keeping his word when he said he was going to do something, helping out around the house and tending to his younger siblings – while never missing a day of lectures or a day at his part-time job. It was a steep curve for him, but it was what he needed to do to make his dream happen. There's a chapter on doing what it takes, i.e. paying the price for your dream later in the book.

Taking personal responsibility for the outcomes of his life led to personal growth for Greg. For one, he grew in self-confidence (not that he hadn't been confident before, but he became more grounded as a person). By the time he graduated, he was convinced that he could do anything he set his mind to, and it was easy to land his first job at one of the best law firms in the city. It turned out Greg made the right choice. I can't imagine that taking personal responsibility to achieve a goal could ever be anything but good.

2. You'll become unstuck

When we don't take responsibility, we feel stuck; we feel as if we are at the mercy of others who decide for us. We feel like forces over which we have no control determine what happens to us and for us. Such forces might include issues from the past, our fears, or our self-limiting beliefs or even other people. There's a whole chapter dedicated to overcoming self-limiting beliefs in this book. Taking responsibility gives you back your power. It gives you the impetus to face these issues head on and overcome them. You stop being a passive victim of circumstance. Instead, you become part of the solution.

When the first man and woman we placed in the garden, it was a wild, unkempt place. But he commanded them that it should not have dominion over them, but that they should subdue it and have dominion over it. They arose without any misgivings, took hold of the responsibility given to them and got on with fulfilling their purpose. It was only when they did wrong that they became stuck. Fear and shame clouded their minds and judgement. It instantly distorted their minds and gave them a victim mindset that rejected personal responsibility. When questioned, neither was willing to take responsibility for their actions. The man blamed the woman.

The woman then blamed the serpent. The serpent couldn't care less; he was already in the worse kind of trouble, with no way out.

But the truth for Adam and Eve was as it still is for us today. They had a choice either to have dominion or be dominated and live at the mercy of external circumstances and forces. To do great exploits you'll need to take control and make the right choices that will lead to the outcomes in life you prefer to have.

3. It will keep you from being casual about your dream

There were once two brothers who received an inheritance from their father. The older one received a parcel of land and the younger received a lump sum of money. The older brother dreamed of turning his land into a source of on-going income. He knew little about investing, and so he poured his energy into attending seminars, reading books, and speaking to people who knew about investing in property. He enjoyed the circuit so much that he started up his own mastermind club of investors and invited industry gurus to come talk to them.

The younger brother craved a lavish lifestyle and also wanted to create an income stream using his inheritance. One day, the older brother came to his sibling and asked to borrow his money. He promised to pay him all of it back with interest. When he heard the interest rate his brother offered, the younger brother gleefully said, 'Yes!' After all, the money was just sitting in the bank and he had no idea how to make it grow. Plus, he had begun to spend it. He'd bought himself a mansion and built a pool in the backyard. He enjoyed having friends over for parties, some of which lasted from Friday night to Sunday evening. Huge bills accompanied those parties. Lending his brother some capital would ensure some of his inheritance was preserved.

Plus, the interest meant income. It was an easy way to make some money.

The older brother used the loan to develop the land he owned. He put up an apartment block and, in no time, it was filled with tenants paying good rent. He was able to repay his brother the loan as well as the interest within the time they agreed. Meanwhile, the young brother had gotten into serious debt to fund his lifestyle. The money his older brother repaid with interest didn't cover all his debts. He asked his brother to help, and his brother generously paid the remainder of his debts as a gift. But after a while, the younger brother found himself in debt again. He was never able to fulfil the dream he had to create income streams using the inheritance his father worked so hard to give him.

Dreaming, wishing, or hoping for a better future isn't enough to get anyone that future. Unless personal responsibility is taken to prepare, plan, and take the appropriate actions, nothing will happen. The younger brother was very casual about his dream, but he wasn't a bad man. In fact, he was grateful for the gift his father left him and wanted to honour his father's memory by making the money work for him. Yet he never got round to translating that desire into reality. For him, it was always, 'One day, I'll do something about it.' Meanwhile, so many things got in the way because he never made a real commitment to create the income he wanted. Personal responsibility is the way to make the transition from having a dream to actually living it. Taking responsibility energised the older brother and he developed a go-getter attitude, which spurred him on to success. He went in search of his dream and found it.

4. It enables you to be a forward thinker and planner

People who do great exploits tend to demonstrate their commitment to their goals by planning and taking actions to achieve them. Planning projects your thoughts towards the future. It lifts you up from where you are and builds a bridge to your goal or dream. Imagining your end result will release energy and motivate you to go forward with your plans.

Another benefit of planning is that it enables you to become aware of anything that puts your dream at risk. Identifying these risks allows you to make the necessary changes or to reprioritise. For example, you may find that you lack important knowledge and skills (like the older brother in the story). He realised that in order to fulfil his dream, he first needed to get an education in property investment. The older brother committed himself to get the training and exposure he needed to become a successful investor. Commitment spurs you on to take control of what is happening in your life and seek solutions to problems rather than be passive or paralysed.

5. People are more likely to believe in you and help you

Have you ever known someone who refused to take personal responsibility for his or her actions or what happened around them? It's very taxing. Most people have a natural tolerance for that to a point. They subconsciously or consciously think, *If I help a little bit, he or she will take up the baton and run with it.* But after a while, when that person doesn't see that willingness to take ownership and responsibility for what is wanted, he or she will lose interest. Even worse, that person will stop believing in you and lose confidence that you can achieve your goals.

After my friend's brother's marriage broke down he found it difficult to keep a job. His drinking got worse and he went from job to job, getting into difficulties with others. Eventually he couldn't pay his rent, so she and their other brothers and sisters decided to help him out financially, to encourage him to get back on his feet. However, instead of getting better, things seemed to get worse. The problem was that he blamed his former wife for his lot in life, and refused to take advice from family who loved him. Eventually, after several years of him asking for hand-outs and continuing to say the state of his life was his ex-wife's fault, people began to withdraw their assistance. His siblings had families and financial responsibilities of their own. It became very difficult to keep financing his bills and expenses especially when he persisted in blaming someone else for his situation and refusing to take personal responsibility for his life.

On the other hand when you have someone who is actively taking responsibility to fulfil his or her goals, even the busiest person will pause a moment to give them the help they ask for.

How to take personal responsibility

Doing everything you need to do on a given day is what leaves you feeling satisfied and content, not loafing around doing nothing.

Here are some of the main strategies for taking personal responsibility.

1. Stop making excuses

The majority of all failures come
from people who habitually make excuses.

Excuses absolve us from taking responsibility for our future – at least in our own minds. But by making excuses, we disempower ourselves and hand over control of our destiny to chance. People who make excuses don't go on to fulfil their dreams.

One of the most common excuses I hear from people when it comes to their dreams is, 'I'm too busy,' or, 'I don't have time.' How is it that people who do exploits manage to do them? Everyone has the same amount of time each day. People who do exploits have the same number of hours in a day as everyone else. They have the same seven days in a week and twelve months in a year … yet they do exploits – and lots of them. This book is dedicated to revealing some of the secrets of those who do exploits. One of those secrets is that successful people use time differently as compared to those who don't do exploits. They understand that time is a resource, just like money or some other asset, and they choose to invest it instead of squander it. They intentionally allocate their time according to their priorities.

Excuses keep people from doing what they need to do in order to do exploits. Moses is a good example of this. Moses had a very important calling: he was born to be a deliverer of Israel. The day he heard it, Moses said something like, 'I can't do that because I'm not good at speaking.' He was thinking about the conversations he would have to have with Pharaoh, the king of Egypt, the leaders of the Israelites, and the people themselves. The thought of speaking to kings and to crowds probably filled him with trepidation, but God insisted that he go. To satisfy Moses, God said his brother Aaron, who was a good speaker, would be there to talk for him. As it turned out, Aaron never had to speak on Moses' behalf. Moses did all the talking himself! He was enabled to do what he needed to do in order to do the great exploits he is now famous for. Therefore, saying he was not good at speaking was just an excuse.

Apart from being shy when it comes to speaking, people create all sorts of excuses for saying no to the call to purpose. Popular ones include not having enough money, fearing people won't like them, and believing that they lack the ability needed. Moses' story shows us that none of these excuses matter when we're called to do something. If you're called, you'll be equipped.

Farmers don't use the weather as an excuse; they go out and sow their seeds. People who do great exploits just go out and do them. Even when the odds are stacked against them, they often choose to try.

2. Stop blaming others

We should recall the past only insofar as it makes us wise to do so.
Life and all its possibilities belong to the future
and the responsibility we take to seize it.

It's very tempting to blame circumstances or others for not doing exploits. But very much like excuses, blaming others takes away our power and renders us ineffective. By blaming, we effectively say that we aren't capable, that we can't be the person we're called to be unless the other person changes. Similarly, we might think we can only do what we're called to do if our circumstances are different. Blaming is saying that people or circumstances have complete control over us – our decisions, our actions, and our destinies are subject to them. But that isn't the case in reality.

Men such as Nelson Mandela have shown us the alternative by their approach to the extraordinary circumstances they experienced in their lives. Mandela had more than sufficient cause to be bitter and vengeful towards those who oppressed him; instead, he remained magnanimous. Twenty-seven years of his life were spent in prison where life was particularly harsh and lonely. Sleeping in cold, damp cells made him unwell from time to time with lung infections. The relentless hard labour he performed in the limestone quarry could have resulted in bitter hatred towards those who kept him captive. If he had allowed his circumstance to break his spirit, he could have given up on his vision of a free South Africa and blamed the people who imprisoned him. But despite everything, Mandela continued his quest to challenge the apartheid system. When he was finally freed in 1990, his attitude was one of reconciliation among all the people of South Africa. While he was alive, I never heard him get into blaming in the media. I believe his vision for a South Africa that was free from apartheid, preserved a powerful sense of personal responsibility that empowered him to focus on the future and promote the agenda for freedom. Mandela eventually rose to become the first president of democratic South Africa.

People who do great exploits don't give any energy to blaming people or circumstances. They usually have a vision they are too busy working towards to pause long enough to attribute blame. Blaming, complaining, or making excuses are counterproductive, energy- draining distractions. They are opposed to taking responsibility for making things happen. Nelson Mandela would not have become the leader he became if he had stopped to blame others for any of the hard times or setbacks he endured.

3. Be accountable

People who don't take personal responsibility also avoid being accountable. One way to keep yourself on course to doing exploits and fulfilling your purpose is to be accountable to a select group of people. Successful people always have someone who acts as a critical friend. Critical friends are those who know what you want to achieve and help you get there by checking your progress. They provide useful feedback and can show you where you need to take corrective action to keep heading in the direction you want to go. In short, accountability keeps you motivated to get things done.

Here's a funny little story about accountability I heard at a seminar – it's a sure way to get nothing done. It's about four people named *Everybody, Somebody, Anybody,* and *Nobody.* It goes like this:

'There was an important job to be done and Everybody was asked to do it. Everybody was sure Somebody would do it. Anybody could have done it, but Nobody did it. Somebody got angry about that because it was Everybody's job. Everybody thought Anybody could do it, but Nobody realised that Everybody wouldn't do it. In the end, Everybody blamed Somebody when Nobody did what Anybody could have done.'

When it comes to doing great exploits, the buck stops with you … not with *Everybody, Somebody, Nobody,* or *Anybody.*

4. Change as your journey develops

My friend Greg talks about the importance of changing to become who you need to be so that you can take responsibility at every stage in your journey. He recalls it was a process of maturation and growth from boyishness to different phases of seasoned maturity. It enabled him to play the new roles and fulfil the new responsibilities that arose in the different phases of his life. There is some scriptural truth in this. After all, in Paul's letter to the Corinthians he said, 'When I was a child, I talked like a child, I thought like a child, I reasoned like a child; when I became a man, I did away with childish things.'[27]

We see David transition through several life stages, boldly embracing the responsibility to fulfil his call to be king of Israel. He did great exploits in every chapter of his life. He was a shepherd and took responsibility to guard his father's sheep, slaying a lion and a bear in the process. He could have allowed the sheep to be taken and then blame the lion; instead, he took responsibility to defend the sheep as was his charge. And then he became a captain of a hundred. As he took that responsibility on, he did such exploits that the women lined the streets and sang, 'David has slain his ten thousands.' As a married man, he took responsibility and became a provider for his wives and children. As a fugitive in exile, when outcasts gathered round him, he took responsibility and became their leader. As a son, he took responsibility for his aging parents and ensured their safety and well-being by relocating them outside of Saul's realm. As a ruler, he bore the title *Israel's greatest king.* Without a willingness to take personal responsibility and adapt to the changes his vision demanded, his story would have been very different.

Don't try to hold on to the past seasons of your life. Samuel the prophet once found himself stuck in an old season, mourning over what didn't go well. He found it difficult to move on. Therefore, he hindered a new and important era for Israel. God asked how long he planned to remain there because there were plans that he wanted Samuel to attend to. While Samuel was stuck, God moved on to

---

[27]   1 Corinthians 13:11 The Amplified Bible.

the next thing. What's the point of lingering when God has already moved on to new and greater things?

To do great exploits, we must be willing to adapt, to lead ourselves through all life's changes on the road of purpose. It's the ability to steer a steady course through the twists and turns of life and still reach our ultimate destination that counts. To do this, you have to be able to let go of past seasons and quickly embrace new ones. People who can't or won't adapt to the inevitable changes along the journey of purpose find it difficult to move forward and tend to get stuck.

Reflection on exploits

Exploits are impossible without someone willing to take personal responsibility. They don't tend to happen unless someone is driving them by taking the necessary actions. Such a person has to be self-motivated and willing to go the distance. The person must be willing to go against the grain when pressures arise. He or she must take a long-term view of life and make the tough decisions in the present that may seem contrary to others. Taking responsibility inspires, empowers, and energises people to do the exploits they dream of doing.

6

People who do exploits
develop their influence

Much of your success in life lies in your ability to get along with others and to influence them. When doing exploits, you'll need people to listen to you, cooperate with you, share information and help you. Your exploits may even depend on partnerships and team working. If you lack the social skills needed to win people over or at least persuade them to give you the help you need to achieve your goal, then you probably won't be able to achieve your goal. It is thought that relationships are more key to our success and progress in life than any other skill we might possess. Likewise, if you're unable to build and maintain relationships you can have all the talent in the world but it will be difficult, if not impossible, for you to do certain exploits. For example studies have shown that the number one reason why people lose their jobs isn't lack of technical ability, but because of poor social skills.

Many years ago, a colleague I barely knew got dismissed from his job as a financial accountant at the private hospital where we both worked. He had too much to drink at the staff Christmas party and got rowdy with a few people, including the CEO. Apparently, he had some concerns with spending on the new wing and used the party as a space to air his views. He was unceremoniously fired the next day. The incident was the topic of conversation well into the next year. The manager had worked for the company for about five years before he got fired and, by all accounts, he was very skilled at his job. He'd supported the finance team and hospital board to bring the organisation out of deficit over three years, which put them in a strong position to raise the money for the new wing. In the period after he was dismissed, no one was interested in the contributions he'd made to the company – he lost his influence in the organisation. Instead, all anyone talked about was that he'd been argumentative and had upset several people at the Christmas party. That lapse in social skills cost him his future with the company and, more importantly, his reputation.

People who do great exploits know that relationships play a key role in their success. If they are unable to build and maintain good relationships many of their goals and long-term dreams will remain unfulfilled. In doing exploits, we usually need to work with others, inspire people with our dream, persuade them to believe in us, and win their help and support. This is what is called influence. Without the ability to influence others to cooperate with you and aid your cause, you will not be able to do great exploits.

What is influence?

Whether we realise it or not, influencing is something we do all the time. In every human interaction we send out messages that get responses from the people in our lives. We can leave them feeling happy, sad, angry, or satisfied as a result of coming into contact with us. This is the normal sort of influencing that may not have any significant implications for us. But when we want to do great exploits, we must ask people to step beyond the ordinary way of thinking or doing to help us – and that takes a bit more thought and effort on our part.

When we influence someone, it means we have persuaded that person to think or act the way we want him or her to. When we influence, we are leading people somewhere – either in their thoughts or their behaviour. Therefore, it's important to understand influence if you want to do great exploits because doing so will enable you to be more effective at getting things done when you need help from other people.

In this chapter, we'll take a look at the power of influence and how to build it if you don't already have it.

Why do we need to influence?

Today, people seem busier than ever before. If you need others to help you or support your goals in some way, you'll have to be able to capture their attention and imagination – perhaps arouse their passion so they can believe that you and your goal are worth their time and effort. It's widely accepted that the ability to influence is a vital skill in life because, when used effectively, you can persuade others to see things your way. When people can see things from your point of view, they are more likely to lend their help and support.

Whatever your dream, it will involve other people at some stage. Authors need good publishers and networks for marketing their books. People decorating their homes must share their visions with the decorators. If you're building a ministry, establishing a charity, or running for political office, you'll need many people from all sorts of backgrounds to assist you. As long as you need people to fulfil your dream, you will need to be able to influence them.

People who do great exploits are skilled at influencing. They can win people over to their way of seeing the world and get them to sympathise with their cause. They can inspire and convince others to buy in to their dreams, goals and plans. If you haven't already done so, you will need to develop this skill to do great exploits. Inevitably, you will have to persuade people to believe in your idea or dream to obtain their help and support.

Effective influencing skills require a healthy combination of techniques, some of which come quite naturally to many of us and some that may have to be acquired. The good news is that all the techniques can be learned and, with a bit of practice, mastered.

Techniques to increase your influence

Usually, all people have to go on is your appearance, what you say, and what you do to develop a picture of who you are. What others say about you can also influence that picture very powerfully. The picture they've formed of you in their minds will determine the extent to which you can influence them.

Thus, to develop influencing skills, start with yourself. Understand the effect you have on others; their perception of you will affect your ability to influence them. Once you have a sense of the effect you have on other people, you can modify the way you present yourself, your views, and your ideas so that they are more readily received by those whose help and support you require for your exploits.

I've listed some of the key techniques needed to increase influence. Anyone who uses them will find that others will become more willing to listen to what they have to say.

1. Communicate clearly and simply so others know what you mean

You'll find it hard to believe how many of us assume other people know what we're thinking or understand what we really mean when we communicate with them. Misunderstanding of instructions is more common than we think. If you need the help of someone else to achieve a goal take the time to really make clear what it is you want them to deliver. Don't make assumptions that they have understood your request.

When communicating your goal or dream, it helps to be mindful of your audience. I once worked for a public service organisation, which served the local community. One of the biggest complaints from our clients regarding communication was the use of jargon. The organisation had to learn how to communicate key messages to different audiences about services in a way they could receive and understand.

People can make themselves available to help us achieve a goal, but if what they're told isn't clear, there's a good chance they'll do what we didn't intend. It helps to remember that regardless of how brilliant your ideas are or how wonderful your dreams are, no one can read your mind. Whatever your thoughts and perspectives, if you don't share them in a way others understand, they won't be able to give you the kind of support you need. Consequently, it's important to help people understand (without patronising them) what you want to achieve and why. Share your ideas using simple messages and encourage others to ask questions. Get them into a discussion so that you can tease out any areas of misunderstanding and address them effectively.

A young intern joined the team of a small local newspaper for the summer holidays. At a staff meeting the editor asked him to prepare a lead for a news release about the financial state of the local health service. She listed the facts: national funding to the local hospital will reduce by 30% over the next five years, the hospital had a deficit of an estimated £15 million, and currently it employed 800 staff providing 80 different services. 'Send it to me in an hour.' She told the intern. The intern went off to complete his assignment. In under an hour he sent it to his boss and waited eagerly for her response. He'd written a lead that arranged the facts and expressed them in one sentence:

'Despite a hospital deficit of £15 million and 800 staff providing 80 services, it is expected that over the next five years, government funding will be cut by 30%'. The next morning at the staff meeting the Editor said, 'I've read your submission. However, the lead for this story is: 'Vital services to be slashed as hospital faces financial crisis.'

When we're seeking to communicate with others, it's not about dazzling listeners with a lot of facts or complex language. Jargon filled language turns many people off unless they're in the same field as you. Likewise, cold facts don't necessarily inspire people. Effective communication is about helping people see the point using language they can appreciate; namely: What are the facts telling us? Ultimately, we must draw a picture of what really matters to people.

2. Communicate the value of your dream

The bottom line is to communicate the value your idea, dream, or goal brings to your listeners or the world. Communicate your dream or goal in the context of how it will change things or bring benefits to other people. People are far more likely to give their help if it's for the sake of others rather than just you. Whatever idea you have, it's bound to have this purpose. Thus, be clear about how it will benefit others so that you can help people understand and get inspired by it … and then communicate it in a way others will understand.

3. Win hearts and minds

> If you want to go fast, go alone. If you
> want to go far, go with others.
>
> African proverb

In chapter 2, I told the story of how President Kennedy galvanised support across America around the vision to land a man on the moon. It was an ambitious dream. How did he mobilise an entire country to believe in it? By appealing to the shared values and beliefs about what it meant to be an American. He spoke to their patriotic pride; he connected the vision to America's spirit of adventure and interest in exploring new frontiers. He also spoke to their national fears by contextualising it against Russia's rapid advancement in space travel. For the sake of humanity and of freedom, it was framed as (virtually) a moral duty that America achieve this monumental goal before the communists did. With the nation's imagination captivated, Americans saw the dream not just as a good idea – but a necessity. It only took the United States eight years to achieve the goal.

People who do great exploits communicate their goals in a way that wins hearts and minds. They make sure they're taking people along with them. They know why their dreams matter to them and can communicate why they should matter to other people. I've endured dozens of presentations and talks in my time, but only a handful inspired me to change my thinking or take action. The presentations were often very professional, and the speakers were articulate, but I remained unmoved, often, disconnected from the core message. People can talk all they want about what's important to them, but unless they bring their listeners along with them, their influence will evaporate.

Whether you're sharing your dream or goals with family, friends, church members, work colleagues, or strangers, bringing people with you is about speaking to what matters to them. Find out what's going on for them and then help them see why your dream or goal matters to them. Once they can grasp the relevance of your goal to their lives, you will have won them over, making it more likely for you to achieve your goal.

4. Get to know your audience

To win hearts and minds, it's important to know your audience. JFK could appeal to the values, aspirations, and fears of the American people because he knew what they were. Some may consider this a manipulative ploy. The reality is that such methods have been used time and time again in advertising, in the news, and (especially) in politics. However, just because some have misused a principle, it doesn't mean the principle itself is bad.

Here's an example of how Jesus used what he knew about Peter to motivate him. After his death and resurrection, Jesus appeared to him. Peter had denied knowing Christ the same night Jesus was arrested. I find Jesus' choice of words really telling. For me, they encapsulate his perfection as an influencer and communicator. He said to Peter, 'Feed my sheep.' Those three words contained his simple and clear message, but they also appealed deeply to what Jesus knew about Peter. Peter was a passionate man. He was passionate about Jesus to the point of following him for three years. He was passionate about Jesus' mission and message. Peter was a fisherman, going into dangerous environments to catch fish that would satisfy hungry bellies. He understood the human need to be fed with good food, and he knew Jesus was the bread of life.

Jesus knew that, following his mistake; Peter was in a deep state of discouragement. Jesus wanted to mobilise him again so that he could become active in the purpose for his life. Jesus' words – 'Feed my sheep' – transformed Peter.

The principle of speaking to the beliefs and values people hold dear is an effective way to influence them. Know the audience receiving your message. Do some research about your bank before you go to the manager to ask for a loan to start your business. Learn about the types of people who may come to hear you pitch your ideas. Ask questions. I was invited to speak to a group of women at a small conference some time ago. I spoke to the Holy Spirit a lot about what he wanted to me to say, but I also had many questions for the organiser: 'How old are the women? Are they married or single? Professionals or students? Churchgoers or not? What do they know about the conference theme? What does the organiser think the women need to hear?' She may have thought I was very particular and demanding but, after my talk, she congratulated me and said, 'You were spot on! You must come back again.' I could only be spot on because I did my best to find out who the audience was and what their needs were and went about preparing to bring something of relevance.

5. Make your dream theirs

The people who do great exploits involving other people are able to communicate their vision in such a way that other people believe it's their own. When they hear these men and women speak, they think, *I believe in that. That's exactly what I want to do!* That's why they get up from where they are and follow them, work for them, and sacrifice for them. If you have a vision or goal that others can believe is also their own, that is the ultimate influence. You won't have to convince or force anyone to help you – they will do it automatically because it's also their vision; you've simply given them the permission they need to take the action you ask them to take to make it happen.

6. Seek companions ready to undertake the same work

When you communicate your dream to others, it's an invitation for them to participate in making it happen. In 1947, Mother Teresa met with the Archbishop of Calcutta in order to tell him that she believed she was called to live and work among the poor. The Archbishop agreed to support her application for permission to live outside the convent while still keeping her vows as a nun. She was granted permission to do so in 1948, leaving the protection of the Loreto convent to give her life in service to the poor and enlist the help of others to do the same.

After a year of teaching an increasing number of children, people volunteered to get involved. Some were students themselves. Mother Teresa decided to start a new order of nuns who would be willing to dedicate themselves fully to serving the poor.

The petite figure dressed in a simple white sari with a blue border and a cross, pinned on her shoulder, called a benefactor to action. An Indian Christian offered her the use of the second floor of his home. In under a year, the number of sisters working with Mother Teresa grew from three to eight. A few years later she had recruited twenty-eight sisters to the cause.

People who do great exploits share their dreams with people to arouse their interest and, if possible, their assistance. They draw people ready to undertake the same work like magnets attract metal. Such people hear a call to action that resonates with their own values and dreams and then use their own influence, resources, and effort to help them make their dreams happen. Often, people have ideas and dreams that are in line with our own. What they're looking for is someone to give them opportunities to get involved.

7. Identify a common purpose

Another way to take people along with you is to identify a common purpose between what you want to achieve and their interests. This can build a strong connection through which your influence can increase. For example, I remember the first time I saw Wendy and Rory Alec, the founders of God TV. They had just launched the channel and gave a talk at the church I attended. I was in the audience, listening to them talk about reaching the world with the gospel message via satellite and cable TV. For someone like me who does not even own a TV, the promotion of a new channel did not hold any interest. But because their channel had a purpose in common with the audience, I, plus many others present were inspired to help. Even though I hardly ever tuned in to God TV myself, because I believed in the purpose, I still contributed financially over several years.

8. Share your passion

Few things stir people to empathise and lend their support than when you share what's in your heart. Even if they're not that interested in your idea, if they can sense your passion and see the value your vision can bring to others, at the very least, they'll listen to you. Your passion may even touch them to the point that they decide to help you.

Sometime ago, I was flicking through the TV channels at a friend's place and stumbled on a documentary about the development of the telescope. I'm not a physicist and didn't enjoy my physics class in high school for one second, but I stopped at the channel because the voice of the narrator arrested me. Her passion for the subject matter was so great that it shone through in her voice; I was curious to see who she was. Finally, she appeared on the screen. Her energy and enthusiasm were so captivating that I watched the entire show.

Unless you're a scientist or enthusiast in a related field, I can't imagine that the creation of a telescope would be that interesting, but because this scientist was so passionate, she caught and held my attention on a subject that I would otherwise consider boring. By the end, I was fully persuaded that the telescope was a great thing. I watched for forty-five minutes, but to me it felt like twenty minutes!

I believe this is one of the reasons Martin Luther King's most famous speech became one of the most recognisable speeches around the world. It takes you right to the heart of the man, his vision, his dream, and the depth of belief and emotion Dr King held for his assignment. It made it difficult for even the enemies of that dream to defend their position. But, perhaps more importantly, it connects with the heart values of decent people. It made his assignment relevant to humanity as a whole by appealing to what people believe is right and good in their heart of hearts.

But you don't have to be as powerful a speaker as Dr King to win people over to your way of seeing the world, and you don't have to have a vision to put a man on the moon like JFK to make a difference with your life ... nor do you have to build powerful telescopes to be a doer of great exploits. You just have to find out what you have been put on this earth for and do that, whatever it might be. It may appear small, like a young woman giving birth to a baby. Mary's baby, though he looked as ordinary as any other baby, changed the world. Never see your dream as inconsequential or small. However, in sharing it effectively, you have to find a way to connect with the hearer in your own authentic way before you can influence them.

Passion increases your influence with other people. Give people a glimpse into just how excited you are about your assignment.

9. Establish your particular expertise

If you have specialist knowledge or experience about your area, be sure to convey it. When people listen to those who know what they're talking about, they are more likely to be influenced by them. The presenter on that TV show about the telescope was passionate, but it was also clear that she knew exactly what she was talking about. Subsequently, I discovered she was an expert who once worked for the Ministry of Defence in the United Kingdom. She developed missile-warning systems and went on to work on hand-held devices to detect landmines. Later, she shifted focus and joined a leading research group at a top university. There she was involved in the development of the Gemini telescope in Chile. That famous telescope enables scientists to study what's happening billions of miles away. Listening to her that one time hasn't convinced me to buy a television but, on occasion, I do think about buying a telescope to gaze at the stars!

10. Network

While you're getting your plans together, you may not have to influence just yet. Still, you can prepare for when you do need to start talking to others about your dream. Doing some groundwork will make things easier when you do step out. A common way to do this is by networking.

To do great exploits you need to seek opportunities to form new relationships and strengthen the ones you already have. Having a network of people with knowledge, skills, expertise, experience, and additional contacts will give you quick access to these resources. When I'm thinking about a new project, one of the first things I ask myself is, *Who do I already know who might be interested in this or know someone who might be interested?* My network links me into the people that I want to influence and get on board with my project. Having a colleague or friend introduce me to someone they know makes life much easier than if I had to approach a stranger and convince him or her to get involved.

Another important reason to build networks is that they can help you develop and refine ideas so that they are likely to be more successful. The ideas we have are simply ideas we pick up by listening to other people. King Solomon said, 'that which has been is that which will be [again], and that which has been done is that which will be done again. So there is nothing new under the sun.[28]' This goes for ideas too. Ideas are simply thoughts we regurgitate after consuming hundreds of pieces of information we receive through listening and observing.

11. Become an effective listener

It shouldn't come as a surprise that the techniques for increasing influence are rooted in the way we communicate with other people. Effective communication doesn't only include the ability to deliver a

---

[28]   Ecclesiastes 1:9, Amplified Bible, Classic Edition

clear, simple message or gain an understanding of what motivates your audience. An equally important aspect of effective communication is being able to listen well.

What better way to understand other people, their needs, wants, and passions than to become good at listening to them? When you listen, give consideration to their ideas and opinions; hear about their experiences, and learn how they have been affected by them. Doing this will help you make vital connections between what they really want and your dream. You will then be able to give them your version of 'feed my sheep' and see them spring into action that is aligned with your purpose.

Actively listening will help you find any common ground. There's little point trying to influence someone who is clear about wanting to head south when you are going north. Effective listening will help you find those whose direction is also north. After that, you can tell whether you can work together to progress together for at least some portion of your journey.

Good listening is also about flexibility. As you listen, you'll find some people have a take on your idea that will make it better. Be willing to change and adapt. Acknowledge their helpful insights and comments and thank them. You'll be amazed at how much help thanking a person can produce.

Apart from increasing your understanding of other people, listening can also expose you to ideas, knowledge, and opportunities that can move you along the path of purpose and exploits.

Winston Langley, a successful businessman who grew up in Louisiana in the 1930s learned the value of listening at an early age. As a boy, he had a job shining shoes outside a grocery store. One day, he happened to hear a customer mention how much he tipped the valets at the club where he was a member. Langley earned about 10 dollars per week at the store and the hours were long. He told the owner of the store that he wasn't coming in one Saturday and instead went to check out the club some distance away. When he got there, he talked the manager into giving him a job as a valet. Langley had never done that type of work before but he observed what the other valets did and followed them. On the first day of working at the gentlemen's club, he earned far more money in tips than he did in one week of shining shoes. Listening had opened up an opportunity that increased his earnings; plus, while he valeted for the businessmen using the club, he also learned a lot about business by actively listening in on their conversations. Langley later cut a successful entrepreneurial path, founding a successful company for himself by applying much of the knowledge and wisdom gained while listening to the men at the club.

Most people are far more interested in talking than they are in listening. The ability to listen puts you in a prime position to receive potentially useful information and insight that may be of benefit to you.

12. Be pragmatic, learn to work with people as they are in reality

In the Bible, Mordecai, the uncle of Queen Esther counselled her saying, 'You have come to your royal position for such a time as this?'[29] It was recognition of her purpose and potential. Influential political forces were working to ensure the genocide of her people, the Israelites. Her husband, Ahasuerus, ruled with absolute power. In order to save millions of lives, Mordecai encouraged Esther to find a way to influence him. Given his treatment of her predecessor, Queen Vashti, Esther was acutely aware that she would have to use wisdom to fulfil her purpose. She studied the ways and attitudes of the king. She developed an understanding of what he liked and disliked. She worked within the protocols required by him and won his favour. Because of this, Esther was able to influence him when she needed to.

---

[29] Esther 4:14, New International Version

You'll meet all sorts of people with different personality types, attitudes and agendas on your journey of purpose. Esther had her Ahasuerus; Moses had his Egyptian slave master (and forty years later, his Pharaoh); David had his Goliath, his Saul, his Absalom; Daniel had his Nebuchadnezzar and his Darius; Samuel had his Eli; Elijah had his Jezebel; Jesus had his Judas and the Pharisees; Ruth had her Naomi; and Rahab had two spies and the king of Jericho. The assignment of each individual was inextricably tied to the challenging personality of the other person or persons. Yet, because they all managed these relationships with wisdom, each of them did their great exploits according to the vision they had in their hearts. Jesus was very sensitive to the personalities round about him and used a lot of wisdom in managing his relationships in order to safeguard God's highest purpose for his life, as the following scripture shows.

> During the time he was in Jerusalem, those days of the Passover
> Feast, many people noticed the signs he was displaying and,
> seeing they pointed straight to God, entrusted their lives
> to him. *But Jesus didn't entrust his life to them. He knew
> them inside and out, knew how untrustworthy they were.
> He didn't need any help in seeing right through them.*[30]

On your journey of purpose, you will also connect you with people you won't have to convince to help you, or strive with, on your particular journey. In as much as David had his Saul, he also had his Jonathan; Esther had her Mordecai; Moses had Aaron, Hur and Joshua; Jesus had eleven other close allies. But, sometimes, almost inevitably, you will meet with those who require more effort and caution on your part to persuade or manage.

It helps to become clear about the role tricky personalities have to play in your assignment. It's important not to be confused about the reason the person is in your life. Avoid being distracted by whether the person is likeable, fair, or right. Many of the young people I coach

---

[30] John 2:22-25 The Message (MSG)

or counsel are often fixated on a boss, or other person in authority, who they describe as, 'Unfair', 'a hypocrite', or 'mean'. I tell them all the same thing, 'Develop the same attitude of the Queen of Sheba when she came to visit king Solomon. If she'd got hung up and judged him for the hundreds of wives and concubines he had, she wouldn't have been able to learn from him and fulfil her purpose for being there. She didn't allow his character issues to impact her personal mission and ruin her future.' You're not there to judge or change that person. If he or she is connected to your purpose, it's because he or she has something that needs to be released to you. In some cases, he or she is the link or bridge to the future.

If you understand the part these types have to play at different points in your life, you can learn how to relate with them for the season they become prominent in your life, like Esther did. Never lose your objectivity like Moses did when he killed the slaver. Learn the strategies you can use to relate effectively with them. Become skilled in those techniques. They will enable you to manage your relationships effectively. Often, it's about learning to manage yourself! Recognise such individuals for who they are in relation to the call on your life and respond to your situation using wisdom. Had Esau taken closer note of his brother Jacob's agenda and personality, he may not have lost his birth right to him. Joseph did not handle his brothers effectively, and he paid a price for it. Some people have close friends they need to be more mindful of too. They can appear very sincere but in fact harbour jealousies and rivalry, which eventually surface when you least expect; and they are quite capable of launching an ambush and even attempting to destroy your reputation and influence with others. Jesus told his disciples, "Stay alert. This is hazardous work I'm assigning you. You're going to be like sheep running through a wolf pack, so don't call attention to yourselves. Be as cunning as a snake, inoffensive as a dove.[31]" When you set about answering the call, you enter into perilous times. You can put your ideas at risk

---

[31]   Matthew 10:16, The Message Bible

by exposing them to the wrong people, or at the wrong time or in the wrong way. Even your best intentions can be misinterpreted or misunderstood. Don't draw any unnecessary or unhelpful attention to yourself[32]. Don't crash and burn; learn to work around people as they are in reality, even the challenging ones.

In the Bible, Ruth influenced Naomi, her depressed mother-in-law, very well. She didn't allow Naomi's bitterness to turn her away from moving towards her dreams. You can read her passionate argument in Ruth 1. Though Naomi had made up her mind about going back to Bethlehem alone, after she heard Ruth speak from the heart about her vision, Naomi changed her mind and decided to help her.

Rahab influenced the spies. Her attitude could have been one of animosity; after all, they wanted to kill her and all her people. But she saw an opportunity and put aside any differences. She offered them her protection from the king of Jericho in exchange for what she wanted. Her service created trust, which she leveraged to get something vital back. She found a way to befriend them and worked with them to build a bridge to her future.

As you seek to grow your influence, you'll notice some people are easier to win over than others. See it as an opportunity to grow in your interpersonal skills. Endeavour to communicate effectively with those people. For Esther, so much depended upon her being able to influence the king. She *had* to find a way to reach him. For the sake of your assignment and those who will benefit from it, you too must find a way to get what you need from challenging personalities.

Even though he was second in authority only to Pharaoh, Joseph was not welcomed to sit and eat at the same table with the Egyptians. Another challenge in life is racism. Joseph didn't complain, (at least to our knowledge based on what the bible says), about being excluded in this way. He got on with the work God had called him to do. Had

---

[32]   2 Timothy 3:1-5, The Message Bible

he let that treatment become a focus for his energy, he would have gotten side tracked from his ultimate purpose in life and may have lost his influence. At times, addressing issues of race and inequalities is critical, but even if it is experienced, it is not necessarily a signal that you're called to address it directly. Think carefully about what specific problems you should spend your energy and gifts on, in a given situation. Choose your battles carefully, always with the bigger picture in mind. Don't be reactive to every little wind of offence; keep your eyes firmly fixed on the ultimate prize that is waiting for you. In the past, someone in authority bullied and harassed me. I didn't make a formal complaint, or talk about it with anyone (although if it was very serious, I would have reported it). I spoke to him about it (of course he denied that he was doing anything wrong and said that I misunderstood him and was being sensitive). After that I made sure that I kept my distance. I remained with the organisation despite that, because I was learning a lot and enjoying my experience there in many other ways. When I moved on it was because the time had come and very quickly the door opened for me to work at the next level. Meanwhile, I had gained the experience I needed in preparation for that next stage of life. Had I left before my time because of that man, I would have missed what I needed at that stage of my professional life and who knows how it could have impacted on my reputation.

Look at this extraordinary exchange between Jesus and a Canaanite woman who came to him seeking a miracle. Jesus ignored her. But as she carried on begging him his disciples told him to send her away because she was harassing them. Jesus replied to them that he was only sent to the lost sheep of Israel. Yet the woman persisted in calling out to him and asking his help, all the more. Jesus turned to her and said, 'It is not right to take the children's bread and throw it to the little dogs.' She said, 'Yes, Lord, yet even the little pups eat the crumbs that fall from their master's table.' Jesus granted her request when he saw that she wouldn't take no for an answer.

I believe the story of that woman was included in the gospels to teach us many things. But for this context of doing exploits, we can learn that our determination to fulfil purpose can be tested by those whose help we need. We are called to persist, to negotiate, to persuade them that we are serious about why we're asking their help. We can't afford to take offence by any rebuffs or put off if they appear not to take us seriously.

People who do great exploits have a certain pragmatism. They have learned how to work with different personalities, difficult people, moody individuals, immature people, critics, people of poor character, etc. Managing relationships will probably be one of the largest investments you'll have to make in terms of wisdom, time, energy, and effort when doing exploits.

13. Always be respectful

Few things have the power to cut off favour and influence like disrespect. In casting your vision, there will be people who disagree with you. It's okay to have different perspectives. Give people space to express their opinions, but you should avoid belittling them or their opinions. Make a decision to be respectful of everyone. You may still be able to influence someone who disagrees with you if you show him or her that you respect his or her point of view. Relationships are built on trust and respect – there can be no influence without them.

14. Be of good character

If disrespect closes the door to influence and cuts off favour, a lack of character is the next big risk to your ability to influence others. In doing exploits reputation goes a very long way. I've known very talented people whose influence was curtailed or destroyed in organisations and beyond, because they broke moral standards. In 2006 the head teacher of a church school in the United States was asked to resign because of his addiction to gambling and alcohol.

His dependency had developed over the course of about 25 years beginning when he was in college. Drinking had helped him relax and manage pre-exam anxieties as a college student. He'd run up significant debt during university and desperate to find a quick fix, he started betting on racehorses. He was quite an ambitious young man and managed to keep both his dependencies out of sight for most of his life. He brought great vision to his job and managed to do exploits turning a failing school around in the first 5 years as the head teacher. In that time there was an increase in the number of students being enrolled in the private school under his leadership. However, after sometime, staff members noticed the odour of alcohol on him. Plus, he became more prone to outbursts of anger. One day, he came to work and it was obvious he was inebriated. Teachers who had become good friends of his were reluctant to challenge his increasingly unpredictable behaviour. Soon, it was obvious, even to the students that he was under the influence of alcohol. The students resisted instructions he gave them. They gossiped about him and he lost his authority with them. They no longer looked up to him as a role model. Many of his staff, were disappointed and hurt, feeling like he had betrayed their trust in him. By the time he was asked to resign by the church board that appointed him, his influence was non-existent.

I know of a pastor who was doing great exploits in a working-class community where he lived and pastored a church. He had big dreams for social action projects to build resilience around families and lift people out of poverty through exposing them to investment opportunities. He was an extremely dynamic and charismatic person. People flocked to his church. Things went very well for many years. He was even gaining influence with government officials and financial authorities. But somewhere along the line he ended up owing dozens of people huge amounts of money. By his influence they had donated money towards building a complex where people could come and be trained and edified. However, that building never materialised and the money disappeared. The pastor and his family went into hiding. His ministry ended. To this day, the situation has never been resolved and he's never been brought to account for what happened.

Credibility and trust are strong drivers of influence. When wanting to influence people to help you do your exploits you need to be able to win and maintain their trust. Trust is built up over time and is dependent on integrity and transparency. If credibility is lost, that person's ability to influence goes with it. Credibility, trust, and integrity are all interdependent. If one of them is lost, the rest are undermined. And the effect is amplified if the person in question is a Christian because a higher standard than the world's is expected.

Good character isn't just doing the right thing in a moment it's in striving to do what's right - as a way of life. People with a lot of influence tend to be looked up to by others. The extent to which an individual is able to influence people, is a direct reflection of how that person behaves all the time. When lapses do occur we must do everything we can to make amends and win back trust. That often includes openly admitting to making a mistake, giving an apology and then making every effort to do better in future. When we are sincere and humble about our errors that can also be a power factor in whether others will open themselves up to our influence again.

15. Help other people achieve their goals

People who do exploits form mutually helpful relationships. They think win–win. This is thought to be an extremely effective way of influencing. As you build your network and step out to achieve your own goals, you'll meet people you can help along the way to achieve their goals. You can form collaborations where you figure out what you can do together to make the difference that is of common interest to you.

The scriptural law of sowing and reaping applies here as much as it does to agriculture or money. When you help people, people will help you. It may not necessarily come from the one you helped, but help will come when you need it. Even if the one you help can't help you, you create a certain level of loyalty in that person towards you.

A man from the Bible, Joseph, offered his help to Pharaoh's cup-bearer and baker, both of whom were thrown into the Egyptian prison where he was serving time for a crime he didn't commit. At the time, there was nothing either convict could do for him in return. But, two years later, one of them remembered his kindness and mentioned him to Pharaoh. The king of Egypt immediately summoned Joseph to the palace to ask his advice. Of all the help Joseph ever received in his life, the cup-bearer's help was the most valuable. Imagine if he had not offered to help him that day in prison?

Help others achieve their goals if you can. There's no telling how helping someone now can influence your future.

16. Share your testimony

Share your testimony. I've had the privilege of reading a number of biographies in my time including that of Richard Branson, the founder of *Virgin*; Howard Shultz, founder of *Starbucks*; Condoleezza Rice, the political scientist and diplomat who served as secretary of state under President George W. Bush, the evangelist Billy Graham and Nelson Mandela. These were the most memorable ones. Years ago I found an amazing complete collection of the speeches, interviews and sermons of Dr Martin Luther King Jr. In it I discovered the depth and breadth of this man's intellect, wisdom and faith, plus the many personal struggles and trials he experienced while doing great exploits leading the civil rights movement in America. It showed me the human side of a hero who laid down his life for his dream.

Though I haven't met any of these people personally, their stories have contributed to the person I am today. They've influenced me to do exploits of my own. Their testimonies are inspiring. They each had big dreams and set about achieving them, doing great exploits as a result. But an interesting thing has come about after reading their stories. For example, when I have to go abroad, the first airline I look to for flights is *Virgin*. Anyone who knows me well knows that *Starbucks* is my favourite place to sit, read a book, think, or write. Often, when challenged by life, I turn to some or more of these books to re-read the problems faced by these individuals and how they were able to overcome them.

This is a form of loyalty that money cannot buy. It has grown in me because of their testimonies. I empathised with their struggles and bought into their cause. What's more, these people and their exploits make their way into my conversations occasionally.

You want people to be so inspired by your purpose that they naturally promote your story, your product, your service, your charity, or your ministry in the same way. But for that to happen you have to let your story be known. Tell people the story of why you're doing what you're doing. Tell them what led you to set the goals you set. Share the circumstances you faced that caused you to develop the vision or dream you have. It will help people to better understand your mission. Your message will resonate more with many of them and they will be more sympathetic towards your vision because they have connected with it on a personal or emotional level.

17. Handle matters with a light touch

You won't be able to influence every single person and bring them round to your way of seeing things no matter what you do. Even the most influential people have had those who disagreed with them, didn't want to work with them, and preferred to actively work against their cause, Jesus met with many such people while he walked the earth. He was unable to influence the Pharisees and Sadducees. He failed to convince the rich, young ruler to join with his cause and become a disciple. In Nazareth, he couldn't do any exploits because no one there took him seriously. He wasn't able to influence them to change their views of him. Still, Jesus never forced his agenda on anyone. He never got riled or bitter when people didn't listen, and he didn't become discouraged when they disagreed or challenged his teaching. Often, he simply moved on.

Use a light touch with those who appear less than interested in your vision. People who do great exploits tend to direct their time and energy where it's more likely to reap a reward. Jesus told Peter exactly where to put his net in order to make a big catch.[33] If you work as hard as Peter did that night and get nowhere with certain people, it could be that you're simply fishing in the wrong spot. To do great exploits be sure to define your target audience or niche market. Ensure you're focusing your abilities in the area where you're called.

The power of using stories

Telling stories can be a powerful tool for influencing others. Jesus himself, told many stories, or parables, to get his point across and help people understand his messages. I was in a meeting where someone was trying to raise funds for a program in the developing world involving young girls. She began by quoting some statistics and talked about the widespread poverty and the number of pubescent girls not having access to hygienic items, which affected their education and future prospects. The charity was raising funds to supply these items. On the surface it seemed a reasonable cause but only got a lukewarm response from the audience. The fundraiser then told us a story. She began with the statement, 'Imagine your daughter or little sister was taken out of school and forced to get married at age 13 just because they started having periods.'

We were then told about a girl called Bezunesh who entered puberty. Bezunesh (and other girls in her school) were routinely sent home from school whenever they were menstruating because they had

---

[33]   John 21:6, The Amplified Bible.

no sanitary towels to use. Though Bezunesh was a bright girl who enjoyed learning, missing school five days out of every month meant that she began falling behind in her classes. It was difficult for her to keep up with the lessons she missed when she was barred from attending school. Having missed 25% of the curriculum, which included key subjects such as math, English and sciences, Bezunesh was held back and made to repeat the year. She continued having to miss school because of her menstrual cycle and eventually dropped out altogether. At age thirteen, with no future prospects, she was forced to marry a man who was old enough to be her grandfather. This man already had two other wives, one of whom was only months older than Bezunesh. His first wife, who was closest to him in age, routinely abused the two newer wives, and used them like house slaves. Just after her fourteenth birthday and effectively still a child herself Bezunesh became a mother.

The telling of that story had a powerful effect on an audience of western women. After hearing Bezunesh's story, and other girls like her, we understood why this issue mattered. It was wholly unacceptable to us that a girl's future could be so adversely affected just for the lack of access to hygienic towels. But the consequences are in fact serious. Everyone signed up to give the £3 per month to the cause. The speaker had won our hearts and minds. By signing up we weren't merely paying for the towels, in our hearts we were rescuing girls' futures.

Your passion for your cause will drive you to take a bold stand on the issues that mean a lot to you. People who do great exploits, seek to influence others who have the means or power to make things happen. They make their cause everybody's business. They capitalise on their network of connections to channel attention and resources where they are most needed. They leverage their name and reputation to attract the types and levels of help that they need, to do exploits and achieve their vision.

Reflection on exploits

In life, doing great exploits is largely dependent upon our inter-personal skills, the ability to interact with others in a positive way and persuade them to cooperate with us. Therefore, the ability to influence others is one of the single most important factors needed for exploits. Jesus, for example, was a master communicator and influencer. He was skilled at relating to people from every walk of life and communicated his mission with effectiveness to anyone listening to him. Knowing your message and who your audience is plus employing different approaches to relay your message make up an important foundation for developing influence with other people. If you want to do great exploits, you must learn how to communicate effectively so that you can influence others.

Part II

Fan into flame the gracious gift of God, [that inner fire – the special endowment] which is in you.

2 Timothy 1:6, The Amplified Bible

Maximise your talents, gifts, abilities, and ideas

Recognise
Overcome limits
Release

7

People who do great exploits recognise their potential

During the 2012 Olympic games, I remember standing in a crowd of about seventy or eighty people who were watching the 100 metre race on a big TV. Although I had heard the name Usain Bolt before, I (not being a sports fan at all – ok, I know!) was never quite sure what the fuss concerning his name was about … until that race.

But even if you're not a sports fan, there's just something about the Olympics and that 100 metre dash that is exciting. I watched while the athletes took their places and waited for the starter pistol to go off. I knew that when that happened, the crème de la crème of world-class sprinters would take off. When I heard the pistol, my attention couldn't help but be drawn to the tall, lean, and long-legged Olympic record holder. Millions of people around the world watched that race; and it sounded like every last one of them was in the room with me when Bolt won. Later, I learned that, not only had he won, but he also broke the record he set in the Beijing games in 2008. He completed the race at an eye-watering 9.63 seconds in 2012. Even I could appreciate the significance of that!

As I said, I'm not a fan of sports, but I am a huge fan of achievement. I have a certain regard for the extraordinary people who accomplish them. People who achieve great exploits are extraordinary because they step off the beaten path, rise above the norm of everyday life, and carve a different path for themselves. At some point in each of their lives, they became aware that they had a gift, talent, or idea that uniquely positioned them to make a difference. One of the many traits such people share is recognition of their potential.

What is potential?

Take my friend's daughter Camille for instance: although she is a very good actress, her first love was singing. Her teacher spotted her potential as an actress during rehearsals for a musical she was directing. She encouraged her parents to get her some acting lessons and take things from there. It took some persuading to get Camille to switch her focus from her voice to acting, but when she did, she suddenly found herself at the start of a trajectory that has already begun to pay off. Almost immediately, her gift attracted the attention of the types of people with the knowledge and experience to help her develop her potential. But it began with that initial recognition on her part that she had something unique to bring to the stage and a willingness to develop it.

In 2014, I attended a play in which she had a significant role. She was only age 13. I was really impressed with her portrayal of the character she was playing. At the end, the production drew a standing ovation from the audience. On the drive home, I told her how great she was at acting and asked if that was something she would do as a career in future. This was her reply, 'I love acting but I still have a lot to learn. It's definitely what I want to do for the rest of my life and I can't wait to see how far I can go with it.'

I believe that, hidden inside every human being, is the potential to do exploits. *Potential* is the future promise contained within something. For example, an apple seed carries the potential to become an apple tree. When they were born every gold medallist carried the potential to become a gold medallist. What potential are you carrying?

Potential is the combination of your ability, gifts, talents, and ideas. It's customised to the unique call on your life. We were created with potential so that we would be able to fulfil the purpose for which we were made. If you have a purpose, a dream, or a mission, you were given the potential to carry it out.

However, fulfilling potential isn't inevitable; purpose isn't always expressed. Not every apple seed goes on to become an apple tree. Not every kid with athletic potential goes on to win medals. The promise of potential is somewhat like holding an apple in our hand. The vast majority of people will consume the apple, enjoying the delicious taste of the fruit. However, they don't take account of the seeds. The seeds are discarded without a thought. They enjoy the pleasure or short-term benefit of their talent but don't think about whether that talent is something they are called to develop in service to a worthy cause. Only someone who cares about the potential in the seed, and looks into the future to see what those seeds can produce under the right set of conditions, will invest in releasing the potential contained in the seeds. If the seeds of an apple are planted in the ground and cultivated in the right way, they will produce countless more apples. Their impact will be multiplied and be a blessing to numberless people. However, if the one apple is simply enjoyed by one person in the moment and the potential in the seed is not released, the apple only blesses the person who eats it.

A huge amount of human potential goes wasted. Many people die without fulfilling their purpose – and that's the reason books like this one are written: to help a person see what he or she needs to do to fulfil his or her potential and purpose.

Why are your gifts important?

I like Usain Bolt's story because its start is not so unlike any of ours. It's about an ordinary boy who was born with potential. The backdrop may be different in that we weren't all raised in rural Jamaica. But at the start of our lives, there's not usually anything to distinguish us in any particular way from other children. In his early years, he probably seemed similar to any other schoolboy with a passion for sports. In reality, however, he had a natural talent that would eventually make him stand out from his peers and lead to great exploits later in life. It was his talent that made all the difference. What talent, ability, or idea do you have that can make all the difference to your life, community or the world? You'll find that it's important for the following reasons:

1. Your gift or idea gives you relevance

Each of us has something we can use to make an impact and a difference in our world. It's what makes us relevant. If you want to order a wedding cake, you don't go to a mechanic; if you want to build a house, you don't go to a singer. To get a wedding cake or build a house, you go to the people who have the relevant gifts, experience, and abilities. Similarly, your particular gift has its own relevance to other people. When you can meet the particular need others have, you become significant to them. If you're feeling irrelevant or insignificant in your circle of friends or at work, it's probably because your gifts aren't being used in that context.

2. What you carry distinguishes you from everyone else

> A man's gift [given in love or courtesy] makes room
> for him, and brings him before great men.[34]

Those gifts and ideas you have, (your potential) are what distinguish you from everyone else. They are what make you different. It's this

---

[34]   Proverbs 18:16, The Amplified Bible.

difference that makes room for you. Your unique difference causes others, who recognise the value it brings, to accommodate you. When you can solve a problem they have or render a service they need, even the busiest and most important of people will make way for you because you have what they need. Joseph was one of countless other slaves in Egypt. Yet he was distinguished from them all when he became the slave of choice and got promoted in Potiphar's house, the prison, and Pharaoh's palace because of his abilities. He solved problems for these great men, and they gave him a special place in the hierarchy despite his ethnicity and social status. For Daniel, it was the same: although he was a slave, he was distinguished from the other slaves because of his gifts and ideas that drew the attention and respect of great men. What would have become of Joseph or Daniel had they tried to blend in with the crowd of other slaves? Had they ignored the natural ability they each carried, they would not have fulfilled the purpose for their lives.

Many people are afraid of their differences. They believe there is safety and security in conformity. Yet it's a lack of conformity that has led to every advance, invention, and progression people enjoy today. Conformity is acceptance of the status quo set by the majority. But it was because Thomas Edison refused to accept the status quo of candle or gas lighting that he developed the light bulb. A woman by the name of Rosa Parks refused to conform to an idea. Because she rejected the status quo of discrimination, the civil rights movement went to another level in the United States. Her simple act of choosing to be different and sit in the 'wrong' place set a chain of events in motion, which eventually changed the culture of a nation. She (among countless others) made it possible for a black person to be elected president forty or so years later. Because another woman called Ruth refused to conform to the societal rules of widowhood in her time, she arose to find a better future for herself. Ruth recognised her difference and chose to honour it. As a result, her name is now remembered thousands of years after her death. She's remembered as someone who didn't settle for what life handed her. Believing she had something to bring to the right man, she offered herself in marriage to a worthy man, making a home for him and giving him an heir. Ruth found true happiness in her search for significance and she's yet another unlikely woman who came into the lineage of Jesus Christ.

Recognition of your difference is recognition of your worth.
It's the understanding that you have something
valuable and useful to offer others.

Blind conformity to a status quo devalues difference and contains potential. It means much-needed service is not released and human need is frustrated.

3. Your potential is given to you for service

When we release the potential of our talents or ideas, it makes a difference in the world. Sometimes, without realising it, we create a ripple effect that never ends. When you exercise your gifts and abilities in service towards your purpose, the effect goes far beyond what you think or imagine. As shown in chapter 1, doing exploits in the form of trophic cascades, wolves and other animals transform their local ecosystems. Such systems contribute to the ecological systems globally. The discovery of the phenomenon has given ecological scientists new knowledge, such as the unexpected impact on the stabilisation of riverbanks and even the way rivers flow. If the potential of wolf packs in nature can have such impact, how much more can a human being do given his or her capacity to dream, imagine, think, plan, and take decisive actions.

Twenty years ago, we all managed without the Internet. Today, we wonder how we could ever live without it. No device, invention, or service you know of would exist if someone had not decided to release his or her potential. Consider the impact the light bulb has had or the cars we drive. How about building a space shuttle to land on the moon or starting a charity supplying sanitary towels to pubescent girls in the developing world so they can attend school and fulfil their potential? What about leading a cell group at your church or turning a hobby into a business? Think about writing a screenplay or salvaging the destinies of young people through mentoring. Your potential is to be used for what you were put you on the earth to do. The gift or idea you're carrying is meant to benefit others. If it's never released, those you were called to render service to will not experience the blessing.

How to recognise the potential of your gift or idea

People who do great exploits believe they have potential. It takes conscious effort to manage our potential well so that it's fulfilled and not wasted. In the process, we learn to master our natural gifts so we become effective – even excellent – at what we're called to do. Here, I share some ways to value your potential.

1. Don't judge by where you're coming from

> But we have this treasure in earthen vessels....[35]

Life has a way of putting people in little boxes based upon certain characteristics they have. For example, if you are from the geographical category labelled *developing world,* the assumption might be that you're poor and lack a decent education. If you're a girl, in some cultures, the expectations about you are lower than if you were a boy. Depending upon your race or ethnicity, various assumptions are ascribed that can be challenging to dispel even when you demonstrate otherwise. As individuals we also have a tendency to put ourselves in little boxes. We assume that our background must be some indicator of who we really are and what we're capable of. In this way, we devalue or negate our potential to impact the world.

But few things are further from the truth. Jesus Christ was born on the floor of a barn and raised in a town called Nazareth. Yet he

---

[35] 2 Corinthians 4:7, New King James Version.

became one of the most famous and influential figures in human history. After Philip met Christ for the first time, he called his friend Nathaniel and told him he'd found the *one* whom Moses and the prophets wrote about. Nathaniel's sceptical response was, 'Can anything good come out of Nazareth?'[36]

After some time away, when Christ returned to Nazareth, the people there couldn't see him as anyone special. Though he had worked many miracles elsewhere, Christ couldn't work a single one in Nazareth because of the people's perception of him as a Nazarene or because they happened to know his family. They refused to recognise his gifts and abilities.

Many people go about their life beating themselves up over where they came from, the family they belong to, or some mistake they once made. I believe that one of the many issues that held Moses back from saying *Yes!* to purpose was his memory of the mistake he made in Egypt some forty years previously. For forty years, he'd lived with the self-condemnation and regret over what he did when he killed the Egyptian slave driver. By the time he had that Divine visitation on Mount Sinai, Moses had fully accepted the belief that nothing good could come from him if he got involved with the politics of Israelite slavery in Egypt again. In a similar way people think, *I want my life to make a difference, but can anything good come out of my family? Can anything good come out of my town? Can anything good come out of me?* They may hold the misguided belief that they have no potential or that they are not worthy of being of service or fulfilling purpose. This is a serious mistake. Many of these very people go to church and consider themselves people of faith. But the bible describes them as, 'holding a form of [outward] godliness (religion), although they have denied its power [for their conduct nullifies their claim of faith]…'[37]

---

36   John 1:46, The Amplified, Classic Edition.
37   2 Timothy 3:5, The Amplified Bible

The power being denied by such people is the power of faith that still makes it possible for to do great exploits in fulfilling purpose.

People who do great exploits never focus on where they came from or where they started. The past has little or no relevance to them. They learn constructive lessons from the past and keep moving forward (see chapter 13). They recognise that what's at stake in the future is far more critical than what may have happened in the past. People who do great exploits are future-oriented people. The thing that gets their greatest energy in life is where they're going, not where they came from.

2. Don't judge your worth by what happened to you

People who do great exploits excel at overcoming challenges. As I've written many times already (and will write again in the chapters ahead), the road to fulfilling purpose is steeped in challenges. Some of the challenges are more potent than others. To manifest the reason for which you were born takes strength, courage, gritty determination, and a certain amount of pragmatism. You have to work through the issues of your life and take control of the way they affect you. Bad things happen to good people. In this fallen world, no one gets a problem-free life. That is the reality. The people who meet their goals in life are the ones who learn to handle the problems that life throws at them. That's how they're different from people who don't do great exploits.

Sadly, child abuse is all too frequent in the world in which we live. The scale of this is much larger than we know. It is often a major barrier to moving forward into a life and future of impact. However, there are many examples of people who, have overcome the strongholds of fear, shame and feelings of worthlessness, that abuse gives rise to. They still went on to do great exploits. By faith they fought for their freedom, not denying its power to transform their lives and make them winners.

For instance, I know of a preacher who grew up in very difficult circumstances in which she was molested. The abuse damaged her sense of worth and caused a lot of emotional pain. Back then it may have been impossible for her to imagine who she was called to be or what the purpose for her life was. Yet, despite those difficult beginnings, she was carrying great potential. This person went on to become a respected bible teacher and is a best-selling author of several books. To hear her share about her early life, you could be forgiven for wondering, *Can anything good come out of such a situation?* Yet it did.

> But we have this treasure in earthen vessels,
> that the excellence of the power may be of God and not of us.[38]

People who do great exploits don't allow the things that happened to them in the past determine the things that will happen to them in the future. They don't see their potential as being subject to what others did or what others said. God who put that treasure in you is more than able to manifest it, regardless of what happened to you in the past. Earlier in the book, I told the story of one of my team members. She learned to conform to what a former boss had said about her, and it would have continued to limit her potential, until someone else challenged her beliefs. She has never looked back. It turns out that she wasn't what people said she was. She began to discover and recognise that she carried a treasure within, i.e. her potential. And the recognition of her potential was a springboard to her great exploits in her career and the organisations she subsequently worked for.

If you took some time to discover and recognise you have potential, what would it be a springboard to for you? What can happen for you if you throw off the labels others put on you, cast aside the things they said about you, and stop focusing on what they did to you? What would happen if you were to just release the past and hold on, instead, to a vision of a wonderful future of impact? What if you were to stop

---

[38]   2 Corinthians 4:7, New King James Version

looking backwards and look forward to where living on purpose would take you? The answer is that you would join the great company of women and men who do great exploits every day.

3. Discover your potential

Stir up the gift...[39]

What gifts, talents, and abilities do you have? What skills and experiences have you already gathered in life? How can you begin to apply all these assets to create a compelling vision for your future? How can you use them in the fulfilment of a purpose that gives God pleasure?

As a young child, when my friends were playing with dolls, I was writing poetry and lyrics. And then I started writing little stories – some of them were only a paragraph long! But I only came to recognise that I might have some talent when I was sixteen. My English teacher was passing back an assignment she'd given the class, a short story. She paused at my desk and said, 'Miss Johnson, when you become a famous author, make sure you tell everyone Valerie Henry was your English teacher.' On that day, Mrs Henry switched on a light within me that has never gone out. I began to treasure my potential as a writer from that moment onward.

Many people never discover their potential; they tend not to see themselves as having gifts or being capable of making the world a better place. Usually, they are more likely to recognise the gifts others have, seeing them as better able to make a meaningful difference in the lives of other people. The majority of us go about daily life not employing our full capacities. We may be aware of being better at doing some things, but many of us don't believe they're worth developing. I've had the privilege of working with a lot of young people over the last two decades. Each time I spot a talent, I tell the

---

[39] 2 Timothy 1:6 New King James Version

person what it is and encourage him or her to begin explore it further because it may well be an integral part of their calling. This is just something I learned from my teacher Mrs Valerie Henry.

There are as many purposes as there are people. Yours may be a talent to entertain – be careful not to undervalue that. Entertaining others is a legitimate reason for living. Everyone has a need to leave their own issues a while and be refreshed through uplifting, inspiring, or edifying forms of entertainment. I enjoy a variety of entertainment. When I hear Leontyne Price, the opera singer, sing, her voice moves me deeply. Inevitably, the power and beauty of her voice leaves me marvelled. Your purpose might be finding a cure for cancer. You could be called to be a scientist in a lab doing experiments on cancer cells, searching for a way to get rid of them. Your purpose might be to demonstrate how challenges in life can be overcome, prompting you to climb Everest and tell your story about how you did it in spite of all the risks. That kind of story always inspires people and mobilises some of them to expect more from their own lives; such stories catalyse action in others so they can achieve personal dreams. Your purpose might be to raise God- fearing children, building within them the confidence that they need to be able to fulfil His purpose in their generation.

Whatever your purpose might be you are equipped with unlimited potential to carry it out. You'll never know just how much you'll influence others unless you try because we do not know who your gifts will touch. For instance, even if your purpose was to meet the need in one person, because of what you poured into that person, he or she might release his or her potential to make a difference to countless others. That's why great teachers are so important. They have an almost sacred power to awaken potential in a child or put it to sleep forever. Because of their authority, pastors and preachers also have this power.

It was a Sunday school teacher who had a passion for speaking to young men about the importance of establishing a relationship with

Jesus Christ who spoke to a young man called Dwight L Moody about Jesus. Moody accepted Christ and went on to preach the gospel in two continents with untold thousands. One night, a preacher made an altar call at one of his revival meetings in Charlotte, North Carolina. One of the people who came forward was a sixteen-year-old boy. He led him to Christ. That boy was Billy Graham. It's reputed that, through his radio and TV programmes, Graham has shared the gospel with over 2 billion people with his own mouth, preaching to more people than any other person (including Paul the Apostle). It's impossible to estimate how many other people those 2 billion people may have shared what they heard with people they met.

We commonly underestimate our potential. My story about my own writing isn't unique. Often, we don't recognise our potential because it hasn't been pointed out. Some people don't recognise their potential because they are told they aren't good enough to do anything, as is discussed in the next chapter.

4. Do everything you can to protect your gifts, talents, and ideas

Having recognised that you have potential, the next thing is to ensure you take care of it. Your gifts and talents are among your greatest assets in life; they are what were given to you so that you can prosper in life and make a valuable contribution to the lives of other people. If you want to take care of your potential, Start by doing the things needed to develop it right now. When it comes to potential, you must use it or lose it.

People who do great exploits cherish the gifts and abilities they have. They know that they can't fulfil their purpose without them. Therefore, they are mindful to preserve what they have been given. One sure way of achieving that is by living a disciplined life. In an earlier chapter, I wrote that people who do great exploits do not live unrestrained lives. They are so committed or 'sold out' to their purpose that they put their gifts to work daily so they may bear good fruit. These people choose their friends and associates wisely; they know that relationships can either nurture or destroy potential.

I'm reminded of the Bible character Samson. He was given a very unique gift on the condition that he never cut his hair. Samson went against the sound advice of his parents and chose to marry a woman called Delilah who did not believe in Jehovah. Delilah's ways were quite different as compared to her in-laws'. More than that Samson had a peculiar call on his life that demanded a particular lifestyle. The lifestyle was prescribed in such a way as to enable him to release the potential of his gift and fulfil the reason he was born. His big mistake was choosing to marry someone who did not fit with that prescribed lifestyle. Delilah and Samson were unequally yoked and that led to disaster in his life. Eventually, she seduced Samson into disclosing the secret of his gift and, while he was asleep, she had Samson bound and cut his hair. When he awoke, he found that he had lost his gift. Though he was shown mercy and his gift was restored, Samson died as a direct result of being careless with it in the first place.

People who do great exploits come to understand that their vision and purpose prescribe their way of life. Purpose dictates their every choice – from what they eat, to whom they marry, to what they think and do. They see cherishing, safeguarding, and protecting their potential as being critical to fulfilling their purpose. They are right because the fulfilment of purpose is dependent upon the use of our gifts.

If you want to do great exploits, be very careful about how you manage your potential. Choose your intimate relationships, friends, allies, and mentors accordingly. Don't take your gifts for granted.

5. Develop your potential and commit to releasing it

There was an Olympic gold medallist who at 8 years old decided she wanted to become a gymnast and win gold medals after watching the games. In the years that followed, she practiced and began to excel at gymnastics until it became clear she had a special talent for the sport. Her parents provided her with a good trainer and, before she knew it, she began winning local meets. But her gift and drive to develop her natural ability meant she needed more advanced coaching and mentorship. Options were limited in her hometown, and she begged her parents to allow her to move to another city where she could train with a coach who had trained former Olympiad gold medallists. Reluctantly, her parents consented to send her to another US state at age thirteen to be trained by this gifted coach. Years later, she recalled what a huge sacrifice it had been to leave home and how much she missed her parents. But with the move a long way from home, she quickly settled in to a challenging training schedule. For two years, she was at the gym for eight hours every day. In the afternoon, she worked on some academics by correspondence. The sacrifice and hard work it took to nurture her potential as a winning Olympic gymnast paid off when she went on to win gold at her first Olympic Games.

Potential must be nurtured in order for it to be released. As long as we leave our potential unchallenged, it remains dormant. No matter how talented you are, without the necessary training your talent won't lead to great exploits.

6. Observe others with similar gifts

If you look around, you'll find that many other people share the gifts you possess. That's why you'll come across more than one pastor, author, business person, architect, computer scientist, doctor, and opera singer in the world! Nevertheless, don't allow that to make you doubt that you can make a difference with what you have. With over seven billion people in the world, there is a market for your particular gift somewhere. Your personality and experiences – the way you view the world – will express themselves in a unique way, and that's what will distinguish you from the others who share a similar gift.

Observe how others use their gifts. Study the market where your particular gifts are in demand and take note of how others execute their ideas. What approaches are they taking? Which gaps can you exploit? What can you do that's different? Identify your niche; find something new that you can bring to the table.

Reflection on potential

One day, a pensioner found an unexploded World War II bomb in the far corner of her back yard when she had her old garden shed pulled down. She didn't know what it was; to her, it looked like a giant bullet. It was about the length and circumference of an adult's forearm. It was rusted on the surface and covered with the dirt and moss that had gotten stuck to it over the years. She thought it was a bit of scrap metal. She picked it up with her bare hands and laid it on a pile of rubbish she had collected to be thrown away. Later, when her son came to visit, he saw it lying on top of the rubbish heap and asked where it came from. She told him where she found it. Immediately, he went inside and called the police. The woman was horrified when she overheard her son refer to the old rusty lump of metal as a *bomb.* Within minutes, the police appeared at her door. Her son led them to the device, still resting on a heap of rubbish from her shed. Soon, more officers arrived, and they cordoned off the entrances to the house and instructed her and her son to vacate the property immediately. The police then went from door to door to evacuate the entire block of neighbours from their houses. Pretty soon, the quiet little street looked like the set of a Hollywood movie. Police officers dressed in anti-explosive gear carted all sorts of equipment into her back yard. It took them hours to diffuse the bomb and relax the cordon so people could return to their homes. An officer explained that it was a specific type of bomb that still carried the potential to explode. If it had exploded, it would have taken out at the entire block – destroyed the houses on the street, potentially killing anyone in them. The old woman couldn't believe that, for all those years, the bomb was dormant in her backyard, quietly possessing massive potential.

Our potential is a force we should use to create and build, but it can also be a destructive force against the systems of the kingdom of darkness. Despite the potential each of us possesses, many of us leave it lying dormant and unreleased because we don't recognise it for what it is. If, like that old lady, you don't understand what you have, you're likely to toss it on life's rubbish heap.

8

People who do great exploits overcome limits to their potential

People who do great exploits break out of every limitation. There are many influences that can either liberate someone to fulfil their potential or put a lid on their potential. There's no limit to where your gifts, talents, or ideas can take you. However, certain influences can affect you in such a way that you put the limitation on yourself. Self-belief is a major influence on the extent to which people do great exploits. We explored this powerful internal influence in an earlier chapter; the influences we'll look at in this chapter are those coming from external sources – the things that have been done or said to us that contain potential.

Influences on potential

Our life experiences, especially in childhood, have a great influence on what we think we're capable of achieving. My teacher telling me my writing was good and suggesting that I could be an author was a turning point for me. I was simply doing what I enjoyed and hadn't thought about whether others might want to read what I wrote. But she sowed in me the idea that not only was my writing worth reading, but also that I had the potential to be good enough to be published. She enlarged my thinking, taking limits off my potential. In short, she created in me a compelling vision of being an author that I have worked on since then to realise.

At his 70th birthday party my friend's granddaughter named him the inspiration behind her blazing her own path as an actress. She'd landed key roles in musicals such as *The Lion King*. As a young man her grandfather had broken the mould and gone into record producing, creating several of his own labels, instead of taking the more traditional route of his family and got a job. His career in the music industry inspired her as a girl to dream about how she could use her own talents to have an impact. She learned from her grandfather that having a love for what you do and becoming a lifelong learner of your trade were keys to success. Passion and continuous learning are needed to fulfil potential. Teachers, friends, or family members can be our greatest source of inspiration and motivation to excel at what we're good at doing. Looking at the lives of others who have done well can encourage us to lift the limits off ourselves and do great exploits. Such people make it a little easier for us to say *yes* to the call to purpose.

But not everyone gets that positive encouragement from others. For instance, bible characters David and Joseph were not encouraged by their families to develop their gifts and fulfil their potential. In fact, David's family didn't see his potential at all; they had no expectations that he could be anything but a shepherd boy. He was one of Jesse's eight sons.

God informed Samuel the prophet that he'd chosen one of Jesse's sons as the future king of Israel and sent him to Jesse's home to anoint the one. Jesse brought all his boys before Samuel, leaving David out.

151

But none of the seven boys that Jesse brought to him was the one. Eventually, Samuel asked him whether he had any other sons. It was only then that Jesse called David. The moment David entered Samuel's presence, he knew, 'He's the one!' It goes to show that people's low expectations are not an indicator of anyone's true worth or potential. If you find yourself being excluded from a certain crowd, it may be a sign that you have something special that they don't (rather than the other way round)!

The low opinions that David's brothers had towards his abilities were so entrenched that, even after they knew he would be their king, they still belittled and dismissed him when he offered his help.[40]

They just couldn't see young David's potential, and they treated him like he was an incapable person. Life's like that. In every family, in every generation before David and after him, lids have been put on children's potential because of a parent, sibling, or relative's limited perspective. In many cases, the child accepts those limitations and learns to operate within that small view. It forms powerful mindsets that make it difficult for some to dream, aspire, or take consistent actions in line with goals. Because incapability is as much a learned behaviour as capability, these limits become self-fulfilling prophecies.

Despite what David's family thought of him, David had a great purpose to fulfil. They may have seen him as nothing more than a lowly shepherd boy, but he carried the potential to become Israel's greatest monarch.

What limitations have the perceptions of others put on you? Are you living like a shepherd boy when you have the potential to be much more? Many people have allowed the things said and done to them to set limits on what they can achieve, but it doesn't have to be that way. I don't believe for a moment that it was easy for either

---

[40]   1 Samuel 17:28.

David or Joseph to be treated the way they were by people who were supposed to nurture them. When Joseph had his dreams, his brothers hated him and tried to get rid of him. They really wanted him dead; instead, however, they chose to sell him into slavery. They may have found comfort in the thought that, as a slave, his potential would be capped and his ambitious dreams would die. But neither happened. Everywhere Joseph found himself, he worked at releasing his potential. Though he was a slave, he exercised his gifts diligently and became the best slave his master ever had. Many people carry these issues from their past into adulthood, and doing so hinders their potential. But David and Joseph applied some of the principles shared throughout this book to get past the rejection. They didn't allow it to hinder them from doing great exploits and fulfilling their purpose.

As I pointed out in the previous chapter, sometimes there are many more voices telling us we're not capable than there are telling us that we are. When we feel the resistance of negative voices, we can make a choice. The examples I've shared of people throughout this chapter prove that this choice exists and is the determining factor of the outcomes of our lives. We cannot help what happened to us, particularly when we were children. But we have a choice to either accept the limitations that negative voices assert, or break free of them. I believe that, in life, everything that feels emotionally uncomfortable to us can be used to help us mature and expand as people (or make us smaller).

How to overcome limitations

Fortunately, there are several effective ways to break the lid off your potential. The strategies shared below – and others – will enlarge your potential and empower you to fulfil your potential despite what has happened to you or what has been said to you.

1. Learn to see yourself the way God sees you

Like David, the way others see you and the way God sees you can be very different. What's most important is the way you see yourself. To break free of the limitations on your potential, let his view become your view; let his opinion of you, become your opinion of you. If you want to do great exploits, you need to be able to see yourself the way he sees you.

We can only know how he sees us by studying his word, which is described as a mirror. In that mirror, the Bible not only reveals what needs improving, but also it reflects all you can be in Christ. Plus, it offers many ways for us to become better human beings, to overcome limits and chains from the past, and to change. The next section is a good example of practical insight from the Bible that involves changing a wrong mindset.

When you look into the mirror of God's word and begin to see all you can be, receive it by faith. Think on it every day to allow your confidence to arise. Any limitations you have will be broken; you will then be able do all that you need to do because you will receive the strength you need.

2. Re-programme yourself

There are various ways to re-programme or renew your mind so that you can maximise your potential for doing great exploits and fulfil your purpose in life. Reprogramming comes through what you look at (observation and imagination), what you hear (inspirational and motivational truth), what you say (affirmation), and the content of your thoughts (meditation). These methods enabled a man called Joshua to maximise his potential so he could do great exploits. They transformed him from being a powerless slave (minimum life impact) into a great leader (maximum life impact).

Sometime around 1300 BC, Joshua, son of Nun, was born into the type of slavery designed to limit or even destroy potential. He came from a long line of slaves. His parents, grandparents and great-grandparents were slaves. They taught him a thousand and one ways to conform to slavery. They programmed him to be a good slave who stayed out of trouble by never challenging the status quo. He was taught to see himself as weak and powerless and the Egyptians as strong and powerful. He was conditioned to be a servant and never a master – a submissive follower, not a leader with aspirations and ideas. Slaves were fearful and intimidated by anyone who was not an Israelite. Slaves had no right to acquire land or property. It was pointless to dream or create a vision for a life owned and governed by the slave master.

But Joshua witnessed the acts of God in Egypt through Moses. He saw how the Red Sea parted when Moses stretched out his rod. He saw miracles happen in the desert when Moses prayed. Seeing these things, Joshua began to think differently about himself. Looking at what was accomplished through one man gave him a new outlook and began to break the limitations on his potential. It reprogrammed his thinking, changing the slave mindset to a God-centred mindset. A new vision of himself was formed that was far greater than the limits placed upon him while growing up in the slave environment. Despite his weaknesses and his past, Joshua learned that, if he would just believe, anything was possible. Though he was powerless in and of himself, by faith he could do great exploits.

Because Joshua made himself available, because he was hungry to discover and fulfil the purpose for his life, he received power to do so. His mindset changed during those wilderness years. One of the things that happened was that Moses, who was never a slave, became his mentor. If you need to enlarge your vision or push the boundaries of potential, learning from someone who has a large vision and is maximising his or her potential is a great way. Continue to look out for those opportunities – they are very easy to miss because people who do exploits look like ordinary people.

But then Moses, Joshua's mentor, died. Joshua was called to step into his place. However, some aspects of Joshua's former slave mentality would always pose a threat to his potential to fulfil his mission in Canaan. That old programme was a powerful one and shouldn't be underestimate it. Don't underestimate the old programmes you may have learned that hindered you from progress in the past; they will always try to interfere with what you're doing. Old programmes, rooted in the past experiences, have a strong gravitational pull and must be actively counteracted by powerful positive words and affirmations. Peter was able to defy gravity and walk on water at Jesus' word, 'Come!' But then Peter's old programme, as a fisherman, involving fear of the sea, rose up within and tried to drag him down. Jesus then reached down and pulled him back up.

God has provided us with his word. None of our old programming is a match for him or his word. Each psychological, emotional or spiritual programme must eventually yield to the consistent building of faith, by the meditation of God's word. Every negative, doubt filled mindset, wrong imagination, piece of knowledge, or erroneous belief must give way to the word. Every programme that is contrary to God's truth about you will fall when challenged by the word. In order to experience the word at work in all its power, we must meditate on it and speak it aloud in affirmations.

From God Joshua received the secret to continuously breaking free of the limitations that slavery had wove into his mind; and to releasing his potential as a leader. The secret was to meditate on the word and learn from worthy mentors and role models. He was told to speak affirmations using the scriptures, meditate on them (fill his thoughts with passages of scripture that counter hindering thoughts) and then make a habit of practicing what the scriptures say. Habitually thinking in a certain way or repeatedly performing actions built Joshua's old programmes.

Breaking them required the same habitual and repetitious activity using words that built new, helpful mindsets.

Like Joshua, our past programmes can create limitations on our potential. But we can break free of them using these methods. They are guaranteed to lift the limits off your life. Is there something that's telling you that you were born for more than what 'they' said to you or did to you?

The experience Moses had on Mount Sinai was one of the factors that inspired me to write this book. I have been in that same place as Moses many times. I've felt called to do many things but hesitated because of the mistaken belief that I didn't have what it took to do the exploits I was called to do. Some I said *Yes!* to. Others I've said *No!* to. When I said *No!* it was usually because of one or more of the same reasons Moses initially said *No!* on that fateful day. I am not unique in that way. No doubt you are reading this book because you have also been in that place where you found it easier to say *No!* But I learned that if Moses, becoming the effective person he went on to become, started out with a host of insecurities, weaknesses, short-comings and mistakes, then it is possible for us all to become what we were intended to be. After all these people of old had a 'nature like ours [with the same physical, mental, and spiritual limitations and shortcomings][41]' yet did great exploits. All Moses' objections to the call were refuted and disarmed the longer he spent laying down his weaknesses at God's feet that day. The longer he remained in his presence, the less those fears and concerns seemed reasonable. In that burning bush experience, all the wrong mindsets that had held Moses back from doing great exploits in fulfilment of the call that was on his life were destroyed. Eventually, those objections had no power

---

[41]   James 5:17, The Amplified Bible

over Moses. He walked away from that extraordinary encounter, a new man.

It was as though he'd been transformed into a new creation and given a new nature, which made him ready to be used. He received a new mind, one of power and love in exchange for the mind of fear and shame. His purpose was revived and he was armed with everything he needed to fulfil it.

> For we are His workmanship [His own master work, a work of art], created in Christ Jesus [reborn from above— spiritually transformed, renewed, ready to be used] for good works, which God prepared [for us] beforehand [taking paths which He set], so that we would walk in them [living the good life which He prearranged and made ready for us].[42]

3. Make a conscious decision to become all you can be

To break limits off your potential, make a decision that you are going to do something great with your life. Some schoolgirls were interviewed about whether they thought boys had better lives than girls. They each gave examples of being told that girls were weak or emotional. One of them said she was told she shouldn't try to be a leader; that it was better if boys led. But one girl said she'd heard all that and more besides. She was asked, 'What did you do about it?' She replied, 'I just decided to prove them wrong!' She promised herself that she would become an *A* student and later run in the elections for president of the student council when she was old enough.

If anyone's told you that you can't do what you're called to do, you can decide to prove them wrong.

Almost a century ago, a woman called Clara Belle Williams became the first African American to graduate from New Mexico State

---

[42] Ephesians 2:10, The Amplified Bible

University in the United States. Though she was enrolled at the university, she regularly had to stand in the hall outside lecture theatres because many of her professors would not allow her inside the classroom because of her race. Even when she passed all her examinations and became eligible to graduate, she was not allowed to walk with her class to get her diploma. Despite those attitudes, Clara went on to fulfil her purpose by becoming a teacher of black students over the course of her career. She lived for more than a hundred years and, after her death, the university renamed the English Department building after her.

People with an unswerving determination to let nothing hold them back do exploits. They don't allow the negative attitudes people have towards them to become stumbling blocks in their lives. They make a conscious choice to see themselves differently as compared to the way others see them. They become skilled at fighting off the constraints of their past. Some even use past experiences as motivation to release the very best of themselves. They turn negative experiences into lifelong goals to 'prove them wrong'.

4. Allow your passion for your gift to eclipse the issues of life

One of the greatest classical composers the world has ever known was subjected to severe floggings on a near daily basis during his childhood. Ludwig van Beethoven was often locked in the cellar of the family home by his alcoholic father and deprived of sleep. As a schoolboy, he was described as average at best, and he did pretty poorly in maths and spelling. He began losing his hearing in his thirties and was completely deaf by his early forties. This chain of negative experiences could have cut short his potential, but his passion for composing was much greater than any of the forces arrayed against him.

Faced with the prospect that he would soon be deaf, Beethoven became very aware of time. He was so driven to release every ounce of his potential he began composing music in lieu of the future time when he wouldn't be able to hear. Beethoven raced against time, intending to get every musical score out of his heart before his world became filled with impenetrable silence. He went on to compose some of his most renowned works during those years, completing over a hundred pieces of music including symphonies, sonatas, concertos, overtures, masses, an opera and a ballet involving a range of musical instruments. Had Beethoven not emptied himself as far as he possibly could, the world would be deprived of all these great musical works.

5. Create a sense of urgency

In life, time is of the essence. Beethoven's deafness caused him to number his days. The Bible describes that as wisdom. Moses put it beautifully when he wrote, 'So teach us to number our days. That we may cultivate and bring to you a heart of wisdom.' 67 When faced with life crises people who did great exploits like Beethoven, learned to use time to their advantage. They stop taking time for granted or assuming they had all the time in the world to release their potential. The threat to their potential made him wise in the use of time. You don't have to wait until there's a clear threat to your potential to motivate you to stop being casual about life's purpose. You can begin now to create that sense of urgency.

Those who allow their past to control them and never find a way to move forward end up losing a lot of time. Years of life become lost to them. Potential is wasted for every passing day we don't give it the best portion of our focus and attention. We can't change the past, but we are always capable of moving forward in new directions. The fact that you're alive and reading this book means that it's still possible for you to fulfil your purpose. Time is given to us so we can release our potential towards the achievement of a worthy purpose.

Great exploits are reserved for those who have regard for time. They have a sense of urgency that pushes them to their limits and forces the very best out of them. Numbering our days causes us to focus on completing our tasks. It helps us put aside the things that happened to us or were said to us because there are greater things to be thinking about and doing. Often, it's through the pains of the fiery furnace that our talents are refined. When we are under pressure of time or resource, the excellence we didn't know was there is forced out of us.

The great body of work Beethoven, and others like him, who experienced trials and yet contributed so much during their lifetime becomes that much more powerful against the backdrop of their personal stories. It's another demonstration that great exploits are not a function of an easy life where everything conspires to smooth the way forward. It isn't a case of everything working in your favour to ease you into fulfilling your purpose. But great exploits can and often do occur in spite of the trials people face, the personal difficulties and suffering, the mistreatment experienced, the humiliation and unfairness that life serves up, and the many other things that can limit potential. Great people are great because of their resolve to release everything within them despite the odds ... and at any cost.

Regardless of all the challenges to his potential, Beethoven's passion for his music was his highest priority and calling. I'm fully persuaded that, with our eyes firmly fixed upward, we are able to overcome any and all things that try to limit our potential.

6. Understand that you may be misunderstood

People who do great exploits are peculiar people and are often misunderstood by others consequently. They may even become controversial figures. Nelson Mandela had a polarizing effect internationally during his years in prison. People who do great exploits create change, and few people are ever happy about things changing – particularly those who personally benefit from the status quo! Game changing types often upset the status quo and, as a result, others feel threatened and often suspicious or resentful towards them.

When you are misunderstood, people will try to limit your potential to become who you are called to be.

Jesus Christ was as misunderstood as much as he was and is adored. He was as much an aggravation to those who resisted change, as he was a beloved teacher to those who received his message as a means of being set free. The following passage of scripture shows the controversy and misunderstanding that surrounded him:

'Then a fresh division of opinion arose among the Jews because of His saying these things.

'And many of them said, "He has a demon and He is mad (insane – He raves, He rambles). Why do you listen to Him?"

'Others argued, "These are not the thoughts *and* the language of one possessed. Can a demon-possessed person open blind eyes?"'[43]

This is not to advocate controversy but to point out the reality that, in life, if you're going to do great exploits, chances are you will meet people and circumstances that try to put a limit on who you are and on what you can do. One of their strategies is to attack you and undermine you with others you are called to influence and serve. In order to do great exploits you shouldn't allow the things your detractors say about you to limit what you're called to do in life.

7. Change your relationships

If you were anything like I was as a teenager, you probably couldn't understand why your parents were so picky about who you spent your time with. I remember my mother always wanting to know where I'd been and who I was with. Now I understand that it was because my choice of friends had a big part to play in how my future would take shape and who I could become. Environment probably has

---

[43]   John 10:19–21, Amplified Bible, Classic Edition.

more influence on who we are than heredity. The examples above show how family, schooling, and society can influence our beliefs regarding what we're capable of and thereby limit our potential. Other key influencers are friends and associates.

Friendships exert a huge influence on how we feel, think, and behave. Therefore, our choice of friends usually contributes to the limits we set for ourselves. Studies from around the world show the effects their peers have on the academic achievement of students in junior school through to university. In very broad terms, friendships with the type of people who have positive attitudes, healthy values, respect, and who work hard encourage us to develop the same attitudes. The effect of this is that our potential is strengthened, making it more likely that we will go as far as we desire to go in releasing that potential. Whereas if we spend time with friends who have poor attitudes, unhealthy values or avoid hard work it tends to have the opposite effect on us in that we become more like them.

The influence the people we associate with is mitigated by a number of factors such as the level of our self-esteem or parental expectation when we're young. If self-esteem is lower or parental influence is low (especially during the adolescent phase of life), social pressure can and does change an individual's beliefs, attitudes, and values forever. At this crucial stage, the person can either build or destroy his or her future as a result of the influence of his or her peer group.

> ...holding to a form of [outward] **godliness**
> (religion), although they have denied its power [for
> their conduct nullifies their claim of faith].
> Avoid such people *and* keep far away from them.[44]

People are important to purpose. They will either be the types who enlarge your vision and motivate you towards achieving it, or they'll be the ones to ease you into a comfort zone that will be difficult to

---

[44]   2 Timothy 3:5

get out of. Jesus seemed very selective about the twelve people he chose to be closest to him. The Bible says he even spent the night in prayer prior to going out and choosing them. They were men who were hungry, men with a strong appetite for bringing solutions to a lost world (all except Judas, of course). Although they each had a profession or were engaged in a trade of some kind, they weren't satisfied with the status quo. They wanted something more. They had a mind to soar into a world of possibilities, to be more than simply having a form of godliness, with no impact on the world around them. They actually wanted to do something with the faith they possessed. Jesus sought those types of people to be his friends.

If you're going to do great exploits, you must associate with people who believe in possibilities. They should also have a dream that they are pursuing. Stay away from the dreamers who never actually take action to pursue their dreams.

Speaking of Judas, even though he was the enemy of Christ, he had his own role to play in Jesus' purpose. Jesus needed someone like him to get to the cross. Those who oppose us can sometimes be greater allies of our purpose than we think. Each of Jesus' close relationships were purpose driven.

8. Fly or become prey

You'll recall the story of the young eagle raised by a family of chickens that I wrote about in an earlier chapter. The young eagle's potential was destroyed for the sole reason that he was hanging around the wrong crowd.

Ever notice that, in nature, the birds that don't use their wings don't get very far? Chickens and turkeys, for example, are bound to the earth. They usually exist in a small territory, never wandering far from home. On the other hand, eagles, geese, and pigeons fly far and wide. Eagles fly the highest of all the birds (between ten thousand

and fifteen thousand feet!). They can reach flying speeds of up to seventy-five miles per hour. Another interesting fact about eagles is that they are the only creatures that can look directly at the sun without damaging their eyes.

An eagle that insists on having chickens or turkeys for friends won't fly as it should. Why? Because, like humans, it will naturally want to be accepted by the group with which it identifies. We all crave a sense of belonging, and the only way to belong is to conform to the norms of a group. We don't want to rock the boat and risk being rejected. Because chickens and turkeys can't fly, an eagle that tries to fit in and conform to these types won't fly either.

The other fact about birds that don't use their wings is that they become prey. The most commonly consumed birds in the world are chickens and turkeys. Life has a way of exploiting and taking advantage of those whose potential is limited.

The old eagle in the story is a metaphor for the challenge life always brings to each of us to step up and fulfil potential. Each of us begins life as a young eagle. We go about the routines of our life, fulfilling the expectations of the people in our environment: family, teachers, friends, and others who are doing the same. And then, at some point, life challenges us to see ourselves in a different way. In fact, that new and different way is who we actually are, but it frightens some people. In their minds, the new visions of themselves are overwhelming, fantastical, impossible. We are faced with a choice to either take up life's challenge to fulfil a much higher purpose or remain as we are, where we are.

Life can call us at any time, at any age. That old eagle shows up in the form of a teacher, a pastor, a friend, role model or a relative. It can show up via a problem that we identify and want to solve or sheer passion for a talent we have. More often than not, it's the inner, still-small voice nudging us to arise.

And so the young eagle, instead of heeding the call, chose to live a very limited existence instead. His decision is tragic for five reasons:

1. He chose to reject the life he was called to live.

2. He chose to live far below his potential, making it unlikely he would ever manifest the gifts and abilities that were already within him.

3. He chose to continue living as something he wasn't. Such a life is usually filled with regret.

4. He chose to reject a mentor who was willing and able to help him reach his potential. Such mentors are rare. It's not every day that a mentor shows up to offer the exact type of teaching and coaching we need.

5. He could just as easily have made better choices, saying *Yes!* instead of saying *No!* to being who he was called to be.

What aspects of your authentic self are you saying *No!* to? What issues might be calling your attention, that you've been resisting? Are you fighting to stay on the ground, when you should be climbing the heights of responsibility to which you are called?

The old eagle imagined helping the young eagle to mature in his potential, teaching him to hunt, and coaching him to handle the strong wind currents in the high places. God promises he will do the same for us when he says that he'll set us securely upon our high places[45].

When we submit to the vision he gives us for our future as discussed in chapter 2, he uses that vision to train us up to new levels of maturity in his purposes.

---

[45] Psalm 18:33 Amplified Bible, Classic Edition

9. Change your environment

> Go away from your country, and from your
> relatives and from your father's house,
> to the land which I will show you.[46]

The Bible relates the story of a man called Abraham who was called to a purpose beyond his wildest dreams. Abraham had dreams about many things about his life in the future. He gave him dreams of prosperity, a great name, countless descendants, and tremendous impact on the world. Through him, all families of the earth would be blessed. It was a very big dream to fulfil, but it was conditional upon Abraham being willing to leave behind everyone and everything he knew. Abraham had to make the decision to trade his past for his future. He chose the latter, saying goodbye to his old way of life in order to run towards his dreams; and, as was said to him, every promise came true.

What holds many people back from maximising their potential are past experiences they continue holding on to. To leave your country and your father's house means letting go of the norms, ways of thinking, and beliefs learned from your relatives, neighbourhood community, education system, and friendships that may be hindering you from moving forward. *Our father's house* is the place where we were schooled about ourselves and about life. It's a place of great intimacy and familiarity to us. Even if it was a loving and supportive environment that fostered the best in us, it was the place where we learned all sorts of coping skills, adaptations, and compensating behaviours for incorrect labels we accepted.

It's no wonder many of us leave home confused about our identity and spend the rest of our lives trying to figure out who we really are.

---

[46]   Genesis 12:1, The Amplified Bible.

Our father's house refers to our mental comfort zones that we should break free of. Earlier, we saw how a talented young person had actually accepted and adapted a part of her life to the label *stupid* even though she was fully capable of learning every skill necessary to fulfil her purpose.

Father's house and *country* are metaphors for the ways we normally operate that inhibit our potential. We must leave them behind in order to learn a new way that will lead to the full release of our potential. The eagle in Kay's fable faced the choice to leave behind things he'd learned in order to learn new things and become everything he could be. But he refused because it frightened him. The prospect intimidated him and may have been a little confusing as well. All his life he'd been programmed to think a certain way; he understood himself and the world around him through that programming. He thought that was all there was to life and who he was. When someone told him that there was much more, all he needed was a little faith to test the claims made by the old eagle. He needed to take a risk. Risk is a big part of doing great exploits, but the young eagle had been programmed not to take risks; and to run from his fears rather than confront them. So his fear and confusion made no room for risks. His view didn't alter the fact that he'd been created to be an eagle and had the ability to do everything eagles do. But he couldn't step out and function as one because he couldn't see himself as having that potential.

So much of what we learned while growing up has conditioned us to put limitations on ourselves. We learned that there are certain things that are impossible for us. In the story related earlier, the school girl said she was told girls shouldn't lead. Leadership would have become impossible to her if she had believed that. Of course, females ably take on leadership roles in every sphere.

Whatever you are called to do is possible for you to do. Therefore, nothing is impossible. To move from seeing our dreams as impossible, to seeing them as possible for us to achieve is a choice. Many people's lives illustrates this well when they chose to move past the limitations ascribed to them and believe they have the potential to fulfil their dreams. Had they continued to believe they were 'stupid' or 'lazy' or 'would amount to nothing', achieving their dream would have been impossible. Their potential would have remained unrealised; they would have eventually gone to their grave with all their unrealised gifts still inside them. What a tragedy that would be – not just for themselves, but for all the lives they were meant to impact. Personal impact can take on a ripple effect. The impact is a far-reaching one, and it is incalculable. The vacuum that's left when we do not release our potential produces a great loss that cannot be determined.

When life tries to bury our potential, we are faced with an important choice: we can either accept the limitation, letting our potential go to waste, or we can decide to break free from it. Instead of living in defeat, we have the choice to cultivate a new attitude. In life, when others say we can't or that we're not good enough, it's always an opportunity to show ourselves, and others, who we really are. Like the aforementioned little girl who was interviewed, we can make the decision to prove all limitations wrong. She chose to turn the things she was told into inspiration and made a commitment to herself that she would release all of her potential in key areas of her life.

We don't often hear about people like Clara Belle Williams. The attitudes she faced existed because some people believed she couldn't possibly have any potential worth nurturing. She was born in a time when severe limitations were placed upon people's potential on the basis of skin colour. It's impossible to know the scale of human potential that went unreleased as a direct result of those foolish beliefs. Its impossible to quantify the impact of that lost potential for humanity. How much further ahead could we all be if we'd had the benefit of those generations fully releasing their potential? But here was one woman who determined that she was going to fulfil her potential even if it meant bearing the humiliation of having to stand outside the classroom to get an education.

We can't always control what other people think of us or say to us, but we have control over whether we accept the limitation or not. We can make every experience work for our good. Those experiences can be valuable to us if we use them as motivators to spur us on to achieve our dreams. Experiences that could have buried us (i.e., cut us off from our potential) could become the triggers that push us to release our potential. All that's required to turn a negative experience into a trigger for achievement is the conscious choice on our part to make it so.

In the next chapter, we'll look at actions we must take in order to release potential and do great exploits.

9

People who do great exploits release their potential

Albert Einstein reportedly said, 'Genius is 1 percent talent and 99 percent hard work.' Even if you're not looking to prove your genius but would be content to achieve success in fulfilling the purpose for your life, you're not off the hook. I've also heard it said that 'Success is 10 percent inspiration and 90 percent perspiration.' This quote has been attributed to Thomas Edison. Whoever, said these words, what is meant is that once you're inspired by an idea, solution to a problem, vision, or particular gift you have, the way to release the potential of it is through perspiration (i.e., hard work); and that talent has a much smaller part to play than we think.

Einstein and Edison are renowned for doing great exploits in pursuing their predetermined purpose and were at the forefront of thought and innovation in their respective times. They would have arrived at this understanding of what it takes to do exploits by experience, which lends their conclusions certain credibility. As I study the lives of achievers, I've found these quotes have a truthful ring. It's also been my experience while pursuing my own goals. To the onlooker, exploits may appear effortless, but they are not. In every sphere where people have done great exploits and achieved what they set out to do, they've done so through hard work and sacrifice. They set about working on their talent, gift, or idea through a process of preparation, perspiration, and hard work (without which, they would never have released the potential of their idea or particular gift).

Your potential is given so that you can materialise the dream that's in your heart and fulfil your purpose. However, people who do great exploits understand that potential isn't something that is released without some work on their part. They accept the reality that great ideas and natural gifts have to be worked on and developed before they can bear fruit. This hard work (or *perspiration*), is one of the reasons many people do not do great exploits. For this reason, they find it is easier saying *no* to the dream they have in their heart, choosing instead to go down an easier route in life.

If you're reading this book, I'm working on the assumption that you want to do great exploits. It was written for people like you, who want to do exploits and want to understand what it takes. Perhaps they have tried before and things didn't work out. Maybe they have had success in the past but want to become better at exploits. It could be that they have started on their road to fulfilling their purpose, reached a plateau, and desire to break through to new levels of exploits in their ministry, their career, their business, or their volunteer service. Whatever is behind your reading of this book, it's important to know that, although great exploits are demanding, you do have what it takes. You have all the potential you need. But it means you'll have to put in the amount and level of effort that it takes.

As a teenager, my friend Greg lost his father (see his story in chapter 5). He was a good student in school and his dream was to become a lawyer. But with his father, the main breadwinner for the family gone, and his mother a low paid worker at factory, Greg had to go to work on fulfilling his dream while helping to support his mother and siblings. He took night jobs that would allow him time to study. Though he recognised he had the potential to get a law degree, he knew his natural inclination wouldn't be enough to make him into the best lawyer he could be. In the day, Greg sat in on extra lectures, he booked time with his professors, he joined the debating team, he sat in the audience in courtrooms listening to cases being tried. He did whatever it took to train his mind to the practice and activities that a career in law would require of him. Greg graduated in the top ranks of his class with first class honours. He's regarded as one of the most skilled lawyers in the country where he lives with his wife and kids.

What it takes to release your potential

Watching Usain Bolt run that afternoon during the 2012 Olympics, I have to say that he makes running one hundred metres in a record-breaking 9.63 seconds look effortless. He finishes his race strides ahead of the competition. He runs his races so well that it's tempting to think it must be easy for him because of his natural talent. But that's not the entire picture, and to credit his victories to talent alone would be misguided.

Leontyne Price, the opera singer's performances seemed effortless, as though she were born singing that way. But she wasn't. What she was born with was a talent. The accolades she received from critics around the world only became possible because she had gone to work developing that talent over many years.

Virgin is one of the most recognizable and successful brands in the world. It includes a range of businesses, employing tens of thousands of people around the world. When you see the company's founder being interviewed or giving a talk, he seems laid back. But he's a man of great ideas and vision. His calm, laid-back, slightly self-effacing demeanour belies the effort he's undoubtedly put in to turning his ideas into the industries they are today. Ideas are like seeds, and they demand a lot of work to establish, and grow if they are going to become successful enterprises.

Bill Gates started his life's work tinkering with ideas to develop computer software. More than thirty years on, millions of people enjoy the benefits of those ideas. Gates took an intangible idea and worked on it until it became a tangible reality. Without that sustained, consistent work, it would have remained just an idea.

Joyce Meyer is one of the most prominent Bible teachers today. She has a worldwide TV and radio ministry. Through her daily broadcasts, she reaches millions of viewers and influences them through Bible-based teaching. But her ministry began with a Bible study group she ran in her living room with a handful of women. In the time between running that group and what she does now, Meyer would have had to put in the work to develop her knowledge of the word, her skill as a speaker, and a range of business skills to run her organisation.

I'd like to also mention one of my uncles, an 'ordinary' man whose life is also a great lesson in regards to doing great exploits and fulfilling purpose. His commitment to the process of working on his intangible ideas until they became a reality and developing a host of relevant skills has transported him from his modest beginnings to multimillionaire status. He started out as a door-to-door poultry seller. He raised the chickens himself in his own backyard, and then he peddled them around town in the form of fresh chicken. Twenty-five years on, he owns several business concerns and is a multimillionaire. When I visit him on the island where he lives, I see him reclining at his poolside, conducting business on the phone. To an onlooker, it looks very easy, but if you knew his journey, you'd know that he worked hard doing exploits to arrive at where he is currently.

I can go on summarising countless other individuals like these, but the point is that they have become adept at making their exploits appear effortless, and this can be slightly misleading. If people think doing exploits just happens out of the blue or through luck, they will experience great disappointment in life. If you have a talent but never develop it, its potential will not be released. If you have an idea yet never work on establishing it, its potential will not be released. The way to release the potential of anything is to use it, train it, develop it, and master it.

Why release your potential?

Your ideas, talents, and gifts must be trained and tested in order to have impact.

1. Stir up the gift

A gift must be activated, roused, agitated, or challenged … otherwise its potential will remain unreleased. While he was imprisoned, Paul the Apostle wrote to Timothy: 'Stir up the gift of God, which is in you.'

Since buying my first John C Maxwell book some years ago, I've read over twenty-five of his titles. Having sold millions of copies of his books around the world, his influence has impacted many lives. Apart from the wisdom and insight in his books, I admire him as a writer. He was doing exactly what I longed to do: writing books that changed people's lives. For a long time, I thought he had written so many books because he had a special anointing. I thought the abilities I admired in him were down to the supernatural. But apparently, writing his first book proved very difficult for him and eventually it took an entire year for him to write one hundred pages.

That story helped me understand that, though there is such a thing as a supernatural enabling or anointing, gifts and ideas need to be worked on and developed by natural acts called *practice* and *study*. Whatever our talents, they must be put through a process of preparation involving practice, focus, belief, and perseverance if we're going to use them for great exploits. Our natural gifts must be developed if we want to use them in service to others. Although Diego Maradona, one of the greatest football icons in history said, 'It's God who makes me play well,' he was known for his dedication to intense training and drills.

You can't do great exploits without releasing your potential; you must go to work developing your talents and ideas.

2. Use it or lose it

There's a well-known story told about a man who had to go on a journey. Before leaving, he called his three servants. To the one he gave five talents, to the second he gave two, and to the third he gave a single talent. He distributed the talents according to the ability of each servant. He instructed them to put the talents to good use because he expected a report on what they had achieved with them upon his return. The servant with the five didn't waste any time. He went out straight away and put the five talents to use. He traded and extended his portfolio of talents by five. Similarly, the one given two talents put his to work and got two more. However, the servant given the one talent did not put it to good use, choosing to hide it instead. Hidden away, its potential remained unreleased.

After a long time, the master returned. He immediately called the three servants for an account of what they did with the talents he'd given them. To the two servants who had exploited the potential of their talents, the master congratulated them. He called them *good* and *faithful*. He promoted them because they were diligent in maximising what they were given. They made the best of what they had and were able to show something for it. But the third, who had buried his talent, started with a series of excuses. Instead of bringing more talents to show his master, he brought reasons why he hadn't gone to work on his talent. Someone else – in this case, the very master who had generously entrusted him with a talent – was to blame for his poor performance. He was afraid to do anything with his talent; therefore, he concluded that, instead of releasing his talent into the world, it would be best if he hid it.

His master was not impressed. He called this servant *wicked, lazy,* and *worthless,* and he took away the one talent, giving it to the one who had the most. The moral of the tale is that those who value their talents will receive more and experience abundance as a result. But those who don't use what they have will not merely lose it, but will be thrown out into the darkness. At some point in their lives, the people who don't release their potential will regret it and experience disappointment over their loss of the associated rewards.

The wicked servant found it impossible to say yes to the assignment he was given because he refused to take personal responsibility for what he was given. He blamed others for his situation and allowed fear to paralyse him. His attitude rendered him unproductive. While his peers got busy working on their talents, he found it easier to say no and do nothing with his. There are many talented people in the world who lose out on great futures for these reasons; it leads to a life of frustration and regret in the end.

3. Releasing your potential has a reward

We can see very clearly from the lives of all the people mentioned thus far that our gifts make room for us in the world. What's more, the story above shows they bring abundance into our lives. The abundance can take various forms. It can be the sheer enjoyment of the gift – the pleasure of playing the guitar or creating a great painting. Actually exercising the gift releases joy to us. When I feel down, I start writing. I know I will feel a lot better through that action. Writing brings immense joy into my life. Few activities in my life feel as good as when I'm releasing my potential as a writer. Whatever your gift is, when you are working it, it should have the same sort of effect on you. That's why so many people are miserable at their jobs. It's not because of their boss or their working conditions; rather, it's entirely down to the fact that they are not operating in their gifts. If your job does not allow you to release your particular talents, you either need to find another one or create avenues elsewhere to release your potential.

The reward is also in the fact that our gift blesses other people. It's one of the primary reasons we were given it in the first place. In the conversation I had with my friend's daughter after seeing her act in a play, I also asked her what did she enjoy about acting. She said, 'It makes other people feel happy and that makes me happy.'

Success is being able to give people what they want or need. When cinema-goers go to see their favourite actor in a film or football fans fill a stadium, they have paid good money to see their team or the star player score goals and win the game. The players who are able to give the fans what they want become the most sought-after and highly rewarded players in the industry. There are countless people out there who need what you carry; your purpose in life is to meet that need. When we bless others through our talent or idea, the blessing is returned to us in many different ways.

One of the greatest rewards of releasing our potential is that it enlarges us. The master in Jesus' story promoted the two good servants and said to them, 'Share in my joy.' Their faithful application of their talents opened doors for them. Their territories were enlarged, giving them greater opportunities to serve. The master described it as 'joy.' He was referring to the joy of progress and all of its rewards. The joy of overcoming the challenges in business, finding solutions to problems, making it possible for people to have what they need or want. He had a vision for them to share in the experience of doing exploits and enjoying all the rewards doing so brings. They were promoted from being mere servants to virtual sons, inheriting a greater stake in his business affairs. Because they had won his respect, he chose to reward them in ways they never expected: they each received greater access to the master by a level of intimate connectedness to him that they didn't have before. They suddenly found themselves possessing more rights, power, and authority, which is dominion. When exercised, our talent increases our value in other people's sight (and we are rewarded accordingly).

Beware the critical space

For the two successful servants and the one unsuccessful servant, something happened between receiving their talents and the outcomes they eventually experienced: time passed. Within that time, a lot happened. Each of them did some thinking and made some decisions. They took actions that were perfectly aligned with those decisions. Their actions bore fruit in line with their personal approach to thinking, deciding, and acting. The results were measurable. They were required to give an account on the results they got. From beginning to end, what happened was entirely the responsibility of each servant. This passage of time between recognising the talent that's in your hand and the outcomes in your life is a critical space.

It's worth studying and understanding the critical space very well if you want to do great exploits in life. I say it's critical because, in that space, we're confronted with the majority of the reasons why it's easier to say *no* to our dreams. Have you ever noticed that the moment you get an idea how, you suddenly become aware of all sorts of obstacles in your path? Before the idea came and you were drifting along doing nothing, these obstacles were not there. When you recognise you have a talent or a good idea, life will immediately begin to challenge you. It's a test to determine how serious you are about making that talent or idea work for you. How we respond to that challenge decides the outcomes of our lives.

People who do exploits face the same challenge everyday too. After all both the successful servants and the unsuccessful servants had the same master. The essential difference between them was that the successful ones choose to go forward and pursue their purpose anyway.

It's worth observing how the people who do exploits respond when met with those challenges that are common to us all. It's worth finding out what they do in the critical space, what their experiences are, how they handle those experiences. It's worth noting how they think, how they made their choices, what actions they took, what it took for them to be able to say *yes* to pursuing their unique purpose in life. We can then see why their lives have turned out the way they have. After that, you can make strides and do exploits just like them.

There's so much we can glean from them that can make it easier to say yes to our own unique call. But it's also worth looking at what those, such as the servant given one talent, did with that space and see where it led. The remaining chapters of this book are dedicated to helping you build that understanding of what it takes so that you can apply it to your own life and become more fruitful in the purpose for your life.

How to release your potential

Below I share some practical keys to releasing your potential so that you can go on to do great exploits.

1. Do all in your power to protect your potential from being destroyed

People who do great exploits don't squander their gifts. They value them and take steps to protect them from abuse. They focus on long-term sustainability, recognizing that, as they grow older, the gift should become richer, not go into decline or be lost altogether.

There are famous singers, particularly in the pop music world, who had great voices when they started but lost the power of their gift to drug abuse or poor health management. In order to release the potential of your gift, you need to take good care of it. Always protect and preserve it so that it can be fully released. Taking care of it makes it more likely that it will serve your purpose well into the future.

2. Find mentors

Because the critical space is often unchartered territory, it helps to have others who can help us navigate it. Solomon, one of the wisest men who ever lived, said, 'There's nothing new under the sun.'[47]

This means that, whatever your purpose in life, there's an excellent chance that someone has done something similar. You don't have to go through the trials and errors of trying to reinvent the wheel all by yourself. Even when it's a pioneering idea and you're forging something new, the fact is that you'll have to build on knowledge that already exists. What we call *new* is usually a synergy of old things. For example, building computer programmes was once a novel idea even though it was just a new way of using numerical data. No one has ever released their potential in a vacuum or in complete isolation of ideas and knowledge that was already out there. Great musicians listen to music made by others; great athletes study other athletes; great artists draw on the techniques of other artists they admire. And business people do the same – these folks find someone who is successful in business and do what they do. They build and expand upon ideas that came before. Likewise, fashion designers feed off each other's styles. Developing your talent or idea, whatever it might be, demands learning from others who have proven themselves in the area of your calling.

A common assumption people make in the critical space is that talent, instinct, or a willingness to take action are sufficient to succeed. But

---

[47]   Ecclesiastes 1:9, New King James Version.

all successful people have been inspired by forerunners in their field and underwent some sort of training that helped make them effective. Mother Teresa is an example of this. After sensing her calling to help the poor at the tender age of 12, she was inspired by reports she read by Jesuit priests in Bengal and other parts of India. At age 18, she took her first vows to become a nun and then worked for several years in a girl's high school near the slums of Kolkata. However, by the late 1940s, she was restless and felt a strong tug to leave the school and convent she belonged to. She wanted to work directly with the poor. To prepare for this, she undertook intensive training in Patna, India. It was the start of an extraordinary life marked by great exploits, setting up missions in centres around the world. Her work included creating schools and homes for orphans, people with HIV/AIDS, and lepers. Also, she built hospices for the terminally ill.

After she retired from teaching, my mother became an entrepreneur. She started up a business building a small fleet of taxis, which she leased out to licenced taxi drivers. When starting up, she turned to an old family friend (a friend of my grandfather's) who had become wealthy himself, through buying and renting properties. His business model was simple. I often heard him saying to mom, 'Invest your capital in businesses where you don't have to do the actual work.' It was a model that worked for him. For a long time, it worked for mom, through her taxi rental business. Uncle Carl was happy to coach and mentor her. He acted as a sounding board when she wanted to test ideas and gave advice when she encountered problems. Through the extensive business network he'd made over the years, he connected her with the kind of contacts she needed to get things in place to start her business. That put mom in a whole new league and with uncle Carl's sound advice, it launched her into other successful ventures.

Great mentors can save us years of mistakes trying to learn things by ourselves. Years ago, I became interested in a new field and wanted to try my hand at it. I took a lateral career move and got a job in an organisation that was very different than the one I had worked in for ten years. Plus, I was now operating in a field I had only nominal experience in. Fortunately, my new manager was just about to leave the organisation for a new job elsewhere. I took the bold step and asked whether she would be my mentor until I found my feet. She agreed. Being able to draw on her knowledge and experience helped me learn my new trade much faster than I would have trying to work things out by myself. She saved me from making mistakes that could have ended any future I wanted to have in the area. She exposed me to people and opportunities that advanced and accelerated my growth and confidence. I will always be indebted to her for coming alongside a complete novice and enabling me to flourish.

After about eighteen months, I was able to stand on my own two feet and make the right decisions. We met less and less, but I remained in touch. One night, we met for dinner and she congratulated me on how well I was doing. She then confided that she'd never been asked to mentor before but was excited at the idea that she could help someone fulfil their potential. It was something she wished she had had earlier on in her career. Yet, at the time of my request, she did not feel prepared to play the role. Therefore, she decided to enrol on a mentorship course so that she could do her best for me. No wonder she was such an excellent mentor! It showed me that whatever you're asked to do in life, a little active learning goes a very long way to releasing your potential to do it.

There's a huge advantage that comes from having a real-life mentor such as I had. Good people like her strengthen you for the task ahead. They can pour their years of wisdom won from experience into you and connect you to the potential or dream you carry because it is also something they carry. In the narrative following Mary's conception of Jesus, she went to stay with her cousin Elizabeth. The moment Elizabeth, who was also pregnant, met Mary, the baby leapt in her womb. Elizabeth sang Mary's praises. She was so happy to know that her cousin was carrying a unique purpose. She could relate because she was also carrying her own unique purpose. Elizabeth was mature enough to know that there was nothing to compete over. And Mary was wise enough not to be so filled with pride that she alienated her potential mentor. Elizabeth affirmed Mary with her words and gave her a safe place to nurture what she carried. She became the mentor or coach who Mary could lean on in that stage of her development. Elizabeth was the type of friend who celebrated Mary's assignment and was a genuine helper of Mary's purpose. These are the types of people we should learn to recognise and draw near to during the critical space.

Opportunities to be mentored come in different packages. Thus, when you're in the critical space its best to be flexible and open minded about the methods. I also had the golden opportunity to be a member of a writers' group where every other writer was already published by a mainstream publisher. Some of them had several published books already. It was an opportunity for me to develop my talent as a writer by learning from real authors. We read and criticised each other's work each month at our meetings. Writing is a very personal process, and it's hard, especially for a budding writer like I was, to read one's work to an audience of critics. It got really painful at times hearing some of their feedback, but they were always encouraging. The fact that they never kicked me out of the group was sometimes the only indicator that they believed I had potential and was worth the effort and time I required from them! But that's one of the benefits of having excellent mentors: they are supposed to refine your talent. They tell you what you need to hear (not what you want to hear) in order to make you better at what you do. Great mentors are less concerned with your comfort than they are with your growth in the area of your ability. They will test your talent, putting it through the fire of criticism so that it comes out as pure gold.

It's great to have the right real-life mentor, but if you can't find such a person, it's not the end of the world. I've had long periods of time when I craved mentorship and couldn't find anyone able or willing to mentor me – especially in the church. Fortunately, I'm very self-motivated and naturally love to research and find information for myself. Thus, during the times when no personal mentor was available, I maintained my learning process by attending seminars, searching the Internet, watching YouTube videos, and reading books written by people with experience in my fields of interest. One year, I even enrolled myself on John C Maxwell's mentoring programme. Back then, there was a one-off fee for one year's mentorship. Each month, I received CDs and a short workbook on a particular aspect of leadership. I never met him in person or spoke with him directly, but I still learned a lot about leadership through that form of mentorship. That programme taught me the importance of lifelong learning.

3. Choose your one thing

In my view, the critical space is all about sacrifice on some level. Through it, we are constantly making decisions about trading something to get something else. Often, the something we're having to trade or give up is what we would rather have or enjoy in that particular moment (for example, giving up a favourite television show to go study). It's really a form of suffering that involves enduring some degree of pain in the present in order to obtain what's better down the line. Greatness stems from exchanging what feels good now to have something great later. But when we develop this habit, it gets much easier over time and we may even stop feeling the pain of sacrifice.

Those who do great exploits have learned to trade what's good for what's best. They make these choices every day. But it's difficult to make the right choices without knowing why you're making them. The smaller choices you make daily that add up to great exploits down the line need to be guided by a bigger, overarching choice about which talent or idea you're going to develop.

As a writer I really wanted to be a novelist. In my twenties and thirties all I ever wrote was fiction. The first two books I submitted to publishers in those early years were novels – one of them, my first completed work was accepted. I was ok as a fiction writer but when I wrote non-fiction, that's when people really seemed to stop and pay attention. Yet I was crazy about fiction. I admired how the novelists I read could evoke powerful imagery and emotion through their descriptions. This was where I learned the power words have in creating characters and worlds out of nothing. Entire worlds have been created by fiction writers, great ones like J.R.R. Tolkien's Middle Earth in *The Lord of the Rings* and Ben Okri's fictional Nigerian city in *The Famished Road*. Not to mention the unforgettable characters conjured up by the genius of such authors and formed in our imaginations through the simple use of choice words that follow a unique order on a page. I really wanted to do that. But more and more I found myself writing non-fiction. More doors opened up for me in that genre. I didn't have to go looking for work; the publishers approached me. Maybe I would have excelled at fiction, but my natural talent shone through non-fiction. In order to release my potential, I had to choose one to focus on and sacrifice the other. I chose (maybe succumbed is a truer portrayal of what happened!) to non-fiction.

Most people have more than one talent and more than one idea. That's probably where the adage, *jack of all trades (master of none),* came from. A person who adopts this strategy becomes a jack of all trades (master of none) when he or she tries to pursue many things and finds it difficult or impossible to excel at any one of them. But when we look at people who have fulfilled their purpose, we discover that they decided to pursue one thing that would produce the greatest value.

Focusing your attention and effort on one area increases your effectiveness and impact in that area – it accelerates your growth and confidence.

People who do exploits don't run off in different directions doing one thing this month and then something else another month. They make a commitment to realise their potential in a certain area and did exploits there. They begin by building a strong foundation in one area. And then, because of their achievements in that one area, they have a platform to do other things.

When starting out, people who pursue many things don't get far with any of them. Consider choosing one thing and focus on developing that. Once you've established yourself in one area, it can provide a great springboard to other things. Another good example of this principle is my uncle. He began selling organic chicken, and when that was established, he started a take away restaurant. Once the take away was strong, he spotted an opportunity to harness the experience he had gained in business to release his potential in another market – providing school meals. He later diversified and now owns a number of different businesses.

I once heard a young woman tell him that she wanted to buy an island in the Caribbean and turn it into a holiday destination for Christians. My uncle replied, 'Fantastic dream, but you've got to have a lot of business experience and know-how to attract the types of investors you'll need for a venture like that. You need to learn to walk before you can run.'

4. Turn away from distractions

Even after I made a decision (or succumbed!) to focus on non-fiction, I still had my work cut out to remain disciplined and focus on it. Distractions were plentiful. I love a good story that's well told – who doesn't? Movies and novels were still my choice entertainments and they made me yearn to write stories of my own. (I spent most of my bible reading time in the Old Testament too, where all the dramatic stories and colourful characters are!). When I gave in to the temptation to read or write fiction, it meant that I was too tired to work on my non-fiction projects. I even missed some important deadlines for a magazine I wrote for. That didn't go down very well with the editor. So, I had to take stock, assess what I was really working towards, return to my vision and head in the direction I had chosen. I put down the novels. At the writing of this book, I think it's been at least six years since I have read a novel. But in that time, I have read scores – and I'm not exaggerating, you should see my library – of non-fiction books. Doing that allowed me to write and publish more, but it was only because I sacrificed the many things getting in the way of my development.

Distractions make it easy to say no to doing what we're supposed to do to make our dreams come true. If we want to do great exploits, we must be willing to give up many of the habits and pastimes that don't really matter in the big picture. Some such activities are not bad in and of themselves, but they may not serve any useful purpose in our lives. To realise our goals we have to reorganise our priorities so we can spend our time on specific activities that will cause our dreams to come true.

…All things are lawful, but not all things are constructive…[48]

Talented people in all walks of life, who want to do exploits eventually, accept that natural talent isn't enough. They need to be coached and trained to develop their skill or idea. If an athlete chose to go nightclubbing instead of getting a good night's sleep or fooling around when they should be training, they would never reach their potential. It's like that for anyone who wants to fulfil the purpose for his or her life. Many people have dreams but spend little time and effort working on them. These people allocate time and effort to the things that entertain them rather than the things that develop themselves as required for their great exploits. For example, the average American spends more than five hours per day watching TV. In the UK its estimated Britons spend about four hours per day watching TV.

---

[48]   1 Corinthians 10:23, The Amplified Bible.

About five hours are spent surfing the internet, playing video games or talking on the phone to friends and family. Added up, that takes it to almost nine hours. That's over a third of each day spent on activities that entertain but may have absolutely nothing to do with the fulfilment of purpose. Add the hours spent sleeping, having meals, travelling to work, and being at work, and that pretty much completes the twenty-four hours all of us have in a given day.

We need to sleep, eat, and work; the nine remaining hours each day are the critical space. The habits formed during those nine hours decide the future. If you want to know what kind of future you'll have, carry out an assessment of your current daily routine. It is going to add up to something. Success isn't something that happens on the day you accomplish your dream; succeeding or failing happens every day on the way to your ultimate destination in life. Daily habits will determine how far you go towards fulfilling your life's purpose.

5. Invest time

Just small changes in the way someone chooses to use those nine hours of critical space will make a huge difference to their future. For instance, it's widely thought that spending three to four hours per day consistently practicing a skill will make you an expert in that area over time. In any field you can think about, the so-called masters in that field are recognised as such because of their expertise. I had piano lessons as a child, which I didn't mind, but wasn't passionate about. I only ever practiced because I had to show progress at my next lesson. Whereas, several of my mother's music students who loved piano or guitar, naturally played their instrument of choice in every spare moment of their time. They would sometimes skip their core classes, English or math, and be found in the music room of the school making music together. Two of the guys I'm thinking of are highly paid musicians in bands today, one of them travels the world. On the other hand I can just about find 'middle C' on the piano even though I had lessons throughout my childhood. It's because I didn't consistently practice, it wasn't my passion and then I gave up the piano by the time I was a teenager.

The point is that to excel at anything, you need to spend time intentionally developing it. Finding the time is nowhere as difficult as we might initially assume. There are about nine hours of time each day that most people spend on entertainments or one kind or another. If they were to use just three hours of that time working on a talent or idea, they will eventually produce good fruit that will bless others.

I have come to the conclusion that some of the exploits we credit to natural talent are actually the product of intense practise or learning from trial and error over time.

Mastering the simple building blocks of your talent or idea is the key to unlocking your potential. Uncle Carl, who mentored my mother in business, was one of my many piano teachers over the years. Because he had businesses where he didn't need to spend time doing the work, his time was given to his next love – Jazz. He was a very good jazz pianist and mom sent my sister and I to learn to play free style from him. He was a great proponent of this approach of learning the basics of your talent. He'd say 'In order to be good at piano, you have to work at practising the basics of music.' So he put us through learning the scales, how chords were constructed. He'd make us look away while he played notes and asked us to name the notes or sing the notes until we knew each note like we knew our mom's voice.

This sort of approach makes perfect sense because excellence comes with a price. We achieve on par with our preparation. Mastering the fundamentals of your work – whether it's sport, academics, music, a ministry service, or your job – is critical to being the best you can be at what you do. That's how people known for doing great exploits were able to do them. Despite his natural musical ability and the advantage that his wide hand span gave him, uncle Carl practised piano every day until he died at age 74. He became known as the 'piano man' because his neighbours could hear his music first thing in the morning and last thing at night. This habit of doing more than what's strictly required is what separates the great from the good, and it always pays off in the long run.

In practical terms, consistently spending three hours per day developing a particular skill is thought to make anyone a master. Three hours per day sounds like a tall order, but when stacked against nine hours of entertainment and other daily activities that make no contribution to your purpose, it suddenly seems doable.

If you want to be like the average person, do what the average person does: spend the full nine hours per day at play. But if you want to do great exploits, put aside the distractions and begin to focus time on your one thing. Spend some time each day developing a ministry, building a business, creating a charity, bringing an idea into reality, inventing things, or innovating on concepts already in existence. Use the time studying, researching, learning, and practising what's required to release your potential in that area. If you do that consistently, you will do great exploits aligned with your vision.

To be effective in developing your talent, the primary focus shouldn't be how much time is spent on your talent or idea; rather, you should ensure that the time is spent learning the right things in the right way. That's why having a mentor, coach, or teacher with experience in the area is extremely valuable. If you have the right mentor, he or she will know what will work and what won't. That person will have expert knowledge of the key aspects you need to cover to aid your development and the most effective schedule for tackling them. If no mentor or teacher is available, study the experts from afar through the avenues available, such as the Internet or the library (as discussed already). Many factors go into whether the time spent actually pays off and to what extent it pays off. Don't focus on the number of hours; instead, focus on spending some quality time daily to work on your dream. The point I'm making is that, if we want to do the great exploits we are called to do, we must use our time wisely.

To use the time in your critical space productively, develop a plan with protected time to spend on your dream every day. Write down goals to work towards and read them four to five times per week, if not every day. This will help keep you on track. It will take time to see some progress in your talent or idea, but don't give up (we'll talk about perseverance and tenacity in later chapters). This is where most people find it easier to say *no*. It's natural to feel frustrated or discouraged when you're sticking to a daily plan but can't see any progress in those early weeks. But understanding that all the great achievers experienced the same frustrations makes it easier to keep saying *yes* to your plan.

Once more: people who are successful at great exploits are not successful because they were talented; it takes a lot more than talent to do exploits and fulfil your purpose in life. These people were eventually able to do great exploits because they overcame all the reasons for saying *no* to their call to greatness. When they felt frustration or discouragement, they pushed past it. When they felt tired, they carried on working. When they made mistakes, they got over them and tried again. That's why they do great exploits today.

6. Find the right environment to develop your talents and ideas

Many people are fortunate to have started their hours of preparation and training from as early on as childhood. One of my mother's students who earns his living playing keyboard for a touring band began formal training in music at age 5 after his mother noticed his interest in the piano. For years, he played in the church band and was asked to accompany singers in concerts, talent shows and other special occasions around our hometown. These can be classed as exploits in themselves: uplifting souls and bringing joy to others by expressing God's particular handiwork in your life. Exploits are about impact and ultimately affect people. They make a difference for the better in people's lives. We are called to do exploits that enrich and bless others, but they can go further towards a transformational impact – whether on one person, a small group, a community, a nation, or the world. It all depends upon what you are called to do and the size of your dream. That young man sensed a call on his life that went beyond the small town on the tiny island where he grew up, and the potential that he carried was great enough to bring to the world.

His critical space stretched between the Caribbean and venues in the U.S., Europe and the Far East. If he had found himself on the stage of such venues at the beginning of his critical space, he would not have had the kind of usefulness he's gone on to have. His potential needed to be unlocked through training, practice and the right types of exposure at certain levels.

It wasn't sufficient to have a big dream or even the passion to see it realised. To possess the dream, he had to be willing to receive the training and experience in the right environment. The soil in which we plant ourselves has consequences in terms of the extent to which our potential is realised. Your environment cannot be underestimated: it continuously transmits signals to your mind (consciously and subconsciously) about what's possible or not. Environments that are wholly conducive to your growth and success are virtually impossible to come across. You have to intentionally create your environment yourself by choosing your mentors, the people you spend time with, the images you look at, the messages you hear, and the thoughts you think. Such environments force the very best out of us. When we're in an environment where iron sharpens iron, it exposes us to new frontiers of ability against which our talent is tested.

Reflection on releasing potential

The whole purpose of the critical space is being trained and prepared to fully release your potential. It's choosing to use your time intentionally to master the technical aspects of your talent or idea, to gather wisdom on how to be effective, and to grow in your experience. Also, remember that the disciples had three years of critical space time with Jesus before he was crucified. He called twelve men who had the potential to carry his message beyond his death and take it farther than he could geographically. In that time, Jesus took them through intensive training. They were with him every day and every night, being coached in the kingdom message, studying his every word, learning how he did things, receiving insight into the ways of his kingdom. After that period, the Holy Spirit took over as the teacher who would lead them into truth and remind them of what Jesus had taught them. Except for Judas, each of them went on to do great exploits using everything they were taught. After all, training is key to doing exploits.

Human nature is such that we tend to embrace only the exciting and stimulating aspects of our talents. But the people the world considers great in their specific areas have developed their skills and abilities in the dark places of trial and error, enduring the pains of endless practise. They worked long, tireless hours mastering their craft or developing their ideas. They transformed their raw talent and ideas into refined, effective weapons used to do exploits, and these weapons set them apart in the world.

Part III

And let us not grow weary of doing good, for in due season
we will reap if we do not give up.

Paul the Apostle, Galatians 6:9, English Standard Version

Never Give Up

Befriend fear
Passion
Pay the price
Keep going

10

People who do great exploits
befriend their fears

Recently, at one of my favourite boutiques, I noticed that a shop assistant, Claire, wasn't her usual outgoing self. Indeed, she seemed preoccupied and sad. When I asked what was wrong, she burst into tears and cried, 'I'm so ashamed of myself!' 'Why are you ashamed of yourself?' I asked.

Sobbing, she told me her story. A week and a half earlier, Claire was at Heathrow Airport with her sisters and two friends about to board a flight to Barbados. It was a dream holiday they had talked about for years, but with work schedules, raising families, and helping to care for elderly parents, there never seemed to be a good time to leave. Plus, money was tight. After their father passed away two years prior, Claire and her sisters decided life was too short to put off their dreams any longer so they set a date to go on holiday and opened a special account. Each month, each of them and two of their best friends paid equal amounts into the account. The fund was to be used to buy airline tickets for all five of them, plus pay for five-star hotel accommodation in Barbados (with some left over for paying for any local entertainment or attractions).

For the last two years, it all went according to plan. And then the day finally arrived – they hired a limo to drive them to the airport and Claire was over the moon because a lifelong dream was about to come true. In fact, she was already planning her next big goal for when she returned from her trip.

The five of them checked in together at the airline counter and passed through the security checks. They enjoyed a big breakfast together. Things were going very well until they got to the duty-free shopping area. Suddenly, Claire felt unwell. She got to the toilet just in time to throw up her breakfast. As Claire turned to exit the cubicle, she was gripped by an overwhelming panic attack. The more she thought of going back into the airport, the stronger her fear became. After a while, she heard her sister's voice calling her name. That gave her the strength to come out.

'What happened to you? Are you okay?' her sister asked.

'I can't go with you,' Claire replied.

'What do you mean you can't go?'

'The plane is going to crash. I can't fly; I'm terrified!'

For the next hour, her sisters and friends gathered round giving Claire support. They coaxed her, they encouraged her, they tried every trick in the book to reassure her. The moment Claire decided not to board the plane, the panic subsided and she felt an amazing calm. *But how can I let my sisters and friends down?* she wondered in despair. With that thought, Claire agreed to go, but the fear rose up again and she felt like she was suffocating. Thus, despite their efforts to encourage her forward, Claire dug her heels in.

Eventually, they spoke to an airline representative and explained the situation. The representative offered all kinds of help to no avail. When it became absolutely clear that Claire was not going to board the flight, the airline agreed to remove her luggage. Because they were among the first passengers to check in, their bags were deep inside the hold. Therefore, *all* the luggage had to be offloaded. The flight was delayed and, meanwhile, Claire insisted that her sisters and friends go on without her. Finally, with moist eyes, they kissed her goodbye. Claire collected her bags and took a taxi home. She cried all the way back to her house.

Fear is the number one reason that keeps people from fulfilling their dreams. But fear can be managed in such a way that it never stops us from doing what we dream of doing. Every human being feels fear occasionally, but the ones who do great exploits have learned how to master their fears and even refer to fear as a friend.

What is fear?

Fear is a physical and emotional response to real or imagined danger. It's important to us as human beings because it helps us protect ourselves from legitimate threats. However, many fears are not life-threatening affairs and, in fact, work against the progress of those who have them. Those types of fears keep people from accomplishing their dreams or plans. It causes them to miss out in life for no good reason.

The kind of fear that arises when we want to pursue our dreams is, more often than not, based on imaginary danger. Claire's experience reflects this well. She believed that the plane would crash, killing her, her sisters, and her friends, but that didn't happen. The four women flew to Barbados and back without incident. Yes, there was a risk that the plane would crash, but that risk is small and exists for every flight. There are a myriad of processes, protocols, and systems that airlines have in place to ensure that such a risk remains small even in the age of terrorist threat. Because those controls are in place, people need not allow fear to stop them from flying.

A popular way of describing fear is as follows: False Evidence Appearing Real (FEAR). The idea is that fear and anxiety are provoked based upon evidence that appears real to the individual but is not actually so. For example, someone wants to start a house fellowship but fears no one will attend. How does she know that without trying? Or another person wants to transform his hobby into a business but fears that, if it succeeds, it will take up all his time. The first is an example of the fear of failure and the second an example of the fear of success. Fears come in all shapes and forms. Someone may have an innovative idea at work but fear it will be rejected; another might crave a promotion but fear he or she is not qualified to deliver at the new level. Some other common examples of fear include: fear of public speaking and fear of what other people might think. These are common fears people live with that hold them back from pursuing their dreams and goals. Yet there are simple solutions to all the imagined dangers that lead to their fears.

Fear is the opposite of faith; after all, faith is belief. It is trust and hope. For the person of faith, anything is possible. For the person controlled by fear, not much is possible. Fear has power to paralyse us, but it can also be a catalyst that pushes us forward. It's all down to how we choose to see it.

It's possible to see fear not as an enemy that overwhelms us and defeats our purpose, but rather as a type of ally. This ally might reveal opportunities, signal to us that what we're facing is significant to our purpose and progress, drive us to take the risks needed to get what we want, or motivate us to reach for excellence in what we do. Fear can also be that friend who gives us no way out so that we have no choice but to move forward.

Fear is the ally who forces you to prepare, to seek the emotional, mental, material, or spiritual reinforcements and measures you need to deal with the task at hand when the stakes are high. Think of the time Jesus appeared to feel something akin to fear: when he was in the garden of Gethsemane. After thirty years of preparing and three years of ministry, the cross and death were just hours away. The overwhelming anxiety drove him to pray, and he received supernatural reinforcement. By the time the soldiers came to arrest him, he was calm, empowered, and ready to go with them. Many of the policies and innovations we live with today have been developed in response to fear. We tend to call that fear 'risk'. For instance the risk that a window cleaner suspended on a hoist outside the 20th story of a skyscraper, might fall, is really the fear of the loss of life, plus the fear of legal repercussions from the cleaner's loved ones. To bring that risk down to zero or next to nothing, window cleaners of responsible companies are fitted with safety belts, harnesses, helmets and other gear so that in the unlikely occurrence they fall from the hoist it won't result in serious injury or a fatality. The fear around this is therefore decreased significantly. But without that fear existing in the first place, safety measures would not be put in place. Fear can drive us to be creative, to design all kinds of tools, devices, innovations, policies and procedures to protect and safeguard our well-being. This is a key way that fear acts as an ally to us.

Some people see fear as a good thing. Fear can tell people what they have to do. It might even be the case that the more fear we feel about our calling, the more we can be sure that it is ours to answer.

The effect of fear in our lives can be quite positive when we learn how to manage it. Fear may give us more value out of life than remaining comfortable ever will. Regardless, the extent to which we learn how to work with fear is the extent to which we will be successful in achieving our dreams. We have the power to decide the role fear will play in our lives.

Why befriend fear?

It's not fear that keeps us from moving forward, it's how we feel about fear. Befriending fear entails changing your perspective about fear, about what it is and what it does. It's like learning how to tame a lion: befriending fear entails recognizing that you have authority over it and understanding that you need not be afraid of it. It's all about gaining the skills to manage fear so that it never stops you from doing what you need to do to achieve your goals and fulfil your dreams.

People who do great exploits have befriended fear in this way. They've acquired the skills and techniques needed to manage it. They feel fear, but because they have tamed it, it doesn't scare them. Fear puts no limitations on them and does not hold them back. It doesn't change their intentions about what they planned to do or immobilise them. They use fear like surfers use waves: to defy gravity, ride the heights, and keep from drowning. The reason surfers don't get swallowed up each time they surf is that they have learned to relate to the sea. When we do the same with our fears, they no longer have the ability to overcome us.

When people stop being afraid of fear and see it as an emotion over which they have control, something they can move past, something that can push them higher, their lives will take on a new level of freedom and power. Paul wrote to Timothy that they had not been given, 'a spirit of fear, but of power, love and a sound mind.'[49] But this doesn't mean we will never feel afraid. A good friend of mine invited me to a conference where she was the speaker for an entire weekend. This person is a very accomplished individual who delivers training to professionals during her normal workweek. Plus, she speaks to crowds almost every weekend of the year. While we were driving to the conference venue, we listened to a lot of worship music, but when we were about thirty minutes away from the venue, she swapped the music for an audio recording of affirmations. To my surprise, the

---

[49] 2 Timothy 1:7, New King James Version.

affirmations all dealt with fear. I would never have guessed that she experienced fear just before speaking. I felt proud of her – proud that she had learned to respond to fear with power and soundness of mind. Without that skill, she would not be able to fulfil that particular call on her life. That weekend, she did great exploits ministering to the crowds.

Fear will appear, but we are called to respond with confidence and power when it does. In order to respond to it effectively, we must first be willing to confront it. Unfortunately, most people are afraid to do so because they think it will overwhelm them. The problem is that, the more they avoid confronting fear, the more fear is empowered in their lives. It's a self-perpetuating cycle. Fortunately, befriending fear can disarm it, and instead of running when you feel it, you can learn how to stand your ground. You'll master how to relate to your fear in an effective way when you experience it. This is how fear is tamed, how you can break free from its bondage.

There are myriad responses we can use to disarm fear, many of them quite simple and practical. The choice of response depends on the particular situation. My friend's response to the fear of public speaking was listening to affirmations. For someone else it might be a long process of preparation, writing up notes, putting together a script, which they take on stage with them. The response of a parent who fears their young child will injure themselves falling off their bicycle, is to attach training wheels to the bicycle. When the child is old enough, the training wheels come off and the parent holds the seat from behind then lets go when the child has found their balance. We can't help fear appearing, be we can control what it does to us by choosing our responses to it. A fearful response would be to never allow the child to get on a bicycle. A response that is not in keeping with power and soundness of mind would be to believe your worst imagined fears will become real and therefore you never accept an invitation to speak. For Claire, whose story I told at the start of this chapter, a response to the fear of flying might have been a mild sedative, which would help her relax and even sleep once she was on the plane. That way she could still go to the Caribbean and enjoy her dream holiday with her sister and friends. That is what Paul meant he wrote we are given a spirit of power and soundness of mind. By faith, we are empowered to drive out fear and move forward in purpose. By the same token, with sound minds, we come up with reasonable responses, which take us into victory instead of being defeated.

> Be sober [well balanced and self-disciplined],
> be alert and cautious at all times.
> That enemy of yours, the devil, prowls around like a roaring
> lion [fiercely hungry], seeking someone to devour.[50]

> So submit to [the authority of] God. Resist
> the devil and he will flee from you.[51]

Peter the Apostle gives a clue about those things that pose a threat to our purpose in the quote above. They are ever–present dangers, always looking for ways to devour, overwhelm and defeat us. But James, the brother of Jesus, shows us the key to overcoming those threats: we are to resist them. Fear is one of these ever-present dangers. It's a part of life. But there is something we can do about it. To resist is to push back or fight back with equal or greater force. The antidote to fear then isn't to run from it, but to face it and apply greater force against it. Fear wants to push you back into obscurity and passivity. The only way to resist is to move forward with greater force. Employ the force of scripture, the force of affirmations, the force of memories and testimonies of how you overcame it last time, the force of definite action in line with your goal. Give up on the idea of praying for God to remove what you fear from your path.

Abandon always wanting to run away. Many people don't do great exploits because they are fasting and praying to make life perfect.

---

[50]   1 Peter 5:8, The Amplified Bible.
[51]   James 4:7, The Amplified Bible.

I don't know anyone with a perfectly problem free life. Some of his best friends in the bible were imprisoned many times, hunted down by enemies, thrown into lions' dens and fiery furnaces! We are not led *around* the valley of the shadow of death, but *through*. David, who wrote those famous words in Psalm 23 pushed back with the force of faith – that God was with him, that his, rod and his staff would defend and guide him through. It is possible to notice feelings of fear and then take specific action, as discussed later in this chapter, to ensure fear either goes away or doesn't stop you from doing what you need to do. For now, here are some reasons why befriending fear is important to your purpose in life.

1. Neutralise the impact fear has on your life

Fear robs people of the great life that can be theirs. It limits influence because it holds them back from taking actions they need to take or even speaking to the people who can help them the most. In an earlier chapter, we discussed the power of influence to accomplish our dreams. Many people are afraid to speak in public or scared to approach others who have the power to help them and share their vision. If we don't find a way to neutralise these and other negative impacts of fear, we won't be able to take hold of the future we dream of.

However, when we befriend fear, it is of no consequence. It can no longer hinder us or harm our future. We are released to do great exploits and fulfil purpose. In other words, we neutralise its damaging impact on our lives.

One pastor I know who oversees six churches shared how he inherited the ministry his father established over the course of thirty years. He grew up watching his father preach, but because of his quiet and reserved personality he was never keen on being on the stage. But one day, when he was old enough, his father did ask him to preach. Not wanting to let his father down he said he would. For the days running up to it, he said he felt physically sick most of the time. Apart from the fear of public speaking, he just couldn't see how he could even stand in the same pulpit as his father, who was a great speaker. Somehow he made it through his first sermon. Afterwards, he expected to never be asked again but instead his father said he'd been great and that he now expected him to preach at least once a month.

His second time round he felt a bit more confident. But he discovered a key secret, a response to his natural fear that worked for him. It involved preparation and talking to himself to boost his confidence. In the days preceding his preaching assignment, he studiously prepared his material and when negative thoughts came to mind he confessed scriptures like, *I can do all things through Christ who gives me strength!* or *I am more than a conqueror through him who loves me!* He also said things like, *They keep asking me to preach. It must mean I am a blessing.* Now that he's running the ministry his father started before he was born, he regularly tells members of his pastoral team. 'You need to act as your own coach and say the right things to yourself.' Had he not learned how to neutralise his fears, he would have forfeited the inheritance his father prepared for him and missed his purpose in life.

Fear-befriending principle: be careful of what you say to yourself. Tell yourself you are the one called to your assignment and able to do it.

2. You'll be in good company with every single person who has done great exploits

In doing the research for this book, it amazed me just how many famous people have a fear of public speaking. The people I know personally who are afraid to speak to a crowd – or even a small group – far outweigh the ones I know who don't appear to be afraid. The ones in the latter group are virtual heroes to those in the former group. Plus, they are more likely to be active in pursuing their dreams and have already accomplished many of their goals. Everyone's more likely to listen to my friends in the latter group, even in social situations. People seem more willing for them to take the lead, Tweet what they said, or seek them out for advice. This comes back to the inescapable reality that a person's ability to influence is critical to his or her success. To influence, people have to communicate. Yet public speaking is one of the commonest fears that stops many people in their tracks.

I read a story featuring a mountain climber who revealed she suffered with a morbid fear of public speaking. She had gone with groups of climbers and tackled some very difficult and dangerous climbs several times over in her lifetime but when she was invited to speak to some 6th form students at a local high school she was overcome with terror. The irony was that her talk was supposed to be about conquering fear! When she got there she was just about overcome by her own personal fear. She stood in front of the class and her mouth went dry plus her mind went completely blank. She'd thought of a few things she wanted to say but couldn't recall them. She dealt with it by taking a sip of water then telling the kids that she had climbed mountains, but in fact was very nervous having to stand in front of them to talk about overcoming fear! Though it wasn't intended to be a joke, the students thought it was and laughed. That changed things for her. She laughed along with them and felt herself relax. Then the things she wanted to say came back to her memory and she spoke. As it turned out, the kids were fascinated by her adventures in climbing and some of the mishaps she'd had to deal with on different climbs. Speaking about an area that she was passionate about helped her forget what she was feeling. Eventually, she completely stopped feeling fear and got lost in telling stories about mountain climbing. She explained that she had faced grave danger at times, but overcame her fear by believing she could make it out alive and remaining very focused on the next step, instead of looking too far down the line.

Fear-befriending principle: make your passion for your purpose, and the things you care about deeply, more important than the fear you're feeling.

3. So it won't make you procrastinate

Fear causes, talented people with a purpose, to play it safe. Because of fear, they let opportunities pass them by. Before they know it, they lose months, years, or even decades. They put off taking action and talk about what they plan to do at some point in the future. Sadly, that day rarely ever comes.

People who do great exploits understand the need to move past their fears and seize the moment. They take action towards their goals every day. They don't put off doing what they can do while waiting for the future to arrive.

4. Fear can be a powerful motivator

Eagles are born afraid to fly. The nest is comfortable; it's safe and warm. Plus, food is delivered to the eaglets in easy, bite-sized pieces. Eaglets are reluctant to leave the comforts of home to soar and be what they were created to be. Indeed, the bald eagle parent has to push its offspring out of the nest if the eaglets refuse to fly!

When their mother finally nudges them off the edge of the nest, they start off by falling. They see the ground speeding towards them and fear kicks in. They probably think, *That's why I wanted to stay in the nest!* Fear tells them that, if they don't fly, they will fall to the ground and die. Suddenly, they start flapping wings they didn't even know they had. And then, as if by magic, they stop falling and begin to fly.

The next time you feel fear, ask yourself, *What is this fear trying to telling me?* Many of us make the assumption that fear means we're not capable or that we should give up because all is lost. But that isn't necessarily the case. Like the eaglets, we should allow fear to help us discover our innate gifts and abilities. Fear sometimes seems to force us to activate our latent powers and resourcefulness.

Again, I think of the harlot Rahab, whose story I told in an earlier chapter. She, like everyone else in Jericho and the whole of Canaan feared annihilation by the Israelites. Fear became the enemy of every individual in her city because they allowed it to corner them in hopeless defeat. However, fear became Rahab's ally. When fear paralysed everyone including the mighty men in Jericho, fear activated this woman's resourcefulness. Her fear gave her the impetus to seek an opportunity to save herself and her family. Fear forced her to look outward, to be more aware, to scan the horizon, and to take a risk that paid off handsomely.

Fear-befriending principle: when you feel afraid, ask yourself, *Is my fear telling me to look for an opportunity for a better outcome or future?*

5. It can make you excellent

Fear is a potential ally because it forces you to prepare. At one stage of my career, my responsibility was to run events for large numbers of people. When I started the job, I had no experience in events management. My first couple of public events flopped, and I felt like I was letting my organisation down. I began to fear the embarrassment of a poorly organised event, plus the criticism that inevitably followed.

To avoid this, I knew I needed to up my game. I decided to take control and began a rigorous process of planning and preparation for each event. I wrote up a protocol and went through every aspect – from the catering, to briefing the speakers, to visiting the venues on the morning before the event to ensure the environments were clean and laid out exactly the way I requested. I met with speakers before the programmes, went over their presentations with them, and answered all their questions. I meticulously oversaw the invitations to stakeholders, even visiting some of them personally to show them why the event mattered to them and why they should be there. I developed relationships with local caterers, venue managers, and all the other people who formed part of the chain. That lifted everyone's performance. We began to work as a team even though we were from different businesses. Prior to that strategy, I just made a phone call or e-mailed one of the suppliers to book what I needed and assumed that people would do their jobs and deliver on their promises; that things would automatically fall into place on a given day. My change in approach really turned things around dramatically. Soon my events were staged perfectly. I became excellent at putting on events and received lots of positive feedback.

Fear-befriending principle: fear can force you to look at what you're doing that isn't working and motivate you to be more effective.

How to befriend fear

1. Make something else more important than the fear

Sometimes, in order to manage a fear, you have to focus on an outcome that is more important than the fear. For example, my friend describes himself as being petrified of heights. He's an engineer with a firm that designs specialised industrial plants around the world in countries such as China. Periodically, he and a team from his firm go out to inspect the plants to ensure that they meet the specifications and that quality standards are being met during the construction process and after the plant is up and running. The consequence of not checking on quality is extremely serious: explosions, fires can result, causing loss of life and damage to the environment.

Often, his inspection protocols require that he climb up the outside of reactors that are anywhere between 60 or 70 metres high. He uses a safety harness and other equipment to minimise the risk of falling, but the fact remains that he is petrified of heights. Yet he pushes back against his terror because lives depend upon him carrying out the quality and safety checks on the reactors. People who do exploits manage their fear even in extreme scenarios such as this one so that they can do what they need to do to achieve their goals.

The people you are called to serve must be more important than any fear you feel. Keep your focus on the difference your talent and skill can create in order to help decrease your fear.

Fear-befriending principle: people who do exploits remain focused on the bigger picture.

> Then I will go in to [see] the king [without being summoned], which is against the law; and if I perish, I perish.[52]

2. Imagine what will happen if you don't just do it

I'm scared to change but terrified of things remaining as they are. When faced with a scary proposition, it's useful to ask yourself,

What will be the likely consequences for me and others if I don't just do this? Sometimes not taking action in the direction of your goal is worse than feeling the fear of taking the action. Of course, if one doesn't take action, one will remain exactly where one was, and for people who do great exploits, that's one of the worst predicaments. Not making any progress or any positive difference in the lives of others can feel worse than any nervousness or anxiety that may arise as a result of taking action.

What would have happened had Queen Esther allowed her fear of the king to defeat her? She faced the possibility of death, but doing nothing was a situation that was even more horrifying.

---

[52]   Esther 4:16, The Amplified Bible.

At the end of their lives, people don't regret the things they finish; instead, they regret the things they didn't complete. Many live their lives feeling empty, wishing they had been bolder and taken up opportunities to pursue their dreams. Due to fear, they played it safe, and this decision makes them wish they had done things differently.

3. *Get real about fear*

Ask yourself one simple question: *What's the worst that could happen?* Once you've identified all the things that *could* go wrong, you can figure out how to prevent them and train yourself to handle the troubles along the way. If you're nervous about speaking in public, write down what you want to say and read it out loud as a means of preparation. Many of the speakers considered gifted orators today do exactly that: they go over their speeches in advance, rehearsing every line until they are very familiar with all the words.

Whatever your fear, remember that it's not unique to you; other people have the same fear. Among those other people, you'll inevitably find some who, instead of being defeated by that fear, have befriended it. Those people will have worked out a system for managing the fear without allowing it to get in the way of their goals – and you could do the same.

4. *Make fearlessness a theme for your life*

When I finally admitted that I had allowed various fears of mine to hinder my progress and happiness in life I made the decision to make fearlessness a theme in my life for an entire year. I made no other resolutions that year, only the resolve to be fearless. This meant that when I was faced with a situation that awakened fear in me, I would do the opposite of what fear would have me do. For example, if I were in a meeting and felt intimidated, I'd make myself speak up and share my ideas. If I had to give a speech but could easily delegate it to someone else, I made myself do it.

As time passed, my confidence grew. In short order, I became bolder, and by the middle of the year, I was transformed: I was a more confident person; I had stopped acting like a timid little mouse. Basically, I was not afraid to share my opinions and expertise. The more I did this, the more I found that people who virtually ignored me in the past began noticing me. They greeted me in the corridors when we passed each other. I could see respect in their eyes, and they invited me to meetings. They wanted to know what I thought about things; they even began referring others to me for my expertise. The unexpected benefit of practicing fearlessness was that my influence grew. I realised I was beginning to make the difference and add value in a way I had only dreamed of in the past. As a result, I felt much healthier, happier, and stronger.

Making fearlessness a theme for my life meant I had to intentionally live it as a life philosophy each day. I had to make sure boldness always won the day. Instead of running away, I forced myself to confront; instead of shrinking back, I made myself face whatever scared me. It was painful at times. On the inside, I often wanted to run away and hide, but I committed to move forward in every situation and not back down. I stopped being the one who made all the concessions so others could have what they wanted at my expense and made sure it became win–win so I also got something out of every process. I stopped caring so much what others thought of me and became far less concerned with whether they liked me. When I met with resistance, I chose to stand my ground, always respectful but firm. In each scenario, my new perspective proved the most helpful to my doing exploits. Every contrary view eventually gave way to the new version of me that was more fearless.

5. *Take risks*

It's impossible to do great exploits without taking risks. Most of us are conditioned from childhood to seek security. Society has prescribed a safe route through life that goes a little like this: get an education, get a job, retire, die quietly. It takes a unique individual to be brave enough to step outside of those lines and do something different. But we know from the countless people who do great exploits that stepping out and taking risks doesn't inevitably result in disaster. If anything, such people learn that true security doesn't exist in a bank balance or a big house. Rather, security comes from faith that, whatever happens, things are going to work out.

The difference between people who do great exploits and those who simply wish they could is that they are willing to take the risks necessary to achieve their goals, to risk failure. Without that risk, they understand that they will never discover whether the vision that burns in their heart is simply wishful thinking. They understand that they will remain stuck in one place if they choose to play it safe. Successful people run towards their fears, not away from them.

> "The lazy one manufactures excuses and
> says, "There is a lion outside!
> I will be killed in the streets if I go out to work!"[53]

6. *Step outside of your comfort zone*

Do the thing you fear the most and the death of fear is certain.

Mark Twain

Earlier in the chapter, I talked about the attitudes of eaglets in relation to flight. Eagles are such beautiful, strong creatures. Most people admire them because of their regal bearing and their ability to fly higher than any other creature. In some cultures, they have become a symbol of strength and dominion. Yet the very thing they were born to do is the thing they start off life trying to avoid. It's almost a human quality!

---

[53]   Proverbs 22:13, New King James Version.

In the early months of life, eaglets prefer the comfort zone of the nest. There, they don't have to do much more than breathe and eat. Life is easy there. There's nothing to scare them because everything is familiar. The ground is firm and secure under their feet; they feel in control. The problem with that picture is that no eaglet will go on to fulfil its life's purpose if it remains there.

To fulfil purpose, we have to be willing to grow. In order to grow, we must be exposed to new things. That exposure takes us outside our comfort zones where risk exists. Risk is uncomfortable, even terrifying. Yet, without experiencing risk, we get nowhere in life. The parent eagle knows this, which is why it forces its young out of the comfort zone of the nest. The moment the eaglet falls, it begins to learn many new things. Its horizon of possibilities begins expanding exponentially. It senses the pull of gravity for the first time and learns how to resist it and avoid failure. It discovers its very survival is now entirely in its own hands and that it possesses latent talents and abilities that distinguishes it from all others. It learns its own resourcefulness in tricky situations. As it thrusts itself skyward, it discovers its unique destiny.

If it had been allowed to remain in its comfort zone, it would never have discovered any of these things.

7. Choose your friends wisely

Many of the fears we have are learned from the people in our lives – not only our parents, but our peer groups too. We may not have chosen the fears we inherited or that rubbed off on us, but we do have power to choose whether to hold on to those fears. For example, I have a relative who has a fear of water. She shared a terrible experience that she and several other friends had while bathing in the sea as young children. They got caught in an undercurrent, which began dragging them out into the deep and needed rescuing by lifeguards. I have always loved the sea and enjoy going into the water whenever

I'm in the Caribbean. I had wondered why this relative never came into the water with us until she told me of her experience. Though I understood and empathised, I felt sorry that she couldn't experience the enjoyment being in the water gave me. Fortunately, I did not buy into that fear. I still go into the water and have lots of fun.

If you have inherited fear others have or been taught to fear something through other people's reactions to it there are ways to break free. Begin by making a decision that you are going to conquer the fear. Then seek to actively forge new relationships with others who don't have the same fear. Watching them do the thing that frightens you can help you take the first steps to get over the particular fear. Constructive friendships inspire us to keep growing and developing so that we are able to fulfil our purpose. In the chapters on potential, I wrote about mentors and other types of relationships that teach and train us, that enable us to become our best selves.

Be mindful of the quality of friendships you keep and the people with whom you surround yourself. They will either inadvertently hold you back or encourage you to keep moving forward in purpose.

11

People who do great exploits
are passionate

People who do great exploits would tell you that it's passion for their purpose that keeps them running their race. Passion is the way you feel about something; how important it is to you. It's a very powerful motivator and driving force. When we are motivated by the love we have for the prize, it fuels our drive and we do exploits. For example, Paul, the apostle had such love for the church that even when he was beaten and imprisoned, he continued to pray for the churches, he wrote letters of encouragement, instruction and exhortation to them. His desire, i.e. his passion was to see people growing in the love and grace of Christ. His passionate letters became books in the New Testament.

In researching people who do great exploits, I have to say that another key common theme that runs through their lives is passion. Whatever it is that they are famous for or have done great exploits in, it was their passion for that cause that motivated them. Great exploits require great passion.

Passion gives rise to a sense of intensity, urgency, and focus that's required for certain exploits. Jesus was so passionate about redeeming us that he was willing to lay down his life for it. A lukewarm attitude, gets you nowhere, as we'll see later in this chapter. We therefore, can't afford to be lukewarm or dispassionate about achieving our life's purpose.

What is passion?

It may be a common assumption that people who do great exploits find their passion easily. It's true in many cases, but not so in others. Some eventually discovered their passion through a meandering road of detours and false starts. Consider Ray Kroc. He impacted the fast food world with McDonalds starting at age 52 after years of odd jobs. Similarly, the man we call Colonel Sanders had already retired before he discovered the one thing that changed everything for him. Yet I would argue that it was an inner thirst, or passion itself, that kept these and others seeking their *one thing*. It explains the restlessness, the searching, and the refusal to settle for what life chooses to hand you. That attitude stems from a desire to express an inner calling that each of us possesses (see chapter 1 and chapter 2). Whatever it is we are looking for is there, but we must look for it to find it. Once it's found, passion stops being a nebulous, restless urge and becomes a fire that fuels our drive to fulfil that calling.

When thinking about passion, the questions to ask yourself include: *What excites me? What can I lose time doing? What wakes me up in the morning? What's the one thing that's always there at the back of my mind? What do I want deep inside? If I had the money or resources I needed, what would I choose to do with my time, gifts, talents, and abilities? What cause gets me angry or moves me?*

Passion is often thought of as the love someone has for a hobby or other interest. For example, one may love gardening or playing an instrument or reading about astronomy. But I would say it's much more than that – true passion is more than a causal interest.

Passion is strong feeling or emotion that we have for someone or something. Passion inspires a sense of urgency, which spurs us on to pursue and try to obtain the object of our passion. It is a powerful motivational force. It drives some people to go all out and leave no stone unturned in their quest for fulfilment. It's what keeps us asking until we receive, seeking until we find, and knocking until the door is opened. The person who won't take no for an answer is a passionate person. Passion is the expression of the level of our need or desire for something. And it is scriptural.

> Because you are lukewarm, and neither hot nor cold,
> I will vomit you out of My mouth [reject you with disgust].[54]

Why you need passion to do exploits

1. So you won't be spat out of the mouth of God

Enough said.

2. Because passion points you to your true purpose

I was very close to my high school history teacher. He taught me for five years in high school right up to my GCE exams. But he became a mentor to me when I handed in an assignment in my third year of being in his class. The assignment was to write an essay about a career that you wanted to pursue and why. I don't know what the other students in the class wrote about, but I wrote that I wanted to be a psychologist. In 2016, in the UK that wouldn't be something considered out of the ordinary for a student to write. However, it

---

[54] Revelation 3:16, The Amplified Bible

was 1983 in Trinidad, and psychologists weren't commonplace. But I remember him calling me aside and asking me where I had got the idea about being a psychologist from. He'd been impressed with my reasons why as I had explained in great detail how I would use psychology to help people – even then I had a passion for empowering and motivating others to be their best selves and to achieve their dreams.

After that he often started conversations with me involving politics, telling me about his life as a degree student in New York in the late 60s and early 70s right after the civil rights movement. My parents also knew him socially because he was married to one of my father's childhood friends and they visited our home often. They knew him well and so I was allowed to spend a lot of time with him. We talked for hours about all sorts of issues of life: politics, race issues, economics, social justice, you name it. He was a great teacher and mentor.

However, by the time I had completed form 5 and passed my GCEs, I had changed my mind about what I wanted to do. I hesitated about telling him because I didn't want him to be disappointed that I was no longer that keen on psychology as a career. I wanted to do something involving English. Perhaps be an English teacher and pursue writing. Days before I left Trinidad, heading to Canada to continue my education, I told him of my change of heart. I was surprised to hear him say, 'Michelle, whatever path you decide to take, make sure you're passionate about it. Find your passion in life.'

If what you're doing doesn't matter to you, if it fills you with indifference – if you are not moved or inspired to solve problems or influence others – it's possible that what you're doing isn't your true passion. Many people experience this lack of passion in their working life and feel trapped. They go to work because they have to, not because they love to. Within a year of that conversation, Valerie

Henry, spotted my potential in this area and her encouragement only served to fuel my passion for writing.

3. Passion is your reason why

Passion is your reason to get up in the morning.

I'm not convinced that loving what you do necessarily guarantees success, but I'd agree that loving (i.e., having a passion for what you're doing) is perhaps the most powerful of motivators. If you have a genuine love for your cause, you'll be more likely to pay the price it demands of you (rather than if you have a lukewarm interest in it). Paying that price is what makes it more likely you'll succeed in achieving your goals and dreams. Passion motivates people to break barriers, conquer giants and push through to new frontiers.

Passion is a conviction about something. It's the determination someone has to do what they want to do or serve as they want to serve. Many people reach the pinnacle of their careers and are considered to have succeeded in life however still feel there is something more, or different, that they want to do. They connect with a passion in their soul for a cause and then focus their attention and find fulfilment in that.

It's also emotional. It can create feelings of joy and contentment even if your purpose takes you through difficult places. It transforms timid individuals into bold figures and gives meaning to the challenging situations they face.

Passion is a hunger for something more, for something greater. The deep yearning creates energy, which fuels focus, intensity, and devotion to a cause. Passion brings people who do great exploits to a do-or-die place. Life seems intolerable without the fulfilment of their cause. It's what made Charles Finney the evangelist cry, 'Give me Scotland or I die!'

4. Passion orders your priorities

All things are lawful,
but not all things are beneficial or advantageous.[55]

In life, there are many good things that we can be doing. But the people who do exploits understand Paul's words and devote themselves to their passion. They lay aside distractions in favour of the things that are important to their dreams. They are much more willing to sacrifice things that fall outside the scope of their purpose – even when they are 'good' things. Their time, energy, and resources are all geared towards the fulfilment of their assignment.

At a business event I attended, the keynote speaker was introduced by the moderator as being 'the single most 'bloody-minded' and focused person' she knew. It was strong language, but I knew what she meant. This person had only started with that particular business four years before and had consistently broken the record for sales in the 12 months prior to the event. She was about to be promoted to the position of senior vice president. In the long history of that company, no one, not even the current president had ever achieved that position in under five years. When the keynote speaker took the stage, her passion for the company and its products was palpable. But her passion to make something of herself, given that she not done particularly well in school also shone through. Wanting to make her family proud of her became her priority and is what drove her to become one of the highest earners in the business

Look at how much Christ achieved in three years of ministry. It's because he devoted himself to certain priorities. Every aspect of his life was built around his purpose, including his friendships and social life.

---

[55]   1 Corinthians 10:23a, The Amplified Bible.

This focus on priorities becomes a natural habit after a while and is a common trait among purpose-driven people. They are known for surrounding themselves with their work but, in reality, they don't view the work of their life's purpose as something separate to them. It's not like a compartment of their life. It *is* life; it's who they are. There is a seamless integrity between who they are called to be, what they say, and what they choose to do. It's what we call personal branding. When most people see certain logos they know exactly what they mean. The brand communicates what those companies stand for and what they're passionate about. The companies' purpose and values are aligned with how they invest capital, time, human resources, and the service or product they provide. Similarly, people who do great exploits are eventually known for what they stand for and what they're passionate about because their lives are immersed in walking out those two things every day. Purpose, time, actions, and even relationships are integrated into one big picture. Less importance is given to things that are not related. This is passion at work.

5. Passion gets you through the rough times

Passion is needed because, although the journey of exploits is one of great victory, it will involve sacrifice, failure, and even loss along the way. Things don't always go smoothly. The journey may be marked by discouragement, disappointment, pain, fear, and self-doubt. When you fall down, you will need to get back up and try again or even start over from scratch. The need for tenacity and perseverance is explored in chapter 13, but the thing that enables you to get back up, to keep dreaming, hoping, and expecting that things will come together is passion. Without passion, it's easier to say no to the call to purpose and give up.

6. Passion empowers people to take the necessary risks

People who do great exploits take risks. Inherent to any dream, plan, or exploit is the risk of failure, the risk of success, the risk of mistakes, the risk that conditions outside our control can upset our best-laid plans. Though these risks are present, men and women who do great exploits go forward despite them.

Of course, passion isn't the same as recklessness. Though risks have to be taken, successful people calculate the risks and weigh them against the benefits. They do their due diligence, taking a close look at all the angles. They seek the truthful reality of things and use that knowledge to inform their decisions.

They do everything they can to mitigate the risks they've identified. If, in their analysis, the benefits clearly outweigh the risks, they are then willing to take the risks. Passion for the prize imbues them with a keen sense of responsibility to not be frightened off by risks but to manage them effectively.

7. Passion makes you commit

There are some people who are so passionate about their cause that they say it feels like a life or death situation for them. For them making a difference or obtaining the prize is a must, just like breathing. This persuasion – *I must or die* – is commitment. People who do great exploits are fully persuaded in this way. On the outside they may look relaxed, but on the inside there is an intense commitment about their purpose that never abates.

A person with a lukewarm attitude is incapable of committing to anything. That person is like a double-minded person: unstable, inconsistent, and unreliable. Ultimately, it means the person is not trustworthy. Someone with a lukewarm attitude might start a project one day – if at all – but take no further action for weeks or months. During that time, all the distractions of the world creep in, which causes them to forget what they started. Therefore, little or nothing is achieved.

It's impossible to do great exploits without a commitment.

8. So others will be drawn to you

If you lack passion, you won't attract the interest of other people. In chapter 6, I talked about the power of influence when doing great exploits. Influence, I wrote, is communication – it's how we relate to others and the impact we can have on their view of the world. Without influence, certain types of exploits are nearly impossible.

Passion is integral to influence. Passion has power to transform individuals into charismatic and influential people who others enjoy and are inspired to be around. Charisma is an expression of passion. My high school Caribbean History teacher was probably one of the few truly charismatic people I've known. When he lectured on history we were transported to Africa; we were herded onto slave ships; we were there on the plantations seeing what was happening to people in that system. Students who were failing in other classes were *A* and *B* students in his. He had a way of speaking to us that made his own passion infectious; we could listen to him for hours. He had that magnetic impact outside class too. When other teachers interacted with him, it was obvious they respected and looked up to him.

Passion has a way of shining through our voice, our mannerisms, and our eyes – it exudes a positive force that captivates and draws others in. People who live out of their passion come across as confident and self-assured without seeming arrogant or cocky. This stems from the fact that they have discovered what they love and have chosen to be true to themselves. In short, we are drawn to confident people who are at ease with who they are. They make it easy for others to be around them because they tend to be affirming instead of critical.

> Light yourself on fire with passion and people
> will come from miles to watch you burn.
> John Wesley

9. *Passionate people make progress*

People who are passionate about their cause tend to make things happen. They don't take *no* for an answer. If a door closes, they move on to find the next door. They don't dwell on the past or the present; rather, they look to the future. Thus, they are more often than not working on their next goal. This has its advantages in that they always have something new on the horizon that they can look forward to. On the other hand, if one is constantly pushing ahead, one runs the risk of burning out. Those who are more seasoned at great exploits have learned the value of balancing the passion for progress with the need to pace themselves. They are adept at balancing forward-thinking with ensuring they also enjoy moments in the present.

How to maintain passion on your journey of purpose

Life can be tough. Doing great exploits is demanding work. It's demanding physically, intellectually, spiritually, and emotionally. Over time, our pursuit taxes us, the resistance wearies us and some of the risks we took will have ended in failure. Our ideas were criticised; some didn't work out. At times, we were misunderstood or rejected by those whose help we craved. Perhaps we managed to attract more adversaries than allies. Even the most passionate of people will find their passion ebbs from time to time. People who do great exploits find ways to sustain their passion but are as susceptible to discouragement as everyone else. If we don't maintain a razor-sharp drive, we run the risk of becoming dull – withdrawing from our appointed race, retreating to a comfort zone where we lose our passion altogether.

I think of David at Ziklag when he and his men returned to the city to find their wives, children, and belongings stolen by a band of mercenaries. That would have been bad enough, but David's men, who had been intensely loyal to him up until that point, all turned on him and threatened to take his life. This was at the point in his journey when he'd spent years in exile, on the run from Saul and sleeping in caves while he begged for refuge from the Philistines, the enemies of the very kingdom he'd been called to rule. The problem was that none of his seemingly endless struggles were adding up to the call upon his life.

People who do great exploits inevitably face circumstances where all seems to be lost. Every human being does. After years of struggle and victory doing small exploits; waiting for the prize understandably takes its toll. However, the difference between those who do great exploits and those who don't is that they find a way to encourage themselves. People who do great exploits rekindle their passion sooner or later. Discouragement may appear to have them for a season but, ultimately, they fight back and recover all (like David did).

There are tried-and-tested strategies people who do great exploits use to reignite, maintain, and intensify their passion for purpose. Here are some key ones:

1. Make a decision to never settle, to never give in to mediocrity

Never underestimate the power of a decided mind. Once you've discovered your purpose, the call that is on your life, the next thing before you embark on any exploits is to make a decision that you are going to fulfil that call no matter what happens. Paul the Apostle said, 'I remained faithful to the heavenly vision.' I suspect it's because, when he was called on that road to Damascus, Paul made a decision that he would fulfil it, whatever the cost. In his writings in the New Testament, we catch many glimpses of what it did cost him. He'd been a rising star of Judaism: a zealot and the pride of the Pharisees. But Paul immediately lost his social status the moment he defected to the other side. He roamed from town to town and was invariably rejected by the Judaist orders he met there. Some of them issued warrants for his arrest and sentenced him to lashes and time in prison.

Without that personal decision to remain faithful to the call no matter what happened, I wonder whether he would have endured.

2. Do like David did

The final straw came for David at Ziklag. Until then, he had faced his difficulties without flinching. He'd worked hard, led his men, and provided for them and their families. He'd politically manoeuvred into a relationship with the Philistines, which gave them some protection. But with the kidnapping of their families, all seemed lost. His men were inflamed with rage against him. David faced deep discouragement. When overwhelmed by troubles and weariness, 'David encouraged himself in the Lord.'[56]

Discouragement is to passion like water is to a fire. When it comes, the remedy is always to go to God, turn to him. Tell him all your troubles. If the call was from him, he will be sure to rekindle your passion.

3. Remember why you started, and be inspired by those who need what you can give

My mother is an amazing woman. She was the music teacher at a high school in the town where we lived. A lot of the kids who attended that school came from impoverished and challenging homes. When I was a teenager mom got the idea to take her choir on tour to Canada to give her students an experience they would remember for the rest of their lives. None of them had ever travelled out of the country before, let alone to North America. The choir was about 70 strong, plus she would need a good compliment of teachers to travel with them, acting as chaperones. Such a venture would require hundreds of thousands of dollars of our local currency.

---

[56]   1 Samuel 30:6, King James Version.

Mom used all the powers of communication and influencing I wrote about in chapter 6, to galvanise support from senior teachers in the school and then take her idea to the school principal. She got his approval to then take her proposal to the Ministry of Education to get their permission for the project to go ahead. Mom did exploits convincing politicians and other government officials that she could safely take 70 students out of the country on a North American tour for two weeks and return them safely to their families.

I remember how excited she was when she finally got the go ahead from all the relevant authorities. She had formed a group of four other teachers to help with the project. Mom invited them over to our house for a celebration. But that was just the beginning. It was a huge responsibility she had taken on and expectations were high. Eyes were now on her like never before. Mom had never done anything like this before. She had to find a way to deliver what she promised, not just to her principal but to the ministry of education. She also had to engage with parents, gain their trust and convince them to entrust their children to her. Plus, she, her team and her students now faced 18 months of fundraising.

They planned all kinds of fundraising activity, from car washes, to bar-b-ques, to raffles, to concerts and sponsored walk-a-thons. She mobilised the students to get involved. She got on the phone and canvassed businesses. Had several meetings with an airline to negotiate sponsorship of some plane tickets. She met with numerous bank managers to persuade them to donate funds. Mom got on the phone and contacted hotels searching for affordable accommodation in Toronto for 80 people. Meanwhile, she had to whip her choir and band into shape. They would have to perform almost everyday at different venues in Toronto.

It was hard work, but mom and her group of teachers were on course to reach the target funds when a key sponsor pulled out just three months before the travel date. That sponsor had pledged $50,000.

It was a serious blow. Mom wondered how she and her team could possibly raise that much in under 3 months. After over a year of working evenings training the choir and on weekends running fundraising activities she was exhausted. Though there were some exhilarating times, there had been difficult times too. She faced a lot criticism from other teachers in the school who never supported the idea. Plus she fielded an endless stream of queries from parents wanting reassurances. With the loss of key sponsorship the setback hit her hard.

One night I heard mom talking with her best friend. 'What was I thinking?' she wondered out loud. 'I don't know if I have any strength left to look for other sponsors. Maybe, it's a lost cause. I'm going to call it off.'

Her friend looked at her, then said, 'You can't call it off. Just think about the kids. Forget everyone and everything else and just think about the kids. You're giving them something no one else has given them before.' Thinking over what her friend told her slowly reignited mom's passion. Her students were depending on her. They were all excited and looking forward to their trip. With them in mind she found the strength again to follow through and deliver on her promises to her students. The tour went ahead. Thirty years on many of those same students still keep in touch with my mom.

4. Remember those who went before you

Seeking out those who are pursuing their own purpose with passion is a great way to get re-inspired to continue your own race. If you're running low on passion, spending time with people who are doing great things will have a good effect on you. Their passion will rub off on you when you hear about what they're doing and sense the energy they exude. You won't want to be left behind when you see the way they are forging ahead. It'll refuel your optimism about the future and motivate you to get moving again.

We can also remember those who have gone before and achieved the dream we're pursuing. That's what my friend did when she was running for elections in local government. She had been a community activist for several years running social projects for young people and became well known to the Member of Parliament (MP) in her borough. One day her MP invited her to a meeting and asked, 'You've been doing a lot of good work here. Where do you see yourself heading with it all?' My friend told me she hadn't been sure how to answer the question because she had never thought of it before. The work she was involved in was her passion, she was good at spotting need and then she simply enlisted the help of people she knew to address that need. She didn't have a 'grand plan' or 'vision' about her own future or of the work she was doing.

The MP suggested she run in the election in the following year. She promised to mentor her and plug her into the right people so that she could begin shaping her vision and planning her campaign. My friend asked for a few days to think it over. 'I never saw myself as a politician,' she told me over dinner one night. 'But that's really what you are,' I replied. 'Politicians do what you've been doing all along – help people. Make a difference. At least the good ones do!'

She talked it over with her husband and he encouraged her to take up the offer pledging his support. That year things began to change very rapidly for her. Night after night, she had events to attend. She had to meet and talk with all types of people, including elected councillors, getting her views about the local situation across. She had to give talks at community events and she felt like she was constantly on the road. Six months in, she became tired of the constant pressures, the venues, the surly audiences, people treating what she said with suspicion, the local media misrepresenting her and was about to throw in the towel. Passion for the opportunity was all but lost. But then she remembered how much her husband believed in her and supported her dream and she didn't want to disappoint him. What's more, she had come quite far and put in a lot work. If she gave in to discouragement, she would also be letting herself down. She asked herself, *After so much hard work, would I give up just because some people are trying to make life difficult?* Finally, she thought of her heroes who had used politics as a vehicle for social change, those who had gone before her facing great opposition: Nelson Mandela, Aung San Suu Kyi and others. Each of them had overcome odds much greater than uncomfortable campaign tours and difficult audiences. My friend felt the fight come back into her and stopped feeling sorry for herself. She went on to run in the election and was voted in by a significant majority. She learned a lot from the experience, including the 'thick skinned bullheadedness' that's needed to be a success.

5. Remember the prize

I hated every minute of training, but I said. 'Don't quit. Suffer now and live the rest of your life as a champion.' Muhammad Ali

Like my mother, when we can't summon enough passion to continue pursuing a worthy goal or are running out of steam, one way to get fired up again is to focus on those who will benefit. That can include you, as the quote from Ali shows. He may have looked into his future and saw he had only two options. He could either be a champion or not. Being a champion would provide a life of benefits and privileges including a platform to make his views heard, and taken seriously, i.e. to influence for the better.

Lay aside thinking negatively about the obstacles, the challenges, and the difficulties you face for a moment and focus instead on the benefits – all the good things that can come out of your exploit if you stick with it, even the benefits that appeal to your vanity. Ali admitted he didn't enjoy training at all. But when he thought about living the life of a champion, passion for that lifestyle gave him strength to run all the miles and complete all the workouts prescribed by his coach.

The example of David at Ziklag shows the power of prayer in transforming a bad situation. He hadn't come so far to die at the hands of his own men. The reason for all his struggles wasn't a shameful death in a Philistine stronghold, it was the prize he'd been called to – to be king and govern a nation. He had to find a way, beyond his own resources, to rise again to the occasion. On the unpredictable and often perilous road to fulfilling the work to which you're called, prayer works. In times of crisis speak to the one who called and he will make his solutions plain. When you experience a crisis on your journey of exploits take some time out to spend in his presence. I have experienced his supernatural touch that brought instant refreshment more times than I can tell. I call it my 'God reset'. In the wilderness, Moses spent as much time as possible in the tabernacle. At times he even retreated up the mountain for days at a time, and isolated himself with God. In those times he recharged his batteries supernaturally. He gained more wisdom. He was refreshed and empowered to continue in the call. He did great exploits.

The Bible states, 'For the joy of accomplishing the goal set before Him [Jesus] endured the cross.'[57] His passion towards us motivated him to bear the extreme difficulties of his particular race.

Reflection on passion

Loving what you do is critical to going the distance with what you do. People who do exploits are passionate about their cause. Their passion drives them, giving them the impetus to push back when faced with obstacles, setbacks, weariness or even fear. They are passionate because the stakes are often high. Their pursuit of purpose will produce great benefits either for others or themselves. They keep their eye on that bigger picture and the desire to win the prize

---

[57] Hebrews 12:2, The Amplified Bible.

set before them. Even when tired, refocusing on that bigger picture becomes like pouring fuel on a fire that's about to go out. Passion is thereby revived. To do great exploits find what it is you're passionate about in life.

12

People who do great exploits
are willing to pay the price

In the 1984 Olympic Games, a new star took centre stage in the women's all-around gymnastics competition, becoming the first American to win a gold medal. Her name was Mary Lou Retton. Retton was an incredibly skilled athlete, who seemed to appear on the world stage achieving success overnight.

But is that really true to say she achieved success overnight? Often people who do great exploits seem to come out of 'nowhere' and achieve success. We come to know about their accomplishments after they've achieved it. Their success appears suddenly and seemingly out of the blue but, in reality, it took them a combination of time – decades in some cases – and working in obscurity before they met with the success that's being celebrated.

The great exploits done by people usually mask the years of effort, dedication, and sacrifice that went into making their accomplishments possible. Consumers and onlookers usually enjoy their performance, invention, or breakthrough without a thought given to the price that was paid to give birth to the dream. Or else it's put down to talent. The contribution of talent, versus hard work, to achievement, is discussed in the chapters on potential.

Every dream has a price. It's helpful for would-be doers of exploits to know this up front; for them to understand that payment of the price is an essential difference between people who do great exploits and those who don't. Success can't be gained on a 'pay later' scheme. The price must be paid upfront in order to produce success.

What does *paying the price* mean?

The price tag on a goal or a dream can be enormous. It depends upon the size and scope of your dream. For example, someone may have a goal to lose fifty pounds. The price for that would include sacrificing foods they particularly love for an extended period of time. They would have to eat foods they don't naturally enjoy in smaller portions than they're used to eating. It may mean they sacrifice going to their favourite restaurants with friends or family. Part of the price is getting active in aerobic-type exercise that accelerates burning calories and fat. The person who has gained fifty extra pounds did so by forming habits that were pleasurable to them. To achieve their goal, the price is to give up what they enjoy and do what they do not enjoy as much. I know from personal experience that that is much easier said (or written) than done! However, if the person actually makes the changes needed and continues in a consistent way, he or she will do exploits by losing the excess weight. If the person is unwilling to pay that price, he or she won't accomplish that goal. It's as simple as that.

Another example is someone whose dream is to become an actor or published author. If he or she is working a full-time job, the price entails giving up evenings and weekends to learn and develop the craft. These are social hours, so in addition to the cost in terms of time, it means losing relationships in some cases. The cost can extend to loss of rest and downtime because time spent on recreation may also have to be sacrificed to the dream. But there is much more involved. Many artists and creative people work low-paid jobs and live in relative poverty while they write or study. The dream will cost them rejection as they try out for roles or submit manuscripts without success. Famous writers, including prize winning authors, commonly tell stories of years of being rejected by publishers before finding one who was willing to take the chance on a new author. Because they were willing to pay the price and didn't give up on their dream, they not only got published, but some also went on to win prestigious literary prizes. A famous actor remarked that his, 'Fame had become the bane of [his] existence.' The fame and celebrity that come with success as an actor might appear very glamorous, but they come with high price tags. Being exposed to the continuous scrutiny of critics can be very difficult. Many famous people eventually succumb to drug use to try to cope with the demands and impact of fame on their emotional health. Some have even committed suicide because the hidden costs of fame proved too high.

Many people are rejected or ridiculed by family members for choosing to pursue their dreams instead of following more secure and conventional paths. They watch their siblings climb the career ladder and settle into home and family life while they live in rented rooms eating toast. They live under the cloud of disappointed or anxious parents. The price for the dream has to be paid up front, and they do all in their power to pay it while continuing to work on their dream.

Supreme moments, such as winning an Olympic gold medal or a prestigious literary prize, can make it seem like the winners achieved success overnight. In reality, it's the culmination of years of long, hard, sacrificial toil that finally paid off. If you want to do great exploits, you must believe it's worth paying the price.

Mother Teresa's dream cost her the relative comfort, security, and predictability of the convent life where she began her early years as a nun. In the safety of the convent, everything was provided for her. In the world of her dream, her responsibilities increased exponentially. She had to fundraise, seek benefactors, and recruit teachers and helpers. The noble and slightly romantic idea of caring for the poor became an industry overnight that required high levels of resource management and organisational and political ability. The joy she would have inevitably experienced spending time with dispossessed children – seeing the smiles on their faces and watching them grow into their potential – came at the cost of leadership and working long hours to shoulder responsibilities she would not have had to had she remained in the convent and lived the usual nun's existence. Yet, for her and those of us who have the privilege of looking back on her life, the price she paid was certainly worth it.

Likewise, business people pay a price for turning their ideas into successful enterprises. They arrive at their business early and work until late. I've worked with researchers working in cancer who arrived at the office or lab first thing in the day, never leaving work until after 7pm. After twelve or thirteen hour days they often went home and carried on working, speaking with colleagues at partner research centres in the US or Europe. I've learned from them that there's a price to be paid for breakthroughs in medical research that goes beyond funding. Their enthusiasm and passion for their *one thing* eclipsed most other things and demanded that they make sacrifices in other areas of their life. You have to have stamina and a high tolerance for hard work to do great exploits in any field.

That adds up to paying the price of your dream, whatever it may be.

Paying the price for the right dream

Looking back over their lives, many people find that they have paid a price, but their sacrifices didn't yield what they expected, that it wasn't enough, or worst of all, what they got wasn't what they wanted. Resist every temptation to sow your life based on anything that isn't your purpose. Your purpose may not meet with societal opinions, family expectations, or even what you might prefer. Deciding how to live your life based on these influences inevitably leads to regret. Instead, make choices based on the still-small voice who whispers his wisdom to your heart. Once you follow the route he reveals, you will sow and reap beyond your wildest expectations and not be disappointed. Joy, satisfaction, and meaning will be yours as you walk through life. This is true success.

People who have done great exploits rarely regret the way they have lived their lives. They became clear about their purpose in life and built their lives around that, balancing all their priorities in a disciplined way. That's why defining your dream and writing down your vision is important: it helps you clarify in your heart of hearts what success would look like to you personally. You're then empowered to count the costs for fulfilling your dream and plan how you'll sow your life into those priorities. Whatever purpose is revealed to you, you must be completely sold out for it so that you can pay whatever price it will demand of you.

The idea for this book sprang from a piece of scripture I was meditating on in Isaiah 53, which reads, '[…] when You and he made his life an offering […].' It was referring to Christ and his sacrificial work on the cross. However, more broadly, it taught me that, like Jesus Christ, each of us has a call or purpose for life, but in order to fulfil it, we must be willing to make our lives an offering to it. In other words, the call cannot be fulfilled if we do not sow our lives into it. This is what we call *paying the price* that the dream demands.

People who do great exploits make their lives an offering to their purpose. Sowing your life is the price you have to pay for getting your purpose fulfilled.

I assure you and most solemnly say to you,
unless a grain of wheat falls
into the earth and dies, it remains alone [just one grain, never
more]. But if it dies, it produces much grain and yields a harvest.[58]

Why pay the price

Dreams require much more than desire. They demand more than
envisioning, talking, or even praying about if they're going to come
true. If you want to realise your dream, you actually have to do
something to achieve it. You must shift from being a dreamer to a
doer, that is, getting yourself mobilised carrying out those actions,
which then purchase the dream. The price has to be paid in full for
you to have your success in hand. The costs of *doing* may be great,
depending on what you want to achieve, but if you persist in doing
the right things, the reward will be worthwhile.

Many of us decided we'd rather not pay the price our dream requires
of us. But there is a price for that decision too. First, if you don't
know your purpose or its price, someone else will choose how you
spend your life for you. The world is full of people whose future and
its attached price have been decided for them by parents, teachers,
spouses, friends, employers, and neighbours. Second, when we're
not doing what we love, life becomes less passionate, the soul gets
dulled, and we enjoy life less. Self-respect slowly erodes; resentment
and bitterness spring up. In the long run, we regret that we didn't
take more responsibility for choosing our course in life. Research
has shown that people at the end stages of life name not living more
boldly and fulfilling their dreams as their number one regret.

Since we will suffer costs whether or not we work on our dreams, we
might as well choose the costs we will pay. We owe it to ourselves to
take control and choose the costs for our fulfilled dreams.

---

[58] John 12:24, The Amplified Bible.

In the Bible, this theme recurs among the personalities that stand out for great exploits. They received a call and paid a price for fulfilling it. Their journey was marked by sacrifice and great reward. Abraham was offered wealth, a great name, many descendants, and tremendous impact and influence in exchange for the life he had with relatives in the country of his birth. He made the sacrifice, leaving behind his country and his father's house to go in search of the dream. Later, he was further tested to see whether he was willing to sacrifice the life of his son to the one who made his dream possible. Abraham's dream was fulfilled in his lifetime and continues to be fulfilled to this day.

Sacrifice – paying the price – is key to getting what you want in life. This is one of the most powerful scriptural principles. For each one of us, the journey of purpose is different and the costs unique. The question is: *What price are you willing to pay to fulfil the purpose for your life?*

Here are some important reasons you should pay the price to fulfil your dream.

1. The best things in life aren't really free

I don't know where the saying, 'The best things in life are free,' came from, but I no longer believe it's true. Everything in life is predicated upon you meeting some set terms. Whatever course you choose in life, it is going to cost you something. Being wealthy has its price; poverty has a price. Getting married has a price; being single has a price. Doing great exploits has a price; doing nothing with your life has a price.

Whether you are intentionally pursuing your dream or not, you will pay a price. There's a price for pursuing a dream, but you will also pay a price for not pursuing it. Doing nothing also comes at a price; and what's the point of paying for nothing?

Don't expect your dream to come true simply because you wish it so. People who do great exploits understand that nothing in life is free.

> There are only two real requirements for success:
> first is to decide exactly what is it you want,
> second is to determine the price you are going to
> have to pay and resolve to pay that price.

> H L Hunt

2. People who do exploits cherish hard work .

Making discipline a habit is key to doing great exploits. Discipline is doing what you should do when you should do it. It's when you do what you need to do even if you don't feel like doing it. It's very similar to what's required for keeping a commitment you make. If you're committed to a dream that commitment shows in your choice to do what it takes to make it happen. Discipline and commitment are independent of feelings. Commitment is dealt with in the chapter on passion.

People who do great exploits work on their passion every day – whether or not they feel like it because they realise that that's what it takes to succeed at whatever it is they're called to do. If you want to do exploits you really need to develop this habit because there's no other way to succeed. The habit of working on your dream in a disciplined way is the most important aspect of paying the price. Consistent action is needed if you're going to achieve your goals.

While the rest of the world is sleeping, window shopping, or watching reality TV, people who do great exploits tend to be at work on their dream. Unfortunately, people who do great exploits can be the objects of jealously because of their effectiveness and success – even though they worked hard to get where they are. Sometimes, those who choose to spend their time less productively attribute their progress and breakthroughs to luck.

When it was suggested that luck had a part to play in my friend Hannah's election (see chapter 11) her husband who had seen her dedication and effort during her campaign mused: 'It took an awful amount of effort and sleepless nights at work to benefit from luck.' He describes the year she campaigned as being merely a single wave in a sea of community work, she'd done over the course of about eight years. In all that time Hannah rarely took any holidays. Her love for making the lives of local people better had made her into a community leader and she became the 'go to' person when they needed help and support. She didn't hesitate when she had to put in all-nighters visiting with families who were bereaved or in the local police station with mothers whose sons had got into trouble with the law or visiting people, she knew who were in hospital. When the opportunity to run for election was presented, she threw herself into it, with the belief that a profile in government would only serve her cause to help those who had no voice. Her success was down to hard work

People like Hannah inevitably do great exploits because they're in a continuous state of availability to their purpose in life and have died to all else.

3. Paying the price can change you for the better

When he was young, Joseph didn't get along very well with his brothers. He was in the habit of giving bad reports about them to Jacob, their father. Jacob favoured him above all his sons, which gave Joseph little incentive to develop himself into a better person. Instead, he majored in pointing out his brothers' faults. Who likes people who love pointing out the shortcomings of others? Instead of correcting Joseph, his father was blinded by his favouritism towards him.

Joseph had two dreams that pointed to his parents and brothers bowing down to him one day. He shared them with his family. It proved the final straw for his brothers. In anger, they sold him into slavery. Joseph spent the next thirteen years paying the full price for the dreams he had. By the time he went through the refining fire as an Egyptian slave who was falsely accused and thrown into prison, he was a completely different person. His character had matured; he was devoid of arrogance and the urge for vengeance. All Joseph wanted to do was serve. His entire focus was on what was in the best interest of the kingdom he was called to serve as the highest official.

4. Paying the price breeds an internal joy, satisfaction, and self-knowledge

Paying the price isn't always about sweat and toil. People who do exploits find much joy and inspiration in the process of giving birth to their dream. Although the dream may demand long hours and other sacrifices, the process of working on your book, for example, engenders a unique joy and satisfaction – part of the reward for fulfilling your purpose. When we achieve the smaller goals we set in line with our big-picture dream, we feel happy. And happy people are much nicer people who are easier to get along with!

It's important to find happiness along the journey of purpose. Happiness shouldn't be put on hold until you reach a specific position in life. We are called to have and enjoy life even as we pay the price of working diligently on the dream he gave us. It's been my experience that doing the little things towards the fulfilment of my purpose creates joy. Walking with God through your paths of purpose also releases joy and pleasure as Psalm 16:11 tells us:

> You will show me the path of life; In Your
> presence is fullness of joy;
> In Your right hand there are pleasures forevermore.[59]

---

[59]   Psalm 16:11, The Amplified Bible

In addition to having joy, you also learn quite a lot about yourself as you live out your life's purpose. People who do great exploits develop a sound knowledge of themselves. They tend to possess a clear appreciation of their personal values, their strengths, and their weaknesses. They also have a sense of their potential capabilities and any limitations they have. They then manage these and other aspects of themselves – such as personality and temperament – to be effective when working with others. In this context, to know is to love. The better you know and understand yourself, the more you learn to love and respect yourself. In short, you can more fully appreciate the handiwork in your life and the fact that you were created for purpose. It then follows that your respect for others grows. When you treat others with respect and sensitivity, they respond to that positively. Developing as thorough a knowledge of oneself as possible produces authenticity, which others sense. The extent to which they perceive that authenticity is the extent to which they will consider you credible and allow themselves to be influenced by you.

Develop a sound knowledge of who you are, where you're coming from and where you want to go in life. This knowledge will enable you to understand the level of commitment you'll need to make personally. It's important to count the cost as Jesus taught, 'For which one of you, when he wants to build a watchtower [for his guards], does not first sit down and calculate the cost, to see if he has enough to finish it?'[60] So develop your knowledge and accept what it will require of you to make success happen for you. For all of us it's going to take paying a price, the size of it depends on knowing all these factors. Knowing empowers us to take responsibility and walk in self-control (discipline) that's required.

4. Paying the price makes you skilled and leads to promotion

> Well done, good and faithful servant. You have
> been faithful and trustworthy over a little,

---

[60] Luke 14:28, The Amplified Bible

I will put you in charge of many things;
share in the joy of your master.[61]

Another great biblical character, David, went through the stages of development needed to be king and shepherd of people. His learning trajectory is pretty clear in the Bible narrative. He started out shepherding sheep. David took his responsibilities seriously, in safeguarding his father's flocks. In confronting a lion who carried off a lamb, he learned a new skill that would see him become a formidable military strategist later in life. He practised his new skill and killed a bear when it tried to steal sheep. (Chances are, David had cause to exercise these specialised skills more than twice and saw off many predators in his time as a shepherd.) By the time he faced Goliath, he was a skilled, wise warrior. David knew Goliath had more experience at hand-to-hand combat and the use of a sword than he did, so he chose a weapon that meant he wouldn't have to come within a sword's length of his opponent. This strategy allowed him to take Goliath down from afar.

Similarly, after he'd gained experience as a shepherd, Saul promoted David to the rank of army captain. He led over one hundred men. His training transferred from leading sheep to leading humans, but encountering the politics of human interactions and interpersonal relationships represented a new challenge. He had to win their trust, put himself at the forefront of danger, and make difficult decisions where men's lives hung in the balance. Later, when he went into exile, three hundred men sought his leadership. He went from leading his band of men to being king of Judah to being the king of a united Israel. The stages in his development are clear. As he paid the price of commitment and diligence, he moved up to new levels that would test him and develop his abilities further. Thus, David did great and mighty exploits time and time again.

---

[61]   Matthew 25:21, The Amplified Bible.

As discussed in the chapters on purpose and potential, I've no doubt that, whatever it is each of us is called to do, we are wired for it. David was a warrior and king in his DNA. When we look at people like uncle Carl, we can see that the ability to play jazz was in his DNA. But at the same time, expressing that innate talent required effort. For example, his ability to improvise wasn't that great when he started playing jazz. He could mimic other players very well, but to come up with his own improvisations took years of practice. He paid the price of learning to improvise by spending hours practising every day. Hard work made him great at it, not merely natural talent, or luck. When you're naturally gifted it takes a certain amount of humility to bring that talent under submission to training.

Star athletes and players regularly suffer dislocated joints or broken bones - yet another hidden cost to fulfilling the dream. Because of their injuries, some of these great basketball players choose to develop different shooting techniques rather than stop playing. They get into the habit of practicing jump shots until they perfect them. When they sustain an injury, instead of retiring, they develop a different jump shot technique and practice until they perfect it.

People who do great exploits are usually skilled at what they do. They gain their skill in exchange for the price of practising or studying, for example, to become not just competent, but extraordinary.

4. Paying the price gives you credibility money can't buy

> And being found in fashion as a man, he humbled himself, becoming obedient even unto death, yea, the death of the cross. Wherefore also God highly exalted him, and gave unto him the name which is above every name; that in the name of Jesus every knee should bow, of things in heaven and things on earth and things under the earth.[62]

---

[62] Philippians 2:8–11, American Standard Version.

There is a level of authority that can't be established except by paying a price. Credibility can't be earned without actually carrying out the tasks associated with success in your particular area. Imagine someone writing dozens of books on leadership, speaking to audiences around the world on leadership, but having no experience of leading anyone himself. People would simply not count him a credible spokesperson on the subject. Talk is cheap. They would have had to pay the price to develop the knowledge and experience of leadership if they were to have any credibility in the field.

In the scripture above, it says that even Jesus had a price to pay to gain the authority he has both in Heaven and on earth, where his name is higher than every name and where every knee must bow to him. The price was to give up the glory he had before the worlds were even made, to become a man and then go as low as any human being could go by dying the death of the cross. His price was his obedience to that call.

Who would believe Jesus when he said, 'No one has greater love [nor stronger commitment] than to lay down his own life for his friends.[63]' yet when it came to the cross he refused to back up his words with the related action?

People are more likely to believe and support the vision of those they know have sacrificed for what they believe. The twenty-seven years spent in prison is perhaps the most important factor that underpinned Nelson Mandela's credibility and authority as a proponent of freedom in South Africa. He paid a price that few would pay. That, coupled with his intellect, magnanimity, and commitment to reconciliation, secured him a place among the great moral leaders the world has known.

A novice is not as credible as a master. An old Bishop I used to know before he went to be with the Lord, used to say, 'Some people want to

---

[63]   John 15:13, The Amplified Bible

tell you how to grow your church, when they've never even grown a daisy!' You don't have to spend a lot of time with someone to sense his or her 'truth.' The depth and breadth of knowledge, experience, and expertise one has in their area of passion filters through their every word. To be credible we need to be able to back up what we say with authentic ability and successful action. Whatever field you're in, you'll find that there's a correlation between credibility and success.

How to pay the price

Christ fulfilled his assignment because he was willing to pay the price for the prize that was set before him. He voluntarily gave himself to doing the work required to complete his assignment on a daily basis. He is the perfect example of how we can fulfil the call by doing whatever is required of us.

The combination of costs in the price of a call is different for each individual. For some people, it may take sacrificing old mindsets for new and more productive ones. The Bible calls this 'renewing the mind.' Others will need to sacrifice daily routines and habits to gain new and more constructive routines and habits that produce specific results in line with a certain vision and purpose (see chapter 2). Yet, for others, it also means sacrificing the distractions that crop up, for keeping their focus fixed on the prize set before them in their vision. Because the costs are so varied, the ways to pay them can't all be accounted for here. To get you started, I've included some foundational costs and how some people have gone about paying them.

1. Be willing to do whatever it takes

People who do great exploits are willing to do whatever it takes to accomplish their goals or fulfil their dreams. They are proactive people who take full responsibility for their future. They accept that the onus rests on them, and so they put in the effort needed to get where they want to go. This isn't as easy as it sounds. Few people are willing to do whatever it takes; most prefer an easier way of life.

But those who have done well and are living their dreams owe such circumstances to their willingness to do what the average person wouldn't do. Long before he became senior partner at a major law firm, my childhood friend Greg (see chapter 5) put himself through University by working nights as a security guard. The ethic of doing whatever it takes to accomplish his goals continues to be a central theme in his life despite being an accomplished lawyer. He works thirteen-hour days at the office and often works more after going home. Greg thrives on his schedule and wishes there were more hours in the day so he could do even more!

2. Living a disciplined life

Venus and Serena Williams seemed to storm the tennis world and become overnight sports stars. Yet the capability they've demonstrated repeatedly was not something that came about overnight. They've been paying the price for their great exploits on the courts since they were young children. Early in life, their routine involved hitting the tennis courts before and after school. While most kids their age were still fast asleep, they were being trained in the disciplined life of champions.

3. Step out of your comfort zone

Stepping out of your comfort zone is the price you pay for doing great exploits. Success is impossible without a willingness to take risks. We must manage our fears in a way that keeps them from holding us back from doing what we need to do to accomplish our goals. In chapter 10, I wrote about the concept of befriending fear. When we befriend fear, we turn it into an ally that gives us more value in life than the safe places we prefer. Making fear an ally empowers us to breach the boundaries of our comfort zone and break into new territory. As we embrace the inevitable changes that come with those new territories, we grow – and our potential for impact expands without limits. As we continue in that vein, we learn to be comfortable with the discomfort of living outside the comfort zone. People who do great exploits do not permit fear to keep them contained within their comfort zones. They pay the price of breaking free. Techniques for breaking free of fear can be found in chapter 10.

4. Accept and embrace unconventionality and necessary change

People who do great exploits are willing to do away with convention, if needed, to follow their dreams. Mary Lou Retton, mentioned at the start of this chapter, like so many others, missed out on what might be called a *normal childhood*. She attended high school but didn't graduate back then. In what would have been her second year in high school, when she would have discovered boys and dating and settled into the normal routines of most teenagers, Retton won gold, silver, and bronze medals at the 1984 Olympics in Los Angeles.

People who do great exploits come from all sorts of backgrounds. What singles them out is a willingness to go against the conventions of culture, peer groups, societal expectations, or family to carve out a route that takes them to the dream they have in their hearts. They often end up going against the flow and decide for themselves what they will do, where they want to be, and how they will get there. And they take responsibility for their choices and the work it takes to get there.

Some years ago, I heard a news story about a woman from the developing world who had climbed to the top of her industry. Right out of university a multinational company hired her and she went on to serve in managerial roles soon thereafter. Within 15 years she was voted in as CEO.

Being female in the male-dominated industry came with many challenges, but she refused to shy away from them. She had learned to navigate challenges from an early age. She'd been raised in a *favela* (a shanty town outside of Rio de Janeiro), growing up surrounded by extreme poverty and crime. She lived with domestic violence in childhood and faced many difficulties in life. Schooling was a challenge for most children living in the *favela* due to the costs of books. Many children did not attend, but she was resolved to do so. As a young girl, she raised money to pay for school by collecting recyclable trash that was dumped in the streets. For her hard work and willpower was the way out for her and her mother. This work ethic, developed in childhood, became her trademark in her professional and public life.

While her peers attended high school, a young gymnast with a dream broke with convention and dropped out. While her peers dropped out of school due to the attendance costs, a girl raised in a *favela* scavenged unsanitary streets for cans to sell so she could get an education. Both did great exploits. What conventions do you need to break in order to fulfil your dream?

5. Bring the most important people in your life along with you

Because of their devotion to their cause, people who do great exploits may find that the relationships most important to them suffer. As they throw their energy, time, and (sometimes) finances into their passion, there is little or nothing left for key personal relationships. My friend's wife was once almost convinced he was having an affair because of the long hours he spent away from home. I told her he probably *was* having an affair ... but with his business, not with another woman! The only thing keeping him away from home was their business. It was a venture they both agreed he would start. Unfortunately for her, she hadn't fully processed what that would mean for them in the early stages of establishing the business. I think my friend also underestimated the price he would have to pay to build his brand and his client list in a challenging market. That price included long hours away from home, not spending time with his wife, and running at a loss for three years, which meant they had to rely on his wife's income to pay their living costs.

People who do great exploits face difficult choices when it comes to their personal relationships. But I like to think that it's possible to have it all (that's one reason for making sure you marry someone who is equally yoked with you – not just spiritually, but having the same vision, similar perspectives on life and what you want out of life). I've known people whose marriage broke down because one person was very ambitious while the other refused to grow. Another couple separated because they each wanted to live in different countries. Equally yoked isn't just about two people being Christians, its also about compatibility, outlook, values, hopes, dreams, direction of travel, etc.

At the same time, however, there are some notable people who made the choice to not have it all and concentrated entirely on the dream. Jesus Christ, for example, remained single. Perhaps the time and focus required to be married, have children, and provide for a family would have hindered him from fulfilling the express purpose for which he was born. Mother Teresa is another person who chose the single life, paying the price of never having biological children in exchange for gaining countless 'children' around the world. The long years of working for a worthy cause can sometimes take a toll on people's marriage despite their shared core values and passion for the cause.

Like the cause itself, key relationships – if they are to be sustained – require commitment, attention and passion. Without that, regardless of how noble or moral the cause, relationships can suffer. If you want to do great exploits, it's worth thinking carefully about how you balance the needs of your passion and the needs of your loved ones – particularly your spouse and children. You're called to honour them too.

Sharing your dream with the significant others in your life might enable them to better understand your choices. They may be more accommodating of time spent away from them, particularly if the dream is in keeping with their own values and desires. It may also inspire them to discover their own purpose and to pursue it with passion when they see you doing that with your life. They may even be willing to partner with you in fulfilling your own dream.

13

People who do great exploits keep going

People who do great exploits develop a long-term view of life. They recognise that even the best laid plans do not always succeed or roll out the way they were intended. Some plans succeed, while others crash and fail. Not uncommonly, people have to go back to the drawing board and start over. If we allow setbacks and failures to deter us, we will not do great exploits and fulfil our purpose. Those with a myopic view of life bow out of the race before it is finished. On the other hand people with a long-term view find ways to keep going. For them every day provides a fresh opportunity to move forward and make progress. They operate from a premise of optimism, even when things are challenging or not going the way they had planned. An important key to their effectiveness lies in never giving up. Whatever life throws at them, they find a way forward and keep going.

It's much easier to give up when faced with challenges, setbacks, disappointments, and stubborn obstacles. The temptation to abandon your assignment can be very strong after you've done all that you can do yet difficulties persist. But giving up is what the average person does. Our lives are the sum of our choices; one important area of choice lies in whether we give up when the going gets tough or persevere until we get our breakthrough. The bible is filled with the testimonies of people who chose the latter. Such heroes of faith like Noah, Abraham, Ruth, David, Paul and many others.

What it means to keep going

In the world countless biographies, feature articles and films have been produced about people who succeeded in fulfilling their life's purpose or in achieving a dream. It's unsurprising because most of us have an appetite for stories about ordinary people who succeed at beating the odds and breaking through. It's particularly inspiring when they fight against seemingly insurmountable obstacles to eventually becoming remarkable people.

The operative word for people who keep going is *eventually.* Dictionary.com[64] defines the word *eventual* as follows: 'a. happening at some indefinite future time or after a series of occurrences; ultimate. b. depending upon uncertain events; contingent.'

Their journey from the humble beginning of having an idea or recognising a gift they had, to fulfilling purpose can be a long one that took place *eventually.* What's characteristic about them is the sheer determination and tenacity they show in their pursuit of a worthy purpose in life. They are passionate about the vision they constructed in their mind for what was possible, and then launched out to do whatever it took to pay the price to manifest their particular vision. After experiencing many setbacks, they eventually achieved their vision and much more ... because they never gave up.

---

[64] Dictionary.com "eventual," in Dictionary.com Unabridged. Source location: Random House, Inc. http://www.dictionary.com/browse/eventual. Available: http://www.dictionary.com/. Accessed: July 24, 2016.

For example in chapter 4 I mentioned the story of Miro, a businessman originally from Eastern Europe who became homeless as a child. Miro never knew his father and before he became homeless, his mother turned to prostitution to try to support them. Unable to cope, she finally handed him over to the care system promising that when she got back on her feet, she would take him back.

After a year in an orphanage Miro was finally placed in his first of many foster homes. He was moved around a lot, growing up in illiterate and impoverished environments. His surroundings were marked by violence, alcoholism, and abuse. As a child he longed to return to his mother. In the early years when he was taken into care, she visited him at foster homes, but over time he saw her less and less and then she stopped visiting altogether. Life was hard and he felt abandoned, yet reflecting on his journey he attributes his success in life to something his mother once told him. She said, 'Just because everyone treats us like we are nothing, it doesn't mean that we are nothing. When you were born, I knew God had given me a special gift. You are special, no matter what anyone else thinks.' Miro was just 10 at the time, but those simple words always remained with him. They turned out to be his mother's legacy to him. They were literally all that she had to give to him, but they proved more than enough because he recalled they led him to believe that his future was worth fighting for.

He refused to accept the fate his background offered and decided he would take responsibility for his life. But things changed for the worse for him one night at age thirteen when he intervened in a fight between his foster father and mother. He was convinced his foster father was going to hit his wife. He got between them and pushed him to the ground. His foster father sprang up and knocked him across the room. That night Miro ran away and spent the remainder of his childhood on the streets of the city avoiding the authorities.

After years of surviving through begging or doing odd jobs, Miro hitch-hiked to a French port and then stowed away on a ferry crossing the channel into the UK when he was 17. He made his way to London. There he found cash in hand work on building sites, cleaning, or making deliveries. In the winter months often times, he found shelter sleeping at the airport in the waiting areas or under cars in the long stay parking lots.

Finding themselves homeless in a foreign city, many people would have given up. It would have been easier for him to accept that this was his lot in life, but instead, he chose to hold on to his mother's words that he was special. He wrote that it gave him a strong desire to find what was special about him.

He discovered what that was when he had saved enough of his meagre earnings to buy a box of scarves at a reduced wholesale price and then sold the majority of them at a Sunday market. That day he discovered that he was a natural salesman. He'd made a profit that was five times what he invested.

Several times during his second winter in London, he repeated the cycle of buying cheap and selling high. But then the season came to an end and he had to find new merchandise to sell. He found a wholesaler selling novelty cups and mugs. Transporting these were more of a challenge because he didn't have a car. He gave a friend some money to help him transport the stock, but in driving across the city, a lorry ploughed into the back of them. The collision destroyed virtually all the mugs and so Miro lost a lot of money. He went back to just working and saving for a while, concentrating on 'stockpiling' the money he made from his earnings. Then one night, while sleeping rough, Miro was beaten up and robbed of several hundred pounds. He realised he had to get serious about getting off the streets.

Miro made a deal to sleep in the back of a shop in exchange for working some hours for free during the day. Since he couldn't open a bank account, having no fixed address, he was forced to get creative about keeping his money safe. He didn't want to be carrying more than a few pounds around in case he got mugged again. So he pulled up a floorboard under a storage cupboard in the shop where he slept every night and hid his money under it when everyone went home.

When he'd built up some capital again, Miro seized an opportunity to buy wholesale jewellery and ladies' belts for 10 pence a piece. There were over two thousand pieces in the crate, which he sold anywhere between £1 and £10 each. It was more money than he'd ever handled in his young life. One evening, before he settled down to sleep in the back room of his employer's shop, he counted out £10,000 in cash, which he'd saved up over about 3 months. He was so happy, that he spread the money across the floor and literally rolled around in it!

Reaching such a milestone in his savings only served to increase his drive to buy and sell as much as time would permit. On the weekends he worked the markets and in the week he took jobs unloading trucks and packing shelves at a few wholesalers in east London. Being around the wholesalers, and capitalising on his sales in the markets, he began to imagine a future for himself in business. In those years, he remembers working sixteen-hour days, seven days a week. He described it as being both an education and yet hellish at the same time. But despite the demands, Miro kept pressing on towards the dream he now had to make it big in business.

Despite the hardships and setbacks he faced on the long road to where he is today, he remained tenacious, refusing to give up on his dream for a much better future. Had he decided to settle and focus on having the jobs his lack of education afforded him, he would never be able to break free from poverty. He'd end up being nothing; and face a life of being treated the way he and his mother had been treated in those early years of his life. He described this period of his life as seeing, 'every box I lifted, every item I stacked and every pound I saved, as taking me closer to owning my own business, to being the one with the vision, to being someone my mother would have been proud of.'

It took him about seven years to realise his dream. During that time, he learned the business of buying and selling wholesale to retailers. He got information on contacts in China, Taiwan and India and studied the import market. Eventually, he developed his own supply chain, importing from the eastern countries and set up shop in east London. When the time was right he broke into London's property market and became a landlord back in the mid-eighties and he's never looked back. Eventually, over the course of twenty-five years, Miro built a stock of thirty-three commercial and residential properties in and outside of London in his portfolio.

His only sadness is that his mother didn't live long enough to see him break through. About five years after migrating to London, he returned to Poland to try to track her down only to discover that she had died about two years after he ran away from his last foster family.

Today, Miro is happily married with three children and involved in a number of charitable initiatives in the areas where he experienced challenges during his personal journey. For instance, he's involved in creating opportunities for homeless young people to find work and affordable accommodation. The article in which he was featured was part of a media launch for a charity he's set up aimed at children living in inner city areas. The charity aims to provide mentorship and training opportunities in business to young people.

Miro has done great exploits in his time and continues to do so through his businesses and community work. Yet he started as an 'ordinary' boy born into harsh circumstances. Such beginnings make certain (negative) outcomes more likely in some cases. They make it easier to give up when faced by situations and occurrences that seem unbeatable. But still, there are many who succeed at breaking with the convention of remaining where they started, or where life drives them; and this businessman is one such person. In fact, he is living a life of impact beyond his wildest dreams.

So what was the difference between him and countless others? What made him the kind of person who would do great exploits? In the feature article about his life, the recurring themes include having a vision and a plan, optimism, being passionate and tenacious.

His life of exploits tells us that what it takes to achieve your dream isn't a strong beginning or tremendous luck; rather, it illustrates that you need to start with defining a clear and compelling vision that you're passionate about. You must take personal responsibility for achieving it, resolve to pay the price, whatever it might be, and then pursue it with such dogged tenacity that there is simply no other end you can arrive at but the dream you set out to fulfil. The examples of people I gave throughout this book show that we need to be willing to embrace the short-term discomforts involved in wandering off the beaten track and stepping out of our comfort zones. To do great exploits demands that we be courageous and even shamelessly fanatical about our dreams.

Why be tenacious?

Let me tell you the secret that has led me to my goal.
My strength lies solely in my tenacity.

Louis Pasteur

Eventual means that at some point in the future, after a series of occurrences, it is possible (and even likely!) that you will achieve your dream ... if you don't give up. It is important to keep working on your vision – even when it tarries – because success might be right around the corner. One certainty is that you won't realise your dream if you give up.

In chapter 1, I wrote that your purpose is basically a desire you have to solve a particular problem. Let's take Miro's story as an example of a purpose fulfilled. The original problem that he set out to solve was that he was homeless and living in poverty. Miro also wanted to do something to turn his situation around so that his mother could be proud of him and so he could give her a better life. Finding solutions to these problems became his passionate purpose, and his fascination with selling was the vehicle that he used to fulfil his passion. Miro paid a price for his commitment to solving each of those problems and eventually fulfilled some key purposes for his life (plus a number of others). Regretfully, his mother didn't live long enough for him to fulfil his dream of providing for her. Instead, he turned his energy to giving hope to young people for the future and helping them to make a better life for themselves.

Finding problems that need solving is very easy. What we do once we've found one is the critical thing, and that's really what this book is all about. What do we do about the problems that attract our interest? Which problems should we invest ourselves in? How do we ensure we position ourselves emotionally and psychologically to work on them until they're solved (or at least progressed as far as we can progress them before handing it over to the next generation of problem solvers)? Every chapter in this book is designed to give some insight into these challenging questions.

Once we have identified the problem we've been created to solve, we're faced with a seemingly endless set of circumstances – both helpful and adverse – in the path between fulfilment and us. To thrive and make progress, we have to be willing to fail, be disappointed, frustrated, and frightened … but still willing to get back on track and keep going. A willingness to keep going and not give up is what sets apart people who do great exploits from the majority of the population who don't. Also, note that tenacity is as important to doing exploits as every other factor mentioned in this book thus far. Here are some key things to bear in mind about the value of tenacity:

1. You won't achieve your dream if you're not tenacious

If you're working towards some predetermined goal but give up somewhere along the line, you won't get to the end point that you had in mind when you started. In order to get to that end point and achieve the outcome you've dreamed; you must engage in persistent action.

Abraham, the biblical hero, is referred to as the father of faith. This was a man who left everything behind to follow a dream. Abraham made one request of God. It was that he would have a son, an heir who he could leave everything he had to. His request was heard and the heir was promised. Decades passed. Both Abraham and his wife Sarah grew very old. Sarah had long since passed her menopause and still the couple did not conceive. But they were tenacious in faith, believing that their dream of having a son together would come true. Eventually, Sarah miraculously conceived a son, who they named Isaac.

Romans 4: 18 says that even when all the human reasons for hope were gone, Abraham continued to hope that he would become a father as God had promised him. His tenacity eventually paid off.

2. Failure is something that happens on the way to success

My uncle has been a great role model to me over the years. I saw him build his empire from scratch. I watched him and learned from him. He often spoke to me, challenging me to do more than I was doing. He'd say, 'Never mind if you fail. Just don't get stuck, get up and try again.' Every person who has succeeded in doing exploits failed, faced numerous obstacles, experienced setbacks, and encountered disappointment. But the reason they ultimately did exploits is because they kept on trying. Brothers Orville and Wilbur Wright, who eventually created the plane, only did so after many failed attempts to create flying machines. They designed prototype after prototype, each of which crashed, and some of which didn't even get off the ground. But the brothers were so determined to solve the problem that they kept on trying new models until they created one that could get in the air and stay there. Had they not been tenacious in pursuing their assignment, they wouldn't have accomplished their dream.

To do great exploits, you have to be willing to fail. And the skills you acquire during those difficult times are perhaps the most priceless pieces of education that you could ever come into contact with. If you persevere through it, you'll not only achieve your goals, but also you'll be much wiser for it.

If I didn't know his story I'd be tempted to think that everything my uncle touched turned to gold, but he has had some business failures in his time too. The fast food restaurant he opened only survived a few years before it folded. He also had a desert shop that went under. Hundreds of thousands of dollars went down the drain on those and other ventures, but such failures haven't stopped him from trying different things or developing new ideas. People who do great exploits do not equate failure with defeat; instead, they put it down to experience gained, learn from it, and move on to the next idea.

Losing is a part of winning, and failure is a part of succeeding. Failing doesn't make us failures. People who do great exploits see their failures as something that happened rather than who they are. They are able to step back and view what happened with an objective eye, identify what went wrong, and then take steps to remedy the problem for the next time. Failure, therefore, isn't terminal; instead, it's part of a process that educates and seasons a person. Many of the people who give up do so because they take their failures personally and make them part of their identity. If you believe you're a failure, you'll drop out of the race. But if you think, *I failed because of the way I ran yesterday,* you become empowered to find out how to run effectively the next time.

When you fail, don't be deceived into thinking it means you should give up. I think of Moses who failed miserably the first time he tried to fulfil the call that was on his life. He was created to lead the enslaved Israelites to freedom from Egypt. However, in his very first action towards that purpose, he ended up murdering a slave driver. Moses ran away from his purpose following that incident. Because he gave up, he set himself back forty years. But he was given another chance. Moses was still so bruised by his early failure that he argued with God, asking him to choose someone better than him to do the job. Of course, no one can fulfil your purpose better than you can, and when all his excuses were refuted, Moses agreed to return to Egypt and fulfil the call on his life. This time, he did great exploits and was a resounding success.

> Failure is only the opportunity to start
> over, with a better plan this time.

3. You'll likely regret not being tenacious

My friend's mother has had a good life. She retired at sixty from a career as an Executive PA for the CEO of a bank. But when she was young, she was accepted at the University of Toronto to do a degree. She left home, travelling to Canada and started the first semester. But she had just gotten married and it was the first time she was such a long way from home. Missing her husband and family, she abandoned her plans, returned to the Caribbean, got a job and started a family. She had intended to return to university at some point in time to do her degree, but never got round to applying.

Meanwhile, she really pushed her two daughters to excel at school. When they were old enough she sent them abroad to study. When they got their Bachelor's degrees, she insisted that they each pushed ahead and got Master's degrees. One of them went on to complete a PhD and the other (my friend) is completing hers as I write these words. Their mother was always very proud when either of them achieved a new qualification. Each time one of them graduated, she threw a thanksgiving party. She is proud of their accomplishments, but also admits that she regrets giving up on her dream to get a degree.

Many people regret giving up on a goal or dream in life. As I wrote earlier, at the end of their lives people don't so much regret what they did, as what they didn't do. It's the dreams that were abandoned for whatever reason that become the source of their regret.

4. Impatience can cut off the future

> Never give up on something before its time.
> Waiting can be painful, but regret is agony.

In waiting for a dream to manifest, the temptation to be impatient can be quite acute, particularly when a long time has passed and progress is slow. However, giving into that impatience can lead you to take actions or express attitudes that can destroy your chances of fulfilling your purpose. Patience is one of the fruits of the Holy Spirit – it's one of the key attitudes needed to protect and preserve your purpose and its rewards in the future. Acting out of impatience can result in costly mistakes and may even disqualify you from fulfilling your call. Indeed, impatient people despise having to wait for anything. They have a desire to grow their own apples, but they end up cutting down the young apple tree in their yard because it's taking too long to mature and bear fruit. Impatience shuts down people's desire to persevere, robbing them of the fulfilment of their dream. Thieves come to kill, steal, and destroy … and impatience is such a thief.

Another area where impatience appears to steal dreams is when hardships and challenges seem overwhelming. Impatient people tend to have a high intolerance for obstacles that get in their way. Also, they are often unwilling to be patient with themselves when they make a mistake. They end up giving up instead of being patient enough to go through the process of learning. Impatient people do not enjoy the hard work that's required to do great exploits. Truly, these types of people get discouraged easily and find it easier to settle for what they have already or give into distractions and lose their focus.

Impatient people often find it difficult to work with other people. I mentioned Moses earlier and how he killed a man who was abusing an Israelite slave. That act of impatience cost him forty years. The consequence was that the very people he had such compassion for ended up being oppressed for an extra forty years. Unfortunately, Moses continued having trouble controlling his impatience, which manifested in fits of anger at critical moments. Forty years after he led the same crowd out of Egypt – just before they reached the Promised Land – the people complained about a lack of water. And again, Moses gave into his impatience with them. When he was instructed him to speak to the rock, Moses struck it instead. As a result, God decreed that he would not be allowed to complete his assignment. His life ended in the wilderness; Moses never entered the Promised Land.

On the road of purpose, we will have to work with others, influence others, and lead others. Plus, we must care for them and negotiate with them in order to advance the assignment we are called to do. We have to learn how to work effectively with people *where they are*. Ultimately, in the working out of our assignment, we remain accountable every step of the way. And it's always possible to do something, which may lead to being disqualified from the race.

5. Because others are depending upon you

Wanting to find his mother and give her a better life became Miro's motivation to keep going even when it was extremely difficult. He believed that he could offer her the happiness that she had never had. He wanted to provide her with all the comforts of life, she would have gone without and that she would not have to work again. He dreamed of bringing her to London, to a different environment than the squalid neighbourhood in which they lived, while he was growing up. He wanted to be able to take care of her and make her proud, to show her that she was right, when she told him that he was special. This clear and compelling vision fuelled his tenacity and kept him from giving up – even when it meant sleeping under cars or in mouldy shop storage rooms.

Nevertheless, everyone who does exploits feels like giving up from time to time. But what often keeps them moving in the direction of their aspiration is the sense of responsibility they carry regarding those who depend upon them to fulfil their purpose. They keep their eye on the bigger picture and know it's not about them. When you're tempted to give up on your assignment, it helps to take a step back and reflect on what it will mean for those you are called to serve.

Strategies for tenacity

It's not that I'm so 'lucky' it's just that I don't give up easily. How can we remain tenacious on our road of purpose? How can we ensure we remain motivated, inspired, and always moving in the direction of our goals? When we face failure, setbacks, hindrances, and temptations to throw in the towel, what can we do to keep on going? How do we remain on course for doing great exploits and fulfilling our purpose? Here are some strategies:

1. Think about what will be lost if you give up

When you feel like giving up, remember why you started.
Unknown

It's unimaginable what would have become of the world if Christ had not been tenacious and endured his cross. The reality is that truly worthy exploits are demanding. Exploits come with great rewards, but they also come with peculiar crosses for us to bear. Accepting that reality is the first step towards being able to stay the course. Focusing on the reward can be a source of renewed energy that helps us endure. Likewise, counting the cost of what will be lost if we give up also brings perspective and is a powerful motivator. What will be lost? Imagine what would happen if you give up.

2. Find ways to encourage yourself

More often than not, the journey of purpose is a lonely one. People who do great exploits don't necessarily have others who cheer them on. In some cases, depending upon the assignment, there are more critics than there are allies. Often, people who do exploits pay the price through long periods of working in isolation. Commonly, they are misunderstood individuals who may be rejected for their single-mindedness and determination to achieve their one great thing!

Because they tend to see the world differently, people who do great exploits inevitably meet with conflict, resistance or opposition. There was a woman who was among the first women to study mathematics at university back in the 1950s. Science and math were male dominated fields of study in those days. But she had always loved math and excelled at it in junior and high school. At university she met with forms of resistance, both subtle and overt. By enrolling she and others like her became forerunners. They were doing something that was not commonplace in culture. It wasn't that she went to university intending to challenge the status quo, which was that only boys should study mathematics. Rather, she attended because of the passion she had for the subject since her childhood. The fact that she was female presented a challenge to the status quo; and the resistance came in the form of a lack of encouragement from her lecturers, who were all male. Despite this she went on to do very well – but life felt quite lonely and many times she felt like giving up because of her experiences. She had to learn to encourage herself.

People who do great exploits often find themselves going against the grain, like salmon swimming against the current. Regardless of how difficult it gets, the key to doing exploits is to keep heading upstream. Salmon were created to swim upstream in order to find ideal environments to lay their eggs; people who do great exploits were created to cut out uncommon paths.

If you want to do great exploits, know that you won't always have others cheering you on. If no one is encouraging you, learn to encourage yourself. People may discredit or even ridicule your ideas and your dreams, but you must ignore the naysayers. Years ago, when I shared that I wanted to be a writer with some people I really looked up to, one of them remarked that I had 'ideas above my station.' I'd be lying if I said that didn't hurt! But more than the pang, it made me see how arrogant and presumptuous that person was. After all, having achieved all that he had in life, why did he think others were wrong to pursue their own dreams? I decided that I would show them. Instead of discouraging me, it made me resolve to throw my energy into developing my talent as a writer. I redirected the energy from the pain of his comment into pure motivation. In times when writing got difficult and I doubted I had what it took to be a published author, I visualised sending that person an autographed copy of my book. That was usually enough to get me energised again!

When no one believes in you or your dream, be your own cheerleader. When you find you have no friends encouraging you, be your own friend. Talk to yourself and say the things you'd tell a friend if you wanted to encourage that person. Let the most important and credible voices you choose to believe be your own and those that are for you.

Remember that others who have done great exploits often revisited their own stories and drew encouragement from recalling their victories. They are human just like you. If they could find a way through, so can you. And if you can believe that, you too will do great exploits.

Know that the Lord is with you. It's striking that a phrase – 'and the Lord was with Joseph' – appears at critical points while he was in Egypt. The first is when he becomes a slave in Potiphar's house, and the second is when he was falsely imprisoned. Those seasons would have discouraged him greatly but, during both times, the Lord revealed that he was present as a way of encouraging Joseph and strengthening him in his journey. The Lord did this to reassure Joseph that he was in control of his situation, and that, despite how things looked, Joseph was on the right course for the fulfilment of his dreams.

It may not have looked like it, but Joseph was given a lot of favour, which then enabled him embraced the opportunities to develop his gifts and skills. When you're moving towards the dream, you'll find such opportunities, mentors, information, and resources. Remember those moments when you feel discouraged, and remember that the Lord made them possible. In short, you should feel encouraged to keep going.

3. Get back up after being knocked down

For a righteous man falls seven times, and rises again, but
the wicked stumble in time of disaster and collapse.[65]

God-loyal people don't stay down long;
Soon they're up on their feet.[66]

A key trait that stands out in people like David and Joseph is their resilience. Both men went through extremes: by being themselves, they angered others to the point of endangering their own lives. They both experienced truly difficult setbacks in life several times over –from the moment they were called to the moment their dreams manifested – everything in their lives turned upside down. But for

---

[65] Proverbs 24:16, The Amplified Bible, Classic Edition
[66] Proverbs 24:16, The Message Bible

every adverse turn of events, they were able to bounce back; when knocked down, they each got back up again.

People who do great exploits are resilient; they always get back up when knocked down. Miro, drew on his mother's powerful words to keep him going throughout his struggles in life. And he was knocked down many times by the circumstances of his life. And yet, defiantly, he kept getting back up.

Make a decision such that, whatever happens, you will never give up on your life's purpose. If you want to do great exploits, you must decide up front that, when you are assailed, you won't give up.

4. Work with passion and commitment while you wait for the fruit

> If I find 10,000 ways something won't work, I
> haven't failed. I am not discouraged,
> because every wrong attempt discarded is another step forward.

> Thomas Edison

While you're working on your dream, developing your ministry, establishing your business, or working on your gifts, you must be willing to wait before you start to see the fruit of your efforts. It's important to continue in your efforts and not give up even if it appears that nothing much is happening. We've all heard stories of starving artists who can't sell their works while they're alive but, after they die, they go on to become famous. Vincent van Gogh was such an artist. He only sold one painting during his life – and that was to a friend for a small amount of money. Van Gogh was considered unsuccessful during his life, but he kept working on his passion regardless and completed over eight hundred works. Today, many of his paintings are valued in the hundreds of millions. His most expensive one sold for over $142 million.

In the Bible, Paul describes a group of people in Hebrews 11. These extraordinary individuals had a vision of greater things. They waited in unfailing faith for the time when those things would be established. Each of them died without seeing the manifestation of the promise, but the promise was eventually fulfilled. I have no idea what the spiritual beliefs of Vincent Van Gogh were, but there is a great parallel lesson we can learn from the people in Hebrews 11 and what eventually happened with Van Gogh's paintings. We never know how or when what we hope for might manifest and be a blessing to other people. We are granted pieces of a jigsaw puzzle, but he sees the whole picture and where each part fits. He's the one who knows how all things will eventually work together for good for those who are called to purpose.

At times, there is a temptation to throw in the towel because we think what we're doing isn't worth anything to others just because it doesn't yield fruit immediately. But try not to give into that temptation. We don't know how God will use us. People who do great exploits continue in faith believing that, though they can't see what they're waiting for, they will ultimately be rewarded if they don't give up.

5. Find your ray of hope

Tenacious people search for an advantage in adversity. Tenacity sometimes hangs on finding a ray of hope when all seems lost. Locating that ray of hope in difficult times enables you to make the best of your situation and can provide the boost needed to face the hardship and come to terms with adversity while remaining buoyant.

People who found themselves at the centre of hard times of old wrote many of the hymns we sing. The hymns they wrote became their ray of hope, which released the much-needed spiritual and emotional bolstering so that they could keep moving forward in the plan for their lives. One such man was Horatio G Spafford, and he penned a famous hymn: 'It is well with my soul.' Between 1871 and

1873, Spafford suffered a series of tragic losses, both personally and fiscally. In a two-year period, he experienced more loss than most people see in a lifetime. It began with the death of his son from scarlet fever in 1871. That same year, he faced financial ruin when all his investments were consumed in the flames of the Great Chicago Fire. Two years later, the family was still reeling from the tragedies so Spafford sent his wife and four daughters on a trip to Europe. Weeks after they left the shores of the United States, Spafford received a telegram from his wife informing him that the vessel they were on had been shipwrecked and all four children drowned in the incident.

Spafford immediately left Chicago to bring his wife home. On his way across the Atlantic Ocean, the ship's captain brought Spafford to the bridge and showed him the area of bellowing sea where his daughters drowned. That night, when alone in his cabin, Spafford penned a remarkable hymn. That hymn, 'It is well with my soul,' still brings comfort and hope to Christians of all denominations, and it's still considered one of the most cherished hymns ever written.

If you want to do great exploits, you need to be able to make the best of every situation, to find that ray of hope (no matter how tenuous). Spafford could not find it in any earthly thing, so he turned to worship. That was his ray of hope.

In moments when it feels like all is lost and you wonder whether it's worth fighting for your dream, find your ray of hope. That small token will remind you why you started and why you must go on.

In Genesis, Moses wrote, 'The Lord regretted that He had made mankind on the earth, and He was [deeply] grieved in His heart. So the Lord said, 'I will destroy (annihilate) mankind whom I have created from the surface of the earth – not only man, but the animals and the crawling things and the birds of the air – because it [deeply] grieves Me [to see mankind's sin] and I regret that I have made them.'[67] But Noah found favour and grace in the eyes of the Lord. Noah became God's ray of hope in those evil times and he decided to preserve mankind by preserving Noah and his family, plus male and female pairs of every species in the animal world. Each of us needs to understand that, even as mortal individuals, we are also his ray of hope. The purpose he calls one to is vital to what he wants to accomplish in his big picture.

6. Become a solution-oriented person

God himself provides us with a great example of keeping going, through focusing on a future orientated solution, when a dream falls apart. We know the story of Adam and Eve and how their sin changed everything for them and for the world. Fundamentally, it had a profound effect on their relationship with God. But he who had created a perfect world didn't turn his back on it when things changed for the worse. He confronted the problem and provided a solution to it. His approaches had to change, Adam and Eve could no longer relate to him in the garden. There would always have to have a blood sacrifice to bridge the gap that was created by their sin. But God had a plan to restore the dream of a good relationship between him and mankind. His was a very long-term view to say the least. Several millennia passed between that fateful day in the garden and the day his plan through Christ brought restoration. Meanwhile, God kept going, working with man through history, to preserve an inheritance among men, for himself. Generation after generation, he has never given up on his dream for us. He just keeps on going.

One striking thing about the passage from Genesis 6:6-7 is that, though God regretted making humans and was not pleased with the way things were turning out, his response was a solution-oriented one. He assessed the situation and saw that it didn't look good, but he didn't decide to give up on his creation. Instead, he identified a

---

[67]   Genesis 6:6-7, The Amplified Bible

way forward and set plans in motion to make it happen. In fact, he is such a master visionary and planner that he had already foreseen the problems that would arise and he prepared the solutions long before they actually occurred. God has been and continues to be tenacious in his plan to restore humanity to its former glory. You must let this same mind and attitude be in you if you want to do great exploits.

7. *Be kind to yourself*

Too often we act as our harshest critic and beat ourselves up when we fail. Negative self-talk is an easy way to kill off the desire to keep going. For instance in the dieting industry it's said that people tend to think negatively about themselves when they give into temptation while dieting. Advice from the experts is that the key to successful weight loss lies in being able to go easy on yourself when you have a dietary lapse. After all, self-criticism often leads to comfort eating, which then produces more self-criticism and more eating. On the other hand, when dieters accept their mistakes without judging themselves too harshly, they are more likely to resume their diets, lose weight, and keep it off. This is a transferable lesson on how to build tenacity; in short, you are more likely to persevere when you are able to forgive yourself of any failures and are kinder to yourself.

Whenever I've failed or suffered a setback, I've learned to cut my losses and move on. I train myself not to give too much focus on what happened. I take responsibility for what I may have done wrong, without blaming myself. I think there is a subtle difference between accepting responsibility and blaming. Accepting responsibility goes back to the idea that I have the power to choose my response, whereas blaming connotes a more punitive or condemning state, which is disempowering. In some cases, I acknowledge the progress I made and may even congratulate myself for having got as far as I did before things went wrong. I practise looking back at the past successes and progress I made along the journey. It makes me feel like I value myself and appreciate my own efforts even though I failed this time, and that makes it easier for me to avoid giving up and to try again.

I recognise from my own experience and from counselling or coaching others, that forgiving oneself can be a challenge to most people. But if you want to go on to do great exploits, you do need to develop the skill of looking at your life in a very objective way. You've got to recognise that you are going to make mistakes. Just as you would be patient with a child or someone that you love, you should embrace being patient with yourself. Choose the way of being honest with yourself, readily admitting when you've made a mistake and then take responsibility for what you will do next. People with that attitude find the strength and power to keep moving forward with their dream.

8. Don't take no *for an answer*

> Do not let the negatives of life control you. Rise
> above them, use them as your stepping stones to go
> higher than you've ever dreamed possible.

> Mary Kay Ash

Yet another strategy for being tenacious concerning your goals and dreams is to resolve to not take *no* for an answer. When the doors do not open as you desire them to, determine not to settle for *no*.

In Luke 18 Jesus told his disciples a parable about a widow who kept going to a judge who neither feared God, nor had any consideration for human beings. She wanted him to offer her defence and protection from an adversary. But he ignored her requests. The more he tried to ignore her, the more she persisted in seeking his help. It could have felt like a very negative situation for her. But she needed to do a great exploit by bringing an end to what her adversary was doing to her. Eventually, the judge thought to himself, *because this widow continues to bother me, I will defend and protect and avenge her, lest she give me an intolerable annoyance and wear me out by her continual coming!*[68] Jesus explained that if an unjust judge could eventually act on behalf of a widow who persisted, how much more would God send help to those who persist.

This type of determination does pay off. It did for my friend's granddaughter, the actress, whose story I told in chapter 9. Although, she now gets lots of good roles, she's been turned down at more auditions than she cares to number. When auditioning for a TV role when she was just starting out, the casting director asked, 'Why don't you just go and become a secretary?' She felt humiliated, but refused to take *no* for answer; instead, she decided to keep knocking on doors until she made it. Eventually, she did make it.

The road to where she is today was long and difficult at times – yet you'd never guess by looking at her. But that's the way of people who do great exploits. What we see are the exploits; we don't see the determination it took to make them happen. You don't know how many rejections they heard and chose to ignore before they succeeded. If you want to do great exploits, you must have determination to make them happen; you cannot afford to take *no* for an answer.

9. Be single minded, hungry, fanatical

People who are casual about their dreams seldom, if ever, achieve them. Doing great exploits takes a bit of desperation (or even fanaticism). Miro, whose story opened this chapter, explained why he never gave up when his journey became rough: 'When I saw my savings begin to grow, it turned me into a fanatic. I started a personal war against poverty.' Desperation is sometimes a good thing – it will keep you from settling for less than the dream that's in your heart.

---

[68] Luke 18:5, Amplified Bible, Classic Edition

Desperation is getting out there at retirement age to knock on the doors of restaurants to get the owners to franchise your recipe. It's driving around and sleeping in your car; it's being rejected over a thousand times before finding your first partner. Had the man we know of today as Colonel Sanders not been desperate enough, Kentucky Fried Chicken would not be sold in over 18,000 restaurants in 118 countries around the world.

Similarly, fanatical about finding a way to make their business dreams come true, many well-known business tycoons experienced failure and bankruptcy when their business ideas flopped. They remained tenacious, though, and eventually hit upon an idea that worked. Today, we're consumers of many of the great workable ideas these people had.

10. Keep going after success

In the Bible, Abram was doing very well in a place called Haran. He got married and was prospering. However, he wasn't moving in the direction of the purpose for his life. God spoke to him and said 'Go away from your country [...] to a land which I will show you.'[69]

Although Abraham was doing ok in Haran, it wasn't the place for the fulfilment of his purpose. There was much more in store for him than Haran, or Abraham's own plans, had for him.

People who do great exploits tend to go from one victory to another, one degree of glory to another. They have an appetite to expand on their service to others, to keep releasing their gifts in service to worthy causes. There's a world full of problems of all types and descriptions out there. The wisdom and skills you may have gathered doing exploits can be utilised to tackle other things. I've worked with people who have done well in their careers, but sitting back after retirement wasn't an option for them. They joined boards,

---

[69] Genesis 12:1, The Amplified Bible.

became trustees, they started mentoring, they started charities – they kept going. One of my former pastors, who had led a large church in London and eventually retired from his job as the general superintendent of one of the main denominations in the UK, said his plan was to spend the rest of his life preaching the gospel. He said he couldn't think of any better way to go but to die while preaching the gospel. At age 80, he was preaching in France, collapsed on the pulpit and went to be with the Lord a few days later. His was a life well spent in exploits right up until the end.

When she was in her early 60s and still successfully running her business, my mom finally answered the Lord's call to go to bible school and become a pastor. It was a call that she had found easier to say *No* to for many years for various reasons. But she eventually found the courage to answer the call. In her 70s she's still running her business and has counselled couples having marital challenges, she's involved in the women's ministry and is called upon to lead in many other areas of church life. She's one of my heroes.

As long as we have breath, we should use it to further his purpose for our lives. What's the alternative to keeping going even to your last breath? While she's motivated by a strong passion for helping other people, mom has made a certain fear of hers an ally that spurs her on to keep doing exploits. Because she fears the image of herself as a frail old lady sitting in a rocking chair with a blanket about her knees, she just keeps on going!

Reflections on keeping going

Every personality whose story I've told in this book has demonstrated the tendency to be fanatical about fulfilling purpose. Many people have developed the right mindset and put in the hard work required to achieve long-term goals. When goals have been achieved, they set new ones. For them the cycle never ends. They value life and the contribution they were created to bring to life and so they just keep going. To do great exploits, you'll find that tenacity is a golden thread that must be present if you're going to move from where you are to where you want to be.

But the path of the [uncompromisingly] just and righteous is like the light of dawn, that shines more and more (brighter and clearer) until [it reaches its full strength and glory in] the perfect day...

Proverbs 4:18, The Amplified Bible, Classic Edition

About the Author

H. Michelle Johnson has written for online and print magazines in both the Christian and secular world. She has a keen interest in what makes achievers different from the indistinct masses, and she has written numerous feature-length articles on those achievers she has been privileged to interview. She uses her broadcasting platform on radio to pursue her passion for helping people become active in the pursuit of purpose for their lives. As a speaker, Michelle is regularly invited to talk to groups of young people and adults, and she has a vision to see twenty-first-century people mobilised for impact and significance.

Visit her website: www.hmichellejohnson.com

Email her at intouch@hmichellejohnson.com

Printed in the United States
By Bookmasters